Into the Breach

The Life and Times of the
740th Tank Battalion in World War II

Paul L. Pearson

Photos and images are accredited to their sources individually throughout the book. Especial appreciation is extended to Harry Miller and Mark Hatchel, to the 740th Tank Battalion Archives, and to the individual tankers or relatives named who contributed from their personal files. And to our Belgian friends—Gaspard Schyns and Marylise Renkens—who chased down a picture all the way to Monseiur Lemaire and the La Gleize Museum.

Thanks also to the Harry Truman and Franklin D. Roosevelt Libraries for the use of their unrestricted images, and to Konecky and Konecky and After the Battle Publishers, to A/P Images, the National Archives and U.S. Army Images.
U.S. Army Signal Corps photos are in the public domain.

ISBN-10: 1-947160-01-X
ISBN-13: 978-1-947160-01-9

Library of Congress Control Number: 2017952022

Published by Write Down the Line, LLC

www.writedowntheline.com

Cover Design: Sarah Flores
Front cover picture by Corporal P. Petroney, U.S. Army Signal Corps.
Back cover picture source: U.S. Army History Images

Revised Edition
2017

For Mother and Dad

And the Girl Who Waited for Me

This book is dedicated to the brave men of the 740th Tank Battalion who fought the good fight in World War II and were killed in action.

And to all those wonderful guys of the 740th, living and dead, who braved the horrors of that war for family, flag and country, and for freedom's sake.

May God continue to bless America.

In Memoriam

Members of the 740th Tank Battalion Killed in Action

Corporal Jack D. Ashby
Technician Fourth Grade Charles E. Boler
Technician Fifth Grade Victor Borelli
Corporal Cecil B. Brown
Sergeant Ira M. Case
Private First Class Noel C. Causey
Sergeant Clayton D. Curtis
Private First Class Angelo J. DeLuca
Staff Sergeant Alton N. Fleming
Private Lawrence W. Gerardo
Private First Class Stanford N Goen
First Lieutenant Warren M. Halverson
Second Lieutenant William H. Hamilton
Private Joe D. Hance
Private Carrol E. Harkey
First Lieutenant Arthur P. Hartle
Technician Fourth Grade Winifred E. Hayden
Private Earl E. Howard
Technician Fifth Grade Herbert Howell
Corporal Raymond E. Johnson
Technician Fifth Grade Carl W. Krempin
Warrant Officer J.G. William Lipsky
Private First Class Raymond Martin
Private First Class Curtis R. Maxey
Sergeant Jack D. McPherson
Technician Fourth Grade John R. Mercer
Corporal Ray T. Merritt
Sergeant J. L. Montgomery
Technician Fifth Grade Grady Morris, Jr.
Corporal Clarence W. Munger
Private First Class Orland D. Myers
First Lieutenant David Oglensky
Private Grover E. Plaunt
Private First Class Eugene H. Pollard
Private First Class Walter E. Poore
Corporal Robert W. Prillaman
Private Clarence W. Provin
Private Ralph D. Rogers
Private Carl A. Schroeder
Private John L. Spieker
Private Neill T. Stancheff
Corporal Herbert V. Sweeney
Staff Sergeant Jimmie L. Wise

Battalion movement though the British Isles and into France.

1. Map courtesy of Daredevil Tankers, by Lt. Col. George K. Rubel

Then, on through France, Belgium, and Germany.

CONTENTS

MAPS, PICTURES, AND ILLUSTRATIONS

Foreword

The author, our Dad, began his book in 1995 when America was celebrating the 50th Anniversary of the end of World War II. He spent the next ten years of his life writing, researching, and interviewing his fellow tankers at their annual reunion, and of course, recalling his own personal experiences.

Into the Breach was initially published in 2007. Almost immediately, Dad began making minor changes in the hopes of further improving the book, with the expectation of publishing a revised version. Unfortunately, Dad passed away in 2009 before he could republish the book. Only recently did we find the working copy of his book along with his notes. Remembering our father's wishes, we decided to publish a new, revised version of *Into the Breach*.

The thirst for information about the life and times of our country at war continues to grow among the general population. New books crowd the shelves. New movies abound, both on the big screen and on TV. *Into the Breach* is a unique portrayal of precisely how it was to be there, and will perhaps add a new chapter to the history of World War II.

While Dad accomplished many things in his life, the one thing he was most proud of was serving his country in World War II. We hope you enjoy his labor of love.

The Pearson Family

Included in the back of this book is a speech titled "Freedom Isn't Free." It was written by the co-founders of the Remember Museum 39–45 in Belgium and delivered at the reunion of the 740th Tank Battalion. This is included to offer you, the reader, a perspective from the Belgian people's experience during the German occupation and the subsequent American liberation of their villages.

Acknowledgments

Following the end of hostilities in World War II Europe, and a brief stint in the U.S. Army's occupation of Germany, I returned to my hometown, Wichita Falls, Texas, "The City That Faith Built," just in time for Christmas, 1945. What a remarkable experience—home, after having been first a gunner, then a tank commander with the 740th "Daredevil" Tank Battalion, through thick and thin from its inception in March 1943.

Soon after my return, I married the girl who had waited for me — we never doubted. After a time, she encouraged me to write about my experiences in the war and with the *Daredevil Tankers,* which was the official code name for the battalion. I became involved and eventually wrote a short piece about the 740th, and I sent it to a major literary agency in New York. They liked it and agreed to market it among the various magazine publishers at the time. Time went on, and they sent encouraging notes from time to time. For whatever reason, the article never connected. I eventually became discouraged and asked that the story be returned.

The years passed, and a lot of water ran under the bridge, until all the publicity hit during the 50th anniversary of the war's end in 1995. As public interest grew, so did my own. I decided to dig into my files, find that old story, dust it off, and try once again.

In the meantime, a number of the old *Daredevil Tankers* had formed an association and were meeting each year around Labor Day. When I attended my first meeting some years ago and began to renew old and lasting friendships and experiences, I was hooked. I had to write that story, which eventually turned into this book. How now do I begin to acknowledge all those comrades-in-arms who sat with me through the years, listened patiently to my questions, struggled to recall very personal situations and circumstances, confided in me, offered anecdotes, pictures, references and books, and helped in so many different ways.

Shortly after the end of the war in Europe, Lieutenant Colonel George Kenneth Rubel, commander of the battalion, authored *Daredevil Tankers, The Story of the 740th Tank Battalion, United States Army.* It was published in Germany in September 1945, and edited by First Sergeant Charles W. Edwards, with illustrations by Private Tats B. Hirasuna. The book listed those who gave their lives and was dedicated to "those of our clan who died that we might live, and to our wives, sweethearts, and friends who awaited [our safe return]." Written basically in three sections, the book had: (1) a chronological history of the battalion, including training, travels, and battle actions; (2) the reliving of "Dark Moments" by a number tankers; and (3) a detailed accounting of the numerous medals awarded to individual members of the battalion, as well as a listing of the battalion membership.

The chronological timeline, dates, places, and actions of the battalion in *Into the Breach*, are based largely on Lt. Col. Rubel's book, and confirmed by written records regarding the 740th from the National Archives, including: the *Chronological History, 740th Medium Tank Battalion (Special), February 1943 to October 1944; Action Against Enemy Reports for the Battalion, January through May 1945; Summary Action Report for Company A, January through March 1945; Journal and Worksheets for the Battalion, March through May 1945; and Reports of Operations, August 1945 to March 1946. Also, General Orders, March through December 1943; January through July 1944; January through November 1945; and January through April 1946.*

I could not have written this book without these particular references. I would especially like to thank Mrs. Hilda Rubel for reading the manuscript, offering suggestions, and granting permission to quote and utilize material from Lt. Col. Rubel's book. Thanks also to Eric Freiwald at The National Archives for taking a special interest in my project, and his invaluable help in securing archival materials.

My heartfelt thanks go to all the (dare I say, old?) tankers who were willing to dig deeply into their very souls in order to bring forth their stories, and with whom I shared both laughter and tears along the way. Thanks as well to the many wives, sons, daughters, and friends of 740th tankers, living and dead, who also shared first-hand knowledge and experiences regarding their tankers, offering materials, assistance, and encouragement, and even translating foreign documents for me as the years went by—wondering all the while, no doubt, *Will he ever finish that book?*

Tankers owed a special debt of gratitude are noted, and you will no doubt recognize quite a number of them living still, as you become more deeply involved in the book. If you follow the documentation carefully, you will also note the scores of citations and awards for their heroic achievement. To a man, these tankers will tell you that all the heroes are dead. But I will tell you that most of them are heroes as well. I think you will come to know that as you meet so many of them in this story.

For their continuing interest, encouragement, and help, my thanks to R. D. Bridges, president of the 740th Tank Battalion Association, and to C. O. "Chigger" Webster, immediate past president of the Association. And finally, especial thanks for the unflagging loyalty and support through the years on the part of Harry

Miller, longtime secretary of the Association and historian extraordinaire, and to Mark Hatchel, current secretary of the Association, archivist, museum director, and son of the late Joe Hatchel.

All four of these men read drafts of the book and have made invaluable contributions of time, thought, and materials to its scope and content. All of them have their stamp on this project. Thank you, my friends and fellow tankers. I will be forever in your debt.

Paul L. Pearson
Benbrook, Texas
2007

And to my fellow tankers for their stories . . .

John A. Amann
Harold G. Bradley
Rudolph D. Bridges
Robert Frank Cole
Dwight R. Davis
Robert F. Fleckenstein
Paul L. Gittings
Harold L. Henry
Clarence R. Horn
J.D. Keen
J.D. Kirkpatrick
Gerard C. Lange
Charlie W. Loopey
James B. Lowrance
Willie F. Morris, Jr.
Frank M. Quick
Billie C. Ritchie
C. B. Seay
Joseph C. Schooley
Rex P. Taylor
James H. Thomas
Homer B. Tompkins
Burtis M. Tyler
John C. Tullier
Hershel B. Wall
C.O. "Chigger" Webster
Lloyd P. Wright

Introduction

Everyone knows that war is hell, but a person cannot possibly know how hellish war really is until he or she has been there. The men of the 740th Tank Battalion were there, most of them boys at the time who fought the good fight in World War II. They are qualified to speak. But you know, most of them don't speak about the war — until they get together. Then, how the words flow. They can't seem to get enough of each other's stories. Old James Thomas used to say that after all this time, they've gotten to where they can even tell each other's stories. At least that's the way it is now when those tankers get together, which a lot of them do each year when the 740th Tank Battalion Association meets, usually around Labor Day.

Of course, there are fewer and fewer of them every year. Somewhat like it was during the war after each clash with the Germans. Always a few who didn't make it back.

What kind of people were these young men of the 740th in World War II? What stories do they tell now when they meet? Stories they never told their families nor talked much about with friends. That's what this book is all about: the lives and times of these young tankers in World War II. *Daredevil Tankers* they were called. This is their story. It is a war story.

It all began a long time ago in Fort Knox, Kentucky. On March 1, 1943, to be exact. These young men came originally from Texas and Oklahoma in the main, but eventually their ranks embraced men from most other states as well. Many of them were drafted from farms, small towns, big cities of the time, and colleges. A number were volunteers. They all knew war was hell. It was common knowledge—even way back then. But they went willingly. Their country was under attack. Their way of life at risk.

My best guess is that none of them had ever seen a real tank up close before that fateful day. Frankly, it is hard to imagine that any of them signed up to be in the Tank Corps. I know one guy who lived in my house that signed up for the Quartermaster Corps.

But there they were, in the Tank Corps. So they began to learn about tanks. And how to fight with them. And they became pretty good at that. After basic training at Fort Knox, however, they were plunged into a top-secret "Special Training Group." Very hush-hush. Suddenly, every last soldier in the outfit was reviewed and frozen in the battalion, sworn to complete secrecy upon threat of fines and imprisonment, then moved into a newly constructed and fenced location called "Cedar Creek." It can now be told that the project was one of the army's most closely guarded secrets at the time: the use of high-intensity carbon arc lamps in tanks to blind the enemy in night fighting, an idea to revolutionize tank warfare.

In short order, the battalion moved en masse on passenger trains to Camp Bouse in the Desert Training Center near Phoenix, Arizona, for months of advanced and highly specialized training, along with other "special" tank battalions and armored infantry. Camp Bouse was an integral part of what would become known as the California–Arizona Maneuver Area, or CAMA, the largest armored infantry training center in the United States at that time.

Lieutenant Colonel George K. Rubel, who helped found and establish Camp Bouse, assumed command of the battalion in November 1943.

By April 1944, the tankers had become the 740th Tank Battalion, Medium Special, and returned to Fort Knox for movement overseas. Three months later, they sailed out into the Atlantic Ocean in a huge convoy of ships headed for England, where the devastation of war crowded in all around them, and where they continued their specialized training in a British tank training center. The last days of October, they crossed the English Channel, packed into GI trucks loaded onto LSTs, and landed in a sea of mud amid the choppy waters and confusion of France's Utah Beach. A rough passage in an ugly sea.

As the battalion began a slow trek through France, they picked up a motor escort in Paris and learned of their assignment to the First U.S. Army in Lt. Gen. Omar N. Bradley's 12th Army Group—not as the 740th Tank Battalion, Medium Special, but as a standard tank battalion with the code name Daredevil. What happened to their top secret project and all that special training? Nobody seemed to know for sure.

Suddenly, they were headed toward the war zone as a standard tank battalion, separate. On November 6, 1944, the battalion pulled into Aubel-Neufchateau, Belgium, just east of the Meuse River, and between Liege, Belgium, and Maastricht, Holland. The Belgian townspeople of Neufchateau and Mortroux took them into their homes and into their hearts, and lifelong friendships were quickly forged. But more about that later.

On December 16, 1944, the Ardennes exploded in a massive German offensive. Hitler's last gamble cracked the weak spot in the Western Front wide open. The attack was so fierce and surprising that entire units were overrun; Americans were falling back, taken prisoner, or dying where they stood. In the northern shoulder of attack, the U.S. First Army Headquarters at Spa was being evacuated. The situation was beyond desperate.

The 740th Tank Battalion was called into the breach. At Stoumont Station, along the Ambleve River, and with elements of the 30th Infantry Division, the 740th smashed headlong into the 1st SS Panzer Division spearhead, *Kampfgruppe Peiper*, led by the infamous Jochen Peiper, who had just emerged from the bloody Malmedy massacre. In the fog and icy rain and snow of the Ardennes, the *Daredevil*

Tankers pounded Hitler's elite SS panzer division and turned it around, forcing Peiper's retreat through Targnon, Stoumont, and La Gleize, in some of the bitterest fighting in the Battle of the Bulge.

On Christmas Day, in hot pursuit of the fleeing Germans, a column of 740th tanks was mistakenly bombed and strafed by a flight of American P-47 Thunderbolts, and a tank was knocked out and several tankers wounded before the planes could be called off.

Four days later, the battalion was pulled out of the 30th Infantry and sent to support the 82nd Airborne Division in the area of Werbomont. Without rest, the tankers continued the fight to drive the Germans back south and east out of Fosse, Odrimont, and Abrefontaine, until the division dominated all the crossings of the Salm River in the vicinity of Grand-Halleux.

It was impossible to walk in the heavy snow, so the tankers loaded the 82nd paratroopers up on the backs of their tanks and rumbled on. By the end of January 1945, they were all the way to Losheimer Graben, with both enemy gunfire and bitterly cold weather having taken a heavy toll on the tankers and troopers.

The battalion attacked day and night, finally battering its way through the *Siegfried Line* in the vicinity of Neuhof and Udenbreth, Germany. Lieutenant Colonel Rubel noted that the only tankers able to get a night's sleep were those who remained alive after their tanks had been hit.

By February 8, the battalion had been transferred yet again, to the 8th Infantry Division this time, near Duren, a scene of utter devastation. Two weeks later, the assault across the Roer River began, and the tanks crossed into Duren on a hurriedly built Bailey Bridge.

From Duren to Cologne was a nightmare of attachment and detachment, from one infantry regiment to another, wherever the need was greatest. The 740th was drastically short of tanks, and there were no replacements. In order to repair a tank, Service Company had to recover a damaged or knocked out tank, often under fire, then hope and pray the parts fit.

With the infantry again on the backs of their tanks, the 740th advanced rapidly until rumbling into a hot spot. The infantry would then dismount and sweep the area, while the tanks covered their movements with machine gun and cannon fire.

By the first week in March, the 740th was across the Erft Canal and meeting serious resistance in the area of Mödrath and Frechen. Still, the closer the tankers got to Cologne and the Rhine River, the tougher the German resistance grew, until at one point, they were under fire from three sides. It was touch and go until they finally broke through.

By mid-March, the 740th had been pulled out and reassigned again—this time to the Seventh U.S. Army in Lt. Gen. Jacob L. Dever's 6th Army Group in the south of France. The tankers were being called upon to breach the *Siegfried Line* again.

The tank crews rode with their tanks on railroad flat cars from Aachen, Germany, to Morhange, France, and hooked up with the 63rd Infantry Division to crack the *Siegfried Line* just north of Ensheim, take the high ground, capture St. Ingbert, and then push on to Homberg. The German West Wall in that area was made up of large dragon's teeth, in front of which, deep anti-tank ditches had been dug. All roads going through the line had been blasted, forming large craters. Huge, concrete bunkers with walls five- and six-feet thick and armed with 75 mm high velocity anti-tank guns overlooked the area. Artillery and mortar fire was heavy when the tankers pulled up into line.

Following a successful mission there, the battalion received word from 12th Army Group to return at once to the First U.S. Army back up north. Their old friends in the 8th Infantry Division were stalled, trying to capture the town of Siegen on the southern edge of the Ruhr Pocket, and were calling for help. The tankers moved immediately to Sarrebourg, France, and on Easter Sunday, April 1, 1945, loaded onto trains once again, and headed for Odendorf, Germany, in the vicinity of Bonn. On April 8, they crossed the Rhine River on a pontoon bridge and marched on to Siegen, eighty miles to the east.

The very next day, the 740th jumped off with the 8th Infantry to spearhead the attack through the center of the Ruhr Pocket. With the infantry on the backs of their tanks again, the battalion roared eighteen miles deep into the enemy lines that first day, at times, fighting day and night. Long lines of prisoners and vehicles began to move past them to the rear of the American lines.

On April 12, word flashed around the world that Franklin D. Roosevelt had died, and that Vice President Harry S. Truman had become president of the United States.

The tanks of the 740th never slowed down. As they fought their way into the heavily populated center of the Ruhr Valley, there were anti-tank guns, machine guns, and mortar fire at virtually every turn in the road. The battalion closed to the Ruhr River at Wetter, turned west, then paralleled the Ruhr as they advanced to Dusseldorf—a grueling and exhausting battle, losing as many tanks as they had in the Ardennes.

The battle of the Ruhr Pocket ended in mid-April. Some 325,000 Germans were caught in the pocket, and surrendered.

In preparation for the crossing of the Elbe River, the 740th was assigned to the Ninth U.S. Army on April 25 and ordered north to Uelzen, Germany, as part of a huge buildup of the 21st Army Group, commanded by British Field Marshal Bernard Montgomery. It was a grueling 350-mile trip overland in their tanks, and the battalion was split up again on its arrival between elements of the 82nd Airborne and the 8th Infantry Divisions.

With his "2,000-year Reich" crumbling around him, Hitler committed suicide in his bunker in Berlin on April 30, 1945. That same day, tankers of the 740th were busy dodging artillery and mortar fire as they crossed the Elbe River on pontoon bridges near Bleckede.

The battalion had moved 760 miles in April and fought under three different armies: the First and Ninth U.S. Armies, and the Second British Army.

On May 1, 1945, with ten doughboys mounted on the back of each of their tanks, and with absolutely no forward reconnaissance, the 740th took off to meet the Russians. They simply barreled down the road until a tank hit a roadblock—a Panzerfaust, an anti-tank gun, or a blown-up bridge. Tank commanders had to radio back and forth to determine whether the troops out ahead were friends or foes. It was a wild ride. German prisoners were sent streaming back down the road to the rear for someone else to take care of.

On May 2, in the town of Gromitz, some four hundred American prisoners of war and an equal number of British were liberated, along with at least two thousand French, Italians, and Poles who had been doing forced labor there.

The tanks machine-gunned their way into Haguenau, then halted the column to shoot down the German airplanes that were frantically trying to take off from a large airfield at the edge of town. In a matter of minutes, thirty or more planes were burning wildly in the area. Just south of Warsow, a small village was so heavily defended by die-hard Nazi troops that the village had to be completely razed. As the 740th column of tanks approached Schwerin, just south of Wismar on the Baltic Sea, the tankers could see literally thousands of German soldiers in every direction, and were more than a little nervous as they barreled into the town at high speed. But the Germans had little fight left in them by then, and tens of thousands came pouring in to give themselves up.

By sundown on May 3, the roads were clogged with German soldiers as far as the eye could see, heading south in full surrender. Even an armored railway train pulled up to surrender.

On May 4, the German forces in Holland and Northwest Germany surrendered. On May 7, all German forces surrendered unconditionally. At midnight on May 8, 1945, all hostilities ceased.

There was a lot of hugging and handshaking and backslapping. *Congratulations! We made it!* But there were no hurrahs. And very few tears. The war was over in Europe, but there was still the war in the Pacific to be won. What next? Would they be called into the breach yet again? Such a turn was very real to the tankers of the 740th. Rumors abounded. But the very idea of fighting another war in another place was almost impossible to comprehend at the time.

Thoughts quickly turned to home. To family and home cooking. To friends and old times. And to how great it would be to get back to the good old USA. *There really is no place like it. Thank God. It's over here. Finally over. What will happen to us now?*

On May 27, 1945, the entire battalion gathered in Schwerin, Germany, in an emotional Memorial Service in memory of their fallen comrades-in-arms—those gallant guys, the real heroes—who had given all they had to give along the way, and would not be going home. God bless them. And God bless America. At last, the tears were allowed to come.

Part I

The 740th Tank Battalion, commanded by Lieutenant Colonel George K. Rubel, was in Fort Knox, Kentucky, on June 6, 1944. It was D-Day in Europe, and the 740th was headed "over there." America was at war on two fronts, and was sending her sons across the seas to defend the freedom which the country holds so dear. Day after day, the battalion moved inexorably closer to war—across the great Atlantic, through England and France, to the front line in Belgium. Suddenly, and without warning, the Germans thrust mightily through the Ardennes, and the men of the 740th were thrown into the breach—into what was to become known as the Battle of the Bulge.

Chapter 1

America at War, 1944

Having completed six months of highly classified tank and crew training in a hush-hush secret project in the California-Arizona Maneuver Area, the 740th Tank Battalion was back where it had started, in Fort Knox, Kentucky, en route to the Big Show. It would not be long now.

The young tankers, commanded by Lt. Col. George K. Rubel, were in a last minute flurry of activity — on the firing range and in outdoor classes under the trees, but still far removed from the killing fields of World War II. Or so it seemed, until the hellish explosion of a 37mm dud at Outpost 6 shattered the tranquility of their otherwise hurry-up-and-wait day.

When the smoke cleared, three from their ranks lay dead or dying, another nineteen wounded. The tragic accident riveted the survivors' hearts and minds on the dead certainty that they were another move closer on the checkerboard of war. **The date was June 6, 1944.**

Across the wide Atlantic, and unknown to the young tankers, the first wave of the mightiest amphibious armada in the history of the world had plunged into the choppy seas of the English Channel for the invasion of occupied France. It was "D-Day."

With the advent of D-Day, the Western Allies began to shift their balance of power to the cross-channel attack, although much hard fighting remained in Italy. The vast war in the Pacific was somewhat stabilized by that time, and the liberation of Europe was deemed crucial. It was a critical decision by the allies.

At the time of the invasion, the Germans were battle-hardened and dug in on the heavily fortified coast of Normandy. Allied casualties were high that day — about nine thousand killed, wounded, or missing in action.[1] For a time, the Allied high command was fearful of being thrown back into the sea. However, the powerful elements of surprise and superior forces eventually turned the tide; tenuous beachheads were won along a fifty-mile front, from the base of the Cotentin Peninsula, east to the Orne River. The battle raged up and down the tangled coast for days. Allied reinforcements and supplies poured into the crowded and bloody beachheads. The British and Canadians engaged heavy opposition on the eastern flank and fell short of their key objective, Caan, a railroad center with wide-open, breakout country to the south. The Germans were tenacious and fought with stubborn courage, determined to maintain their reserves at the Pas de Calais, where they were certain that the main Allied invasion was yet to come.

American troops on the British right were extremely vulnerable in the French "bocage" country, thwarted amid small fields, virtually impenetrable hedgerows, sunken roads, and overhanging trees. There was little chance for tanks to maneuver or breakout. Ambush lay in wait at every turn.

On June 13, back in England, Hitler's first flying bomb, the V-1, materialized and thoroughly frightened the populace just outside of London, as it dived to the earth and exploded with a ton of TNT. The small "rocket" putt-putted in at nearly four hundred miles per hour, and dived hell-bent for earth when the fiery exhaust cut out. It was the first of Hitler's "secret weapons" to be launched. The fearful allies could only guess what was next to come.

A storm of hurricane proportions battered the invasion coast in mid-June, severely disrupting the Allied timetable, and sinking hundreds of landing craft, severely damaging the artificial "Mulberry" harbors at both the British and American beaches, and totally frustrating the critical build-up of men and supplies. The saving grace was that the Allies had nearly 750,000 troops ashore by the time the storm bombarded their defenses.

There was great excitement at Fort Knox, among the men of the 740th, as word rocketed through the battalion that their endless training was at an end—that their time had come. They had missed D-Day, but now they were going Over There. The young citizen-soldiers boarded the long, olive-drab troop train for Camp Kilmer, New Jersey. It was July 19. Their great adventure had begun.

As the Allied invasion grew in depth and intensity, a wide-ranging group of German generals and politicos who were deeply opposed to Hitler and the Nazis, determined that it was time to strike. They plotted to kill the *Führer,* then petition for a peaceful settlement with the West—perhaps even enlist the support of the Americans and the British in their struggle with the hated Bolsheviks from the East.

July 20: At the Wolf's Lair, in East Prussia. Hitler and his staff were gathered around a huge oak table in a packed conference room at the Wolfschanze headquarters in a forest near Rastenburg. A powerful bomb, secreted in an aide's briefcase, exploded, shattering the table, blowing out windows, and creating havoc throughout the Lair. Although many senior officers were killed and injured, Hitler seemed to be only superficially wounded and took survival as a measure of divine providence and the invincibility of his cause.

What happened then could only be described as a bloodbath. The conspiracy was quickly broken. The generals involved, and thousands more of those believed guilty of complicity, were eliminated or dispatched to concentration camps. The most hated were hung from meat hooks until dead — their suffering recorded on film.[2]

July 25: Breakout in Normandy. After weeks of bitter resistance, the German line west of St. Lo finally buckled under massive American pressure, and the U.S. forces poured through the gap toward Coutances and Avranches. The Allies had established themselves on the mainland and had finally broken out. Excitement was high back in America.

On July 26, the 740th Tank Battalion, along with five thousand other troops, sailed out of New York Harbor aboard the USS General William Mitchell, and joined a huge convoy of gray-clad troop ships and tankers. They were protected by a destroyer and a number of destroyer escorts.

The convoy system had proved to be quite effective against the menace of the German submarines, which swarmed in "Wolf Packs" across the wide Atlantic. Still, the journey was hot and slow and cumbersome, and by the time the 740th sailed safely into the Irish Sea and finally docked at Liverpool, England, it was August 6. Eleven long days had elapsed since they had left home and country behind. The war loomed ever closer to the young tankers.

By early August, American troops in France were striking west into Brittany toward the port of Brest, driving south to Angers and the Loire River, and wheeling east for Paris and the Seine. Allied air superiority battered enemy supply lines and frustrated a massive German counterattack at Mortain. American tanks were at last on the move. The first pipeline under the channel became operational, and precious fuel began to flow to Cherbourg from the Isle of Wight.

On the home front: The war had brought an end to the brutal economic depression in America, and times were generally good — except for those families with a loved one overseas and in the fight. Almost everyone who wanted to work had a job with an average annual income of $2,378.00.[3] Still, the country was in a war on two fronts.

America had proved that it could provide both guns and butter. But war production devoured astronomical amounts of the country's resources. Real estate was high. There were hardly any new cars to be had, even at the outrageous price of $975.00, and only retread tires. A loaf of bread was only ten cents, but everyday commodities were scarce. And almost everything necessary, from food, clothing, shelter, and transportation, was rationed. A brisk black market had developed in gasoline stamps.

The fog rolled in layers as the men of the 740th Tank Battalion filed cold and exhausted from the troop train, which had brought them from the ship at Liverpool in England, south into Wales, at Glynderwen. They were attached to the 9th Armored Group, then moved by truck to a tent camp on a windy, rocky hillside, continually blustering with mist and fog and rain near the small town of Rosebush, Wales. Welcome to the war.

Conditions smoothed out considerably, however, when the battalion was transferred two weeks later to Castle Martin, a British tank training center on the sea near Pembroke. There, they had plenty of room to stretch out and begin working with the specially equipped tanks designed for surprise night action against the enemy.

In off times, the tankers visited Cardiff, Pembroke, Tenby, and other nearby sites of interest, and gradually became acquainted with the country and the people —whom they knew only from their geography books and history lessons. The people were warm and friendly to the "Yanks," appreciating that they were all in this thing together.

August 15: Invasion of southern France. Against strong British opposition to the plan, the American forces invaded the French Mediterranean between Cannes and St. Tropez, to keep the Germans in the area from moving up to the main battle in the north. More importantly, the Americans desperately needed the major port of Marseilles to bring in the reinforcements necessary to protect their southern flank.

Fortunately, the German lines were spread thin through the bunkers and pillboxes in the area, and the fighting there was comparatively light. French Resistance fighters, with and without weapons, thronged to the fray, harassing the German withdrawal. Divisions of the Free French Army, equipped and supplied by the U.S., landed the next day and headed for Toulon, and thence to Marseille, while the Americans attacked toward Cannes. With the capture of southern seaports by late August, additional troops, tanks, and supplies came on-line for an Allied thrust into the south of France.

In the meantime, the British and Canadians smashed through at Caan and pushed south to link up with the Americans at Argentan-Falaise. The German troops who escaped from that pocket began a frenzied retreat toward Paris and the Seine River. After two-and-a-half months of bitter fighting, the Battle of Normandy was over.

Since the Allies had landed, German casualties totaled nearly half a million, but Allied losses were high as well—some 200,000 killed, wounded, or missing in action. Two-thirds of them were American.[4]

The race for Paris and the Seine: Following the Normandy breakout, Allied columns began to pour into France in hot pursuit of the fleeing German army. As the invasion forces neared Paris, the men and women of the French resistance took to the streets to do battle with the German garrison occupying their beleaguered city. Hitler decreed that Paris should be defended to the last man, and should not fall into the hands of the enemy, except in ruins. But the German garrison commander, *Generalleutnant* Dietrich von Choltitz, steadfastly refused Hitler's orders to lay waste to the historic city. Therefore, his defense was sporadic and half-hearted at best. He surrendered on August 25 as the people took to the streets, and French and American forces swept into the city.

In spite of scattered sniping, and large numbers of German soldiers still determined to hold out here and there, General Charles de Gaulle led the French forces in a somewhat fitful, but jubilant parade down the Champs Elysees the very next day.

As the last of the Germans were rounded up or fled the city, the enthusiastic Parisians continued their celebration in the streets, as did the French forces, who disappeared into the more pleasurable environs of the city. On August 29, two American divisions marched in triumph down the Champs Elysees, through the city, and on their way to the front.

A crisis of supply: General Dwight D. Eisenhower, Supreme Commander of the Allied Expeditionary Force, was worried. With his armies breaking loose across France, and the entire population of Paris now to be fed, logistics had become a very real problem. The Allies had planned to hold at the Seine in order to expand the Normandy beachhead into a much larger "lodgment area," so that the Brittany ports could be opened, airfields built, and supplies and service troops assembled. With the Germans on the run, the high command had decided to push on across the Seine and head for Germany. As a result, the front became ever farther from the mountain of food, gasoline, and ammunition, building steadily on the invasion beaches. The French railroad network was of little use: it had been bombed and sabotaged almost out of existence. The "Red Ball Express," a one-way truck route from Normandy, was bumper to bumper with the supplies and still could not keep up with the demand.

Having pushed all the way through Belgium and Luxemburg by the first week in September, the Allies nearly ground to a halt for lack of gas, just short of Germany's *Siegfried Line,* the infamous Westwall.

A crisis of command: With the Americans predominating in troops and resources, it was understood that General Eisenhower would move to France from his London headquarters and assume direct command of all field operations, as soon as practical, after the invasion forces had secured lodgment and breakout.

General Bernard L. Montgomery commanded the invasion troops —British, Canadian, *and* American —and was to continue in command of the British Second Army and the Canadian First Army, comprising the 21st Army Group after the breakout.

Lieutenant General Omar N. Bradley commanded the U.S. First Army during the invasion. Lieutenant General Courtney B. Hodges took over the U.S. First

Army, and Eisenhower moved Bradley up to organize the 12th Army Group, which, in addition to the U.S. First Army, now included the newly formed U.S. Third Army, commanded by Lieutenant General George S. Patton, and later, the U.S. Ninth Army, under command of Lieutenant General William H. Simpson.

After the breakout in Normandy, the two army groups, Montgomery's 21st and Bradley's 12th, were to form a two-pronged attack across France, and into Germany.

The British and Canadians were to push through the northern route across France and into Belgium, and capture the important port of Antwerp to relieve the supply problem, then on into the vast German industrial area of the Ruhr. The Americans were to drive through the center, south of the heavily forested Belgium/Luxembourg Ardennes, and into the strategically important industrial region of the Saar.

Later, Lieutenant General Jacob L. "Jake" Devers formed the Sixth Army Group, which included the U.S. Seventh Army, commanded by Lieutenant General Alexander M. Patch, and the French First Army, commanded by General Jean de Lattre de Tassigny. This army group was organized from the invasion troops coming up from the French Riviera to protect the Americans' right.

Together, these army groups were to form a united, "broad front" attack against the length of the German border, from the North Sea to Switzerland, all under Eisenhower's command.

However, when the Supreme Commander arrived in France on September 1, the change in active ground command, even though previously agreed to, quickly began to draw sparks from the British. Montgomery argued that he should retain ground command, and that all available resources be thrown behind his "single, full-blooded thrust" through the northern region, to the Ruhr, then on to Berlin—with the Americans primarily guarding his flank and maintaining an "aggressive defense" in the south. The British Chiefs of Staff agreed.

2. Photo courtesy: U.S. Army
Signal Corps
General George C. Marshall

Eisenhower knew that neither the American Chiefs of Staff, nor the American public, would hold still for this, so he continued to push forward with his broad front strategy. Montgomery's obstinacy continued to be a burr under the supreme commander's saddle for months to come. And, although the British high command appreciated "Ike" Eisenhower's unique ability to politically hold things together between the armed forces of the two countries, the British never placed much faith in him as a tactical strategist.

Eisenhower prevailed only with the support of President Roosevelt and the commanding presence of General George C. Marshall on the British and American Combined Chiefs of Staff. British Prime Minister Winston Churchill persuaded King George to promote Montgomery to the rank of field marshal to ease his transition from overall ground commander, placing him at the same four-star level as General Eisenhower. For his part, Ike put together four airborne divisions, including the American 82nd, 101st, and the British 1st, and placed them under Monty's command as the First Allied Airborne Army. In addition, he agreed to have Bradley position elements from his 12th Army Group north of the Ardennes in order to strengthen Monty's right flank.

Bradley and the American generals were outraged at the splitting of American armies and believed that Ike was being overly influenced by the British. But in order to reinforce and shorten allied supply lines, Ike needed the Belgium port of Antwerp, so he gave Monty's 21st Army Group priority until this could be accomplished.

Still, Montgomery never relented in his determination to regain basic ground command, nor on his ambitious "full blooded" thrust through the north, with him leading the charge—even though, because of the supply situation, such action would have brought the American forces in the south to a screeching halt.

Ike finally told him that the American people would not allow that to happen. Ultimately, he had to threaten Monty with a "me or him" approach to the Combined Chiefs of Staff if he didn't back off. Montgomery bowed to the reality of the moment, but, characteristically, he never gave up. The long months of top-level disagreement were known to Hitler, and undoubtedly energized his momentous decision to counterattack through the Ardennes in December, with the intention of making a headlong dash for the sea and splitting the British and Americans. Then, he believed, he could sue for a separate peace and make a deal with the Allies to join him in throwing back the barbaric Russians. In his opinion, there was no way that history would allow three conflicting and disparate governments—the United States, Great Britain, and Russia—to come together as a cohesive and compelling force and defeat him.

The British liberated the Belgium capital of Brussels on September 3, and entered Antwerp on September 4. The prize port, essential to allied victory, was still intact. Its large capacity and proximity to the German border assured that the allied supply problem would be solved. The only problem was that the Scheldt Estuary—sixty miles of canals and waterways linking Antwerp to the North Sea, including the key Walcheren and Beveland Islands—was still under tight German control.

Instead of going all-out to clear the Scheldt in order to activate the port of Antwerp, Montgomery somehow pressured Ike into a grandiose scheme that came to be known as Market Garden. The plan was to hopscotch the rivers and canals, and nearly one hundred miles of natural barriers, dropping the First Airborne Army at strategic points all the way to Arnhem, in Holland. Hopefully, this would pave the way for elements of the British Second Army to flank the *Siegfried Line* and force a bridgehead on the Rhine.

The controversial project jumped off on September 17 and demanded much of the available allied resources. The explosive operation ran into a German buzz saw, and although a sixty-five mile corridor and a couple of bridgeheads were wedged into the Netherlands, eight days and nearly twelve thousand casualties later, the allies acknowledged the failure of the plan and withdrew. All the while, the Germans were busy reinforcing their defenses in the Scheldt. As a result, it was November 28 before the channel area was swept free of enemy troops and mines, and the first allied convoy could make use of the vital port of Antwerp in Belgium. Months of bitter campaigning were sure to come.

Meanwhile, on September 16, back in the Wolf's Lair, Hitler's most trusted generals—Keitel, Jodl, Guderian, and Crêpe—whispered back and forth, waiting for the Fuehrer to appear. Hitler's health had not been good since the assassination attempt in July, and they were not surprised at his appearance when he came in wearily and slumped in his chair at the head of the conference table. He was obviously ill, shaken, and appeared much older than his 54 years. Still, they were astonished at what he had to say.

The *Führer* had made a momentous decision. He was sending troops to the offensive in the Ardennes. As soon as five hundred thousand men and supplies could be readied. Although the enemy was at the fatherland's gates, and the *Wehrmacht* was reeling after enduring close to a million casualties in the past two months alone, Hitler was going to attack in total surprise, through the rugged Ardennes region of Belgium and Luxembourg, across the Meuse River and on to Antwerp, splitting the British and American forces, and causing them to petition for peace. It was obvious to him that the allies were having trouble getting along anyway.

Thus was born the *Wacht am Rhein* (Watch on the Rhine), which became known to the Allies as the Battle of the Bulge, the most decisive battle on the western front during World War II. The citizen-soldiers of the 740th Tank Battalion—still in England, still light of heart and filled with youth and adventure, but untested and untried—were headed straight for the Ardennes.

The tankers were on the move—first to a camp at Longbridge Deverill, near Warminster, England, on September 24, where they were billeted for the first time in facilities that were already established. There was a large recreation hall, coffee and doughnuts every night, warm beer, and dances with the local girls. The war seemed off in another world somewhere.

On October 6, troop movement emptied Camp Sutton Veny nearby, and the 740th took charge—brick buildings, movies, even hot showers. Recreation parties reached out as far as Gloucester, Bath, and Stonehenge. Many of the troops visited London and saw the unbelievable devastation of war for the first time. They were surprised at the depth of their feelings over the blackout in the huge old city, the chilling sound of air-raid sirens, and the bizarre behavior of buzz bombs putt-putt-puttering overhead, then becoming suddenly silent in the night—just before the frightening explosion.

Suddenly, the battlefront seemed closer than before.

Franklin D. Roosevelt was 62 years old and in extremely poor health. He was bone-tired in body, mind, and spirit, but hitting the hustings in an all-out fight for an unprecedented fourth term as president of the United States. The appearance of this exhausted man was shocking even to those who were close to him. Rumor had it among those in the know that he would not live out his term, even if elected.

Still, he was determined to see the worldwide war to a successful conclusion, and the United Nations organized after the conflagration had ceased, in order to guarantee the peace.

He was supremely confident of his reelection, and he was pushing for a Big Three meeting in November with Churchill and Joseph Stalin, the Russian chief of state and head of world communism. But Stalin was being obstinate.

Believing in his personal powers of persuasion, Roosevelt felt that he could handle "Uncle Joe" (as he and Churchill called Stalin privately) one-on-one. But Churchill wasn't so sure. It was evident that the intractable Generalissimo had his own agenda, and the Prime Minister was now more fearful of the Red Army's spreading subjugation of Eastern Europe than he was of the Germans.

Having finally turned the Germans back from their heartland, the Russian legions had stormed through the Balkans and were in the process of crushing resistance in Poland, where Stalin wanted his own puppet government. Although the Soviet turnaround was due in large part to American productivity and lend-lease, Stalin was now an independent power with which to be reckoned.

On the western front, the Germans were fighting with dogged determination. As the Allied thrust toward Germany and the Rhine River began to slow, General Eisenhower considered going on the defensive until Montgomery could clear the Scheldt and Antwerp could become operational. The Allies were desperately playing catch-up on supplies, and infantry replacements were almost non-existent. At the same time, the weather was worsening.

The rumor mill was grinding its way through the 740th. The tankers knew, of course, that they were one of a small group of battalions classified as "special," but the scuttlebutt was that the secret project in which they were so deeply involved was being scrapped. At first, they heard that they were to be thrust into combat as a mine exploder outfit. Then, it was as a standard tank battalion. Hearts suddenly began to beat a little faster. Imaginations ran wild. Were they ready for this? What was going on here?

The uncertainty did not last long. In a matter of days, orders came down to convert to a standard tank battalion. And, even before they could fully comprehend their new responsibilities and organization, they were ordered to turn in their special project equipment and were moved en masse to the port of Weymouth, England.

On October 29, the 740th Tank Battalion was loaded onto two LST's and barged across the English Channel the next day. It was a rough and emotional journey.

October had been bloody on the continent. In spite of the difficulties of supply and replacement, General Eisenhower determined that it would save lives and shorten the war if the Allies continued to press the attack, when and where they could, in order to keep the Germans from regrouping effectively. Therefore, the early winter of 1944 involved vicious fighting and a real test of the courage and the resourcefulness of the Allied armies.

After a number of fitful starts and stops, Hodges' First U.S. Army finally assembled the power to push through the Westwall at Aachen, the first major German city to fall. The fighting raged from building to building, house to house, and even room to room before the final surrender on October 21.

Aachen was a holy city for the Nazis since the Emperor Charlemagne's tomb was there. And, according to Hitler's view of history, Charlemagne had founded the First Reich, the Holy Roman Empire was the second, and his was the Third Reich.

On the First U.S. Army's right, the Third U.S. Army's George Patton's slashing, smashing dash across France, ground to a halt as his gasoline and supplies dwindled. Under his breath, Patton cursed Ike for giving Montgomery the lion's share of resources and settled down to the merciless infantry slugfest he hated—dug-in Germans near Metz, an important road hub and the capital of Lorraine.

Further south, Dever's French and American armies were not faring much better. They were fighting in the mud and rain and struggling for supplies as well. His 6th Army Group's communication and supply line stretched five hundred miles, all the way from the Vosges Mountains on the western side of the Rhine River Valley, to Marseille on the French coast. Up north, Montgomery had given the First Canadian Army the job of clearing the Scheldt, but resisted the pressure to get Antwerp operational. Instead, he continued to press the Supreme Commander to concentrate the available transportation and supplies behind his 21st Army Group for a thrust to the Ruhr and Berlin. None of the Americans believed Monty's grandiose scheme would work.

After a rough passage across the English Channel, the tankers of the 740th reached Utah Beach the evening of October 30, but the sea was too rough for landing. Sleeping fitfully or not at all, they rode the swells overnight, and their LST was finally able to get close enough for them to roll onto the beach in G.I. trucks the next morning, October 31. The beach was a mass of mud, debris, vehicles, men, and equipment in every direction. The excitement of the moment was quickly replaced with reality. "This is it. This is where it all begins." They were in France.

The battalion bivouacked that night at a marshaling area at Saint-Germain-de-Varreville. No orders awaited, and a real SNAFU (Situation Normal All Fucked Up) developed. A hundred important things were happening, and the commandant of the yards had his cup completely full. He had never heard of the 740th Tank Battalion. And he had no idea what he was supposed to do with all of these people.

It became quickly evident to Lt. Col. Rubel that this beach was a place the 740th did not need to be. He could see no reason to hang around in such a dispirited location when the war was going on in Belgium, where a lot of brave American soldiers were fighting for life and country and needed all the help they could get.

He requested immediate permission to head for the European Theater of Operations' headquarters in Paris to find out what was going on, and to get the 740th outfitted for the long haul across France. The commandant was undoubtedly relieved at the prospect of solving this one problem without major complications and quickly gave his blessing, warning the 740th's commander to stay clear of the route of the Red Ball Express.

Rubel immediately sent an aide to Paris to pave the way for the move, and early the next morning sent the order down: "Move 'em out!"

In the meantime, General Eisenhower had been under pressure from the Combined Chiefs of Staff to launch a major offensive before winter set in. With Montgomery still trying to clear the vital Scheldt approaches to Antwerp on the North Sea, but with logistics somewhat improved, Ike decided that Bradley's 12th Army Group would make the main effort.

Bradley shifted Simpson's new Ninth Army to the First Army's north flank, between the First U.S. Army and Montgomery's British/Canadian 21st Army Group. The First and Ninth U.S. Armies, both north of the Ardennes, were to join and jump the Rhine River south of Cologne, with the Ruhr as their objective. Patton's Third Army, well south of the Ardennes, was to push northeast through the Saar and provide strategic support for their right flank. Dever's 6th Army Group heading north from the invasion of southern France was assigned to clear the upper Rhine.

However, the Roer River flowed sullenly between the Americans and the Rhine, and Germans claimed the high ground at Schmidt overlooking a series of dams on the upper Roer, which could easily flood the valley crossing. The First Army sucked in its gut and pushed off. Only the Huertgen Forest stood in the way.

Just south of Aachen, the Huertgen Forest turned out to be a green hell **for** the Americans. The forest was a dense and formidable half-hundred square miles of jagged, hilly terrain, crisscrossed with pillboxes, mines, and determined defenders. As the weather turned harsh, one division after another was chewed up and turned back. Fifty-percent casualties were not unusual in the Huertgen. It became known ultimately as the "Death Factory."

The First and Ninth U.S. Armies were seemingly bogged down in a grinding war of attrition. Patton's Third U.S. Army initially faced weaker opposition, but then the fighting stiffened. The weather worsened every day, and by the time the Americans reached the Roer and the Saar, the November drive ground to a halt. A determined enemy would yield no more.

The Germans were backed up against the border of their homeland. As a result, their own lines of supply were considerably shortened. The infamous *Siegfried Line* lay dead ahead and behind that, the formidable Rhine River. The western allies knew that they were in for a tough winter.

Chapter 2

The 740th on the Move
And FDR's Re-Election

On November 2, the 740th began to move across France, south to Carentan, then to Coutances, and on to Brécy, where they bivouacked that night in a muddy pasture. The ravages of war were everywhere.

The next day, they rolled through Sees and Chateauneuf to Maintenon, where Lt. Col. Rubel's advance party met the battalion with orders to join the United States First Army in far-off Aubel, Belgium. Next stop—Paris.

The sight of American troops moving toward the front still exhilarated the people of the newly liberated country. The French people lined the roads here and there to cheer on the tankers as their convoy of G.I. trucks trekked through the countryside, then rolled with a motorcycle escort into the outskirts of the Capital City. A thrill of excitement and anticipation swept through the battalion.

They set up camp on the eastern edge of Paris Saturday night, November 4, and hard times were forgotten for the moment as the tankers dreamed heroic dreams of victorious marches, barelegged mademoiselles, and tumultuous times to come. It was a hectic, sleepless night.

The battalion broke camp and moved northeast through Soissons and Laon, then into Hirson, where they bivouacked in another wet, muddy field. It had rained the entire day.

The next day brought more bad weather as they rumbled west through Rocroi, then northeast again into Belgium. The rain and cold had left the tankers depressed and dispirited, but spirits quickened as more and more of the villages and towns they pushed through had been noticeably shattered by bombs and gunfire. Suddenly, they began to see abandoned and shot-up enemy vehicles along the road or back in the trees. An exciting and sobering spectacle.

The battalion arrived at Aubel, Belgium, on November 6, and set up camp for the night in an apple orchard near Neufchateau. Just as they were getting settled in, a German V-1 flying bomb trailing orange flames roared a few hundred feet over their heads. Awestruck, they watched in horror as the motor cut out, and a nerve-wracking wait began for the pilotless craft to dive for the ground. Fortunately, the explosion came some minutes later, well past the encampment.

During a jittery night, they counted at least fifty more of the monsters as they roared overhead. Their best guess was that the rockets were headed for Liege or Antwerp, and that the 740th's bivouac was directly in the fly path. Devilish things. The tankers never knew when one of them would go wrong, turn, and dive right into their midst. It was something they had never really gotten used to. And it was their welcome to the war in Europe.

3. Photo credit: A/P Images

With its engine cut out, a German buzz bomb heads earthward.

"Damn!" exclaimed the President of the United States. First, he had trouble closing the curtains behind him in the new Hyde Park voting machine, and then he could barely read the local referenda from his wheelchair. The members of the press standing nearby were undoubtedly shocked at the profanity; the first lady certainly was. It was November 7, 1944—Election Day in the United States of America.

When he got home, he ordered everything readied for that evening—the dining room table laid out with pencils and tally sheets, a radio for The Associated Press, United Press news tickers, and a direct line to the Democratic National Headquarters in New York.

Later, a torchlight parade and band from the village made its way to the estate, and Roosevelt was wheeled out onto the porch to welcome them and say a few words. Then he was back with his tally sheets, checking the late returns. Finally, in the wee hours of the morning, Thomas E. Dewey, the Republican candidate, conceded.[1]

A man who could not walk was chosen by the American people to carry the flag for them in a worldwide war. F.D.R. had been elected to an unprecedented fourth term of the presidency.

Of the forty-eight states, he had won thirty-six. He had 25,602,505 of the popular vote to Dewey's 22,006,278, and he held 432 of the electoral votes to the Republican's 99. He immediately scribbled a telegram of congratulations to Harry S. Truman, who had been chosen at the last moment to replace Henry A. Wallace as vice president.[2]

Headlines told the story across the world. In an election extra, the November 8 edition of the G.I. newspaper, *The Stars and Stripes,* had a quarter-page picture of a broadly smiling President Roosevelt with the caption, "In War as in Peace—the Champ."

The men of the 740th were smiling too. Although it was just another cold and misty day in Belgium, they were pulling up stakes from the miserable conditions of the countryside and moving to billets in Neufchateau and in the neighboring village of Mortroux. The battalion was about halfway between Liege, Belgium, and Maastricht, Holland—a mile or so east of the Meuse River and just north of the Ardennes. The Ardennes, a somewhat mountainous and heavily forested area, was shortly to become the site of the fiercest battle of the war, and the 740th's baptism of fire.

Meanwhile, Lt. Col. Rubel was heading for First Army Headquarters in Spa, Belgium, about fifteen miles to the south. Once there, he found that there was no immediate assignment for the battalion, since there were no tanks available. It was there he learned that "Daredevil" was to be the battalion's code name.

Apparently, there were only thirty or forty medium tanks in the whole army reserve, and the best information was that it could possibly be the first of the year before any Shermans would be available to the battalion.

Rubel wasn't one to sit around waiting for something to happen, so he promoted the loan of a dozen tanks. At least the battalion could do some re-training, and practice firing and driving in the heavy mud with which they would be faced. They also had to reorganize as a standard tank battalion.

A light tank company had to be organized, and assault gun and mortar platoons formed. A number of officers and non-commissioned officers were sent to visit with the outfits on the prowl in the vicinity of Aachen, where they could get the feel of enemy fire and observe tank tactics on the front lines.

Written orders came shortly, relieving the battalion from their general assignment ETO and assigning the 740th to Lt. Gen. Omar Bradley's 12th Army Group, and specifically to Lt. Gen. Courtney Hodges' First U.S. Army. They were placed in army reserve, and their first combat was expected sometime after the first of the year. It seemed that an attack was to be launched in the spring where the battalion might be utilized, and they were tentatively attached to the 99th Infantry Division, which was then carrying on a holding action south of Monschau, Germany.

Not being involved in the fighting set Lt. Col. Rubel's teeth on edge, and except for the battalion's capture of an occasional enemy paratrooper, the relative quiet of the next couple of weeks wore on his nerves considerably. Finally, on December 14, he decided to pay the 99th a visit to find out first-hand what was going on. En route, he got sidetracked, and the upshot was that he ended up back in camp. Suddenly, things began to pop. Instructions awaited for the 740th's commander to report to the First U.S. Army Headquarters at Spa immediately, if not sooner.

Enemy patrols and activity were escalating. But First U.S. Army intelligence was not overly concerned. They were just taking precautions for what could've been a spoiling attack. The Germans were certainly in no shape to launch a major offensive, least of all through the Ardennes. They had taken quite a beating during the Fall Campaign, and the Allies were hoping for a winter slowdown so the supplies could catch up.

Of course, the Fall Campaign had been costly to the Americans as well. As November turned into December, and the winter snow and sleet descended on the action at the front, the First and Ninth U.S. Armies, fighting side by side, had lost 57,000 killed or wounded, and another 70,000 to battle fatigue and exposure to the wretched weather. Five hundred fifty tanks were lost in the First Army alone.[3]

Still, the Allies had by then liberated almost all of the territory that had been under German occupation, and there was talk back in the States that the war would be over by Christmas. The Germans appeared to be in real trouble. So how could enemy activity be escalating anywhere at the front?

The Soviet Union was looming dark and large in the east, with heavy fighting in the northern region, and a massing of its legions in German Group Center for a major winter offensive after the first of the year.

Although the British and Americans were somewhat stalled on the western front, General Eisenhower was counting on the just-opened port of Antwerp to inject new life into the Allied push.

Montgomery's 21st Army Group of British and Canadian armies was pressing for the *Siegfried Line* in the north. Bradley's 12th Army Group of three U.S. armies was in the center, and covered, by far, the most territory. Devers' 6th Army Group of one U.S. and one French army was nearly to the Rhine on Bradley's right flank, extending the "broad front" advance from the North Sea all the way south to Switzerland.

With General Eisenhower in agreement, Bradley had concentrated his forces in the north and south of the center sector, straddling the Ardennes —an eighty-mile front along the German/Belgian border. It was a calculated risk, stretching the American lines rather thinly through the Ardennes. Heavily forested and mountainous terrain made the region difficult for military purposes, and it was deemed a "quiet" sector, unlikely to draw enemy action.

North of the sector, Bradley had Lt. Gen. Simpson's Ninth U.S. Army covering Montgomery's right flank, above Aachen. Just south of Aachen, Lt. Gen. Hodges' First U.S. Army, still recovering from the bloody Huertgen Forest ordeal, was concentrating for an attack on the Roer dams, using the Ardennes as an R&R area for beleaguered or newly formed divisions. The Germans had been ostensibly utilizing the opposing area for the same purpose for some time. Below the Ardennes, Lt. Gen. Patton's Third Army was preparing to launch an attack against the Saar River.

All in all, the Allied High Command was feeling pretty good about the situation. All was quiet on the Western Front.

Then, all hell broke loose.

Chapter 3

Counteroffensive: In the Ardennes

Although Hitler found himself with astounding losses in both men and equipment, and backed up to his own border on all sides, he still had ten million troops in uniform. The draft was soon to be extended to 16- and 64-year-olds. And German industry, much of which was underground, was still at almost full production in spite of the Allied bombing.

In total secrecy, the German *Führer* had amassed his powerful forces for the breakthrough. Two Panzer armies of twenty-four divisions were poised and ready to strike out of the mist and fog of the Schnee Eifel—a heavily forested and protected area adjoining the Ardennes—with an additional army on each flank to take up the slack.

Bringing troops, tanks, and planes from the Eastern Front, Hitler increased his manpower in the west from 416,000 on December 1 to 1,322,000 on December 15.[1] His goal was to "go over to the counterattack" with such force as to overwhelm the few American divisions in the Ardennes, drive across the Meuse River, split the American and British forces, and re-capture Antwerp. Hitler believed that the western alliance was about to destroy itself anyway. It was evident that they couldn't get along because of their national pride and differing politics and philosophies. His powerful counteroffensive would be the decisive blow. The hated British and Americans were bound to sue for peace and then join Germany in its holy war against the Bolsheviks.

That dark Saturday morning broke bitterly cold in the Ardennes. The soldiers' breath frosted in the thick, wet air, and the trees of the dense forest hung heavily with snow. A six-inch blanket of white covered the forest floor, crunching underfoot in the early morning shadows. The chilling mist created ground fog so thick as to seem almost impenetrable to those who were awake. It was 5:30 a.m., December 16, 1944.

Up and down that sixty-mile "Ghost Front," from the quaint little community of Monschau on the German side of the Belgian border in the north, to the antiquated Luxembourg town of Echternach in the south, the Ardennes came alive.

At first, whistles in the distance alerted the American outposts that something unusual was happening. No real pressure for the last couple of months —a few patrols, a few snipers, an occasional burst of big gun fire, and only a few hundred casualties. And, of course, the weather took its toll —frostbite, trench foot, even pneumonia.

But suddenly, after the alert, pinpoints of fire flickered from afar, and the German heavy artillery opened up and came whistling in at the main points of attack. In the distance, the sky lit up like the Fourth of July from the explosions of nearly two thousand big guns —88s, rocket launchers, huge fourteen-inch railway monsters, even some V-1 buzz bombs. *Shriek! Crump! Zizzzz!* The ground literally shook from the thunderous fire. The ear-splitting noise was deafening, resonating through the forest.

In total disorder, the Americans came out of their sleeping bags and scrambled for whatever cover they could find, as huge holes exploded in the ground all around them —great splotches of black against the stark white of the snow. Few of the Americans, even the most experienced, had seen anything like this before. It was a devastating bombardment, seemingly from out of nowhere.

Huge, ugly black holes appeared suddenly where wide-eyed soldiers in sandbagged foxholes had been just moments before. Checkered bodies lay sprawled about, twisted and torn in a kind of grotesque abandon. A jeep turned topsy-turvy, its wheels spinning crazily in the air.

Some sleepy-eyed soldiers emerged from what was left of their liberated houses, struggling with their clothes and guns in an effort to find out what kind of hell had broken loose. Others just ran, desperately trying to escape. But jagged shell fragments, slicing through the trees and ricocheting wildly, caught too many of them in the open and hacked off an arm or a leg, or left them pinned helplessly against a wall or a tree. Up and down the line there was total disbelief —and literally no place to hide.

Finally, the thunderous artillery fire and the screech of the Nebelwerfers ended or moved on, and the German searchlights blinked on, reflecting off the low clouds and onto the snow, producing an eerie twilight effect.

Suddenly, the woods began to move right in front of the Americans' eyes. From out of the mist and fog, the Wehrmacht came, filtering through the shadows, and the mist and fog, in white camouflage and gray-green greatcoats and helmets. Two hundred thousand strong in the first assault alone. The odds against the Americans were nearly three to one all up and down the line, and six to one where the spearheads were concentrated.[2] The *burrrp* of the German rapid-fire machine guns and the sharp crack of their Mauser rifles were heard everywhere.

Then came the panzers. They were clanking in the distance at first, but were suddenly on top of the Americans before they could even react. Machine guns chattering. Cannons belching fire. Wide tracks cutting a jagged swath through brush and trees and snow, crushing everything in their way. The doughboys, frozen with fear, watched in cold sweat as their small arms fire zinged harmlessly off the German's protective armor. Those who could not jump and run fast enough screamed in horror as the huge tanks clambered up and over their foxholes. The wounded, if not quickly spotted and dragged to safety, simply froze to death within the hour.

Amid the devastation and panic at the front was a brigade of German soldiers dressed in American uniforms and equipped with captured American weapons and vehicles. They slipped through the lines to seize bridges and create havoc with sabotage and misinformation. Many of them spoke fluent English. The German operation, code-named *Operation Greif,* was commanded by *Obersturmbannführer* (Lt. Col.) Otto *Skorzeny.* Cutting telephone lines and switching signs as they went, one team succeeded in directing an entire U.S. regiment down the wrong road. Another, feigning terror and certain death up ahead, convinced a number of American tankers to back up and get the hell out of there. As luck would have it, one group managed to break off the cable link between Army Group headquarters in Luxembourg and First U.S. Army's command center in Spa, which was in danger of being overrun.[3]

Although the GIs caught on quickly and began to demand a lot of ID (along with a goodly knowledge of baseball, Mickey Mouse, and Betty Grable) from anyone they didn't recognize, the saboteurs did a lot of mischief behind the lines. Those who were caught red-handed in American uniforms were shot as spies.

Behind the lines, information was scary and scarce. The scuttlebutt drifting back was bad. There had been a massive breakthrough. The Germans were coming — and in great strength.

The 740th Tank Battalion was ordered to hand over the handful of medium tanks which had been assigned to them, and which they knew like the backs of their hands. These familiar Shermans were needed elsewhere — now! Rumors of bitter fighting in crushing force and coming their way ran helter-skelter through the battalion.

The next day, the situation grew even chancier, and Lt. Col. Rubel was informed that the battalion would probably have to fight with what it had — two 105mm assault guns and three M5-A1 light tanks. Tankers without vehicles would likely go into battle as infantry. This sent collective shivers up and down 740th spines.

Back at the front, the massive German juggernaut ground forward, literally crushing everything in its way. Overwhelmed, and with their communications cut, many isolated American units became confused and gave way. Here and there, individual and small group action hung tough in spite of the fierceness of the attack, but there was mostly slaughter and chaos up and down the line. The entire front was perilously close to collapse.

The Germans' main thrust exploded out of the Schnee Eifel at the Americans' weakest point — the Losheim Gap. Entire American regiments were outflanked or overrun on the first day of the onslaught.

To exploit the breakthrough of the German Sixth SS Panzer Army, *Kampfgruppe Peiper* was created to spearhead the attack. This regiment-sized task force included about half of the *Leibstandarte Adolf Hitler* 1st SS Panzer Division's armor, along with Panzergrenadier troops, engineers, and artillery in tow. *Obersturmbannführer* Joachim Peiper ("Jochen," as he preferred to be called) was a favorite of the Führer, and had been personally chosen by him to lead the Sixth SS Panzer Army's main attack. At the age of 29, young for his rank of Lieutenant Colonel, Peiper was widely recognized for his competence and leadership ability. He came to command in the Ardennes with significant combat experience in Russia, and a reputation for both ruthlessness and heroism in battle. He wore the Nazi's top award for valor — the Knight's Cross of the Iron Cross.

Sunday, December 17: Breaking out on the second day of the blitz, Peiper overran one small town after another, bypassing strong points and heading hell-bent for leather for the Meuse River. His massive column snaked for miles through the winding country roads. His tanks and troops took no prisoners, even shooting civilians who got in the way.

As the column clawed its way toward Malmedy, Peiper's troops ran headlong into a passing convoy of American field artillery observers at a little road junction at Baugnez. The atrocity that followed came to be known as the "Malmedy Massacre."

After shooting up the convoy, the Germans commandeered the vehicles that were not destroyed, and then disarmed some one hundred thirty survivors and crowded them together in a nearby field. In short order, shots rang out, and a number of the Americans fell. A couple of German tanks opened up with machine guns, and the helpless Americans screamed in horror and scattered in panic. No more than forty-six Americans were able to scramble to the safety of the forest, and many of them were wounded and blood-spattered, and several died. None of them would ever be the same. The slaughter was over in minutes. Still, the Germans were not through. They moved among the bodies in the field, kicking them in the head or groin to make sure they were dead. Those who cried out or moved or even moaned were shot at close quarters with pistols and rifles.

A few, face down in the mud or burrowed in beneath their buddies' bodies and literally afraid to breathe, lived on for a time. But only a heartbreaking few survived to tell the story.

The bloody few shivered and shook, and somehow managed to survive the target practice of the passing German tanks and troops for the next couple of hours, until they were finally able to drag themselves away in the darkness.

Numbers vary, but at least seventy-two American soldiers were slaughtered in the mud and slush of that field. Another fourteen were found frozen or dead in the snow nearby, although some of them may have been killed in the attack on the convoy.[4]

By this time, Peiper's armored columns were more than fifteen miles deep into the American lines and were headed for Stavelot and the Ambleve River. From there, the Meuse seemed vulnerable, and the roads to Antwerp were wide and clear. As the powerful *Kampfgruppe* ground forward, the German atrocities mounted. Word got around that Peiper's troops were executing American prisoners and murdering Belgian civilians who witnessed the killings.[5]

The chilling news of the German rampage through the Ardennes began to echo through the rear echelons the next day. Word was that the breakthrough was gaining momentum and that entire units had been completely overrun. Nothing much was known for certain because communication was completely impossible in so many places.

The men of the 740th were still billeted in the homes with the people of Neufchateau and Mortroux in the vicinity of the Meuse—and getting along famously. The Belgian citizens very much appreciated their newly won freedom and the safety provided by the presence of the Americans, and the GIs recognized the heartache and suffering their newfound friends had been through, and valued the warmth and acceptance of the citizenry.

Life for the 740th was about to change drastically. On December 18, orders flashed through from First U.S. Army headquarters and turned their citizen-soldier world upside down. The battalion was to field a reinforced company immediately. They were to move to the ordnance vehicle depot at Sprimont, Belgium, equip themselves with whatever combat vehicles were available, and advance to Aywaille. There, on the Ambleve River, just a few miles southwest of Spa, they were to take up defensive positions and slow the deadly German thrust.

Captain James D. Berry's C Company got the nod and prepared to move out. As the tankers climbed into their GI trucks, they couldn't help but wonder at the turn of events. They felt body-and-soul naked and afraid. Where was the armor with which they had trained? Those prized Sherman tanks that fit them like a glove, the ones they knew like the backs of their hands? The 75mm cannons that could tear out the side of a building hiding the enemy? The .30 caliber machine guns that would chop to splinters any place a sniper could secret himself? The 50s that could ravage all but the thickest German steel?

They were tankers. This was no way to go into battle. It was life and death against an enemy force so powerful that it was spreading panic up and down the front, and literally crushing everything that stood tall enough to get in its way. How could they be expected to fight like this?

4. Photo credit: From the files of Harry Miller

Le Château Regout at Aubin-Neufchateau, Belgium, in 1944. Headquarters of the 740th Tank Battalion before the tankers went into combat in the Battle of the Bulge. Raoul and Bernadette Regout owned the chateau at the time.

Word had just reached Ike that he had been promoted to five-star General of the Army, so he was all smiles when Lt. Gen. Bradley arrived at Supreme Headquarters Allied Expeditionary Force (SHAEF) in Versailles, France, the day that the Germans broke through. Bradley was there to press for some help with the acute shortage of infantry replacements at the front. Heavy casualties in the fall campaign had taken their toll on the foot soldiers, particularly riflemen, as had a terrible onslaught of trench foot in the ice and snow of early winter.

Later that day, they received word that the Germans were counterattacking in a number of different areas along the First U.S. Army's front, and their initial reaction was that it was just a spoiling attack to relieve First and Third Army pressure on the *West Wall.* Both men were concerned, but not overly so. Ike took the news more seriously than Bradley, but he still took time out to attend a wedding reception for his orderly who had married a WAC driver that morning. When he returned to his headquarters, they popped the cork on a bottle of champagne and sat down with some associates to play a few rubbers of bridge.[6]

As the evening wore on, however, the reports coming in to SHAEF became more alarming. Ike quickly became convinced that the situation was serious, that the German commander in the west, Field Marshall Gerd von Runstedt, had managed to mount a major attack through the Ardennes with what appeared to be at least three full armies. He and Bradley immediately set about to break off the American offensives above and below the "bulge." They turned the main strength of Hodges' First Army south, and Patton's Third Army north toward the center of the Ardennes, in order to hold the shoulders of the attack. They swung into action.

The XVIII Airborne Corps, in reserve and under the command of Major General Matthew B. Ridgway, was also thrust into the line at strategic crossroads—the 82nd Airborne Division at Werbomont, and the 101st Airborne Division at Bastogne. At the same time, the 30th "Old Hickory" Infantry Division was ordered down from the Ninth Army, elements of which were to go into the line as part of Ridgway's corps.[7]

With the 740th's C Company on the move by truck toward the ordnance depot at Sprimont to grab what armor they could find, Lt. Col. Rubel took off with his liaison officer for Aywaille on the Ambleve to report in and then scout out the area to be defended. He quickly learned that an armored task force was coming their way and was no more than a dozen miles away. As quickly as Company C could be equipped with combat vehicles, the company was to take up a defensive position at Remouchamps, just east of Aywaille.

The ordnance depot at Sprimont was sheer bedlam as the men of C Company worked desperately to make something to fight in from the leftover tanks they found there.

The depot was there to repair and make serviceable tanks lost in combat, and there were perhaps twenty-five tanks of different types in the depot. But only three were in any shape to fight. Fortunately, these three were M4 Shermans, medium tanks in which the tankers had trained. Unfortunately, even these were without essential equipment.

What was left in the pile ranged from M5 and M24 light tanks, to the old M7 and the open-topped M10 assault gun motor carriages, and even an M36 tank destroyer with the high-velocity 90 mm gun (which, strangely enough, turned out to be a blessing in disguise). They all had parts destroyed or missing—engines, starters, generators, breechblocks, wheels, tracks, radio transmitters, and receivers. None had combat loads of ammunition.

Throughout the night, the tankers spent miserable hours cannibalizing parts and pieces of one tank or vehicle to make another one work. It was demoralizing, backbreaking, heart-wrenching work, with absolutely no light at the end of the tunnel.

One medium tank crew worked frantically all night long making a light tank ready; a tank which they had never been in before and knew next to nothing about—not even how to drive or aim the gun. At the very last minute, several Shermans arrived from out of nowhere, and they grabbed one. Alleluia! There was life after death.

By this time, Lt. Col. Rubel had, on his own initiative, ordered the balance of the battalion to Sprimont, and there he established the Battalion Command Post. The battalion's Service Company took over the ordnance depot.

Although the tank situation was still pretty hopeless, a regular tank crew was assigned to any type of vehicle they felt they could get into action. However, so few of the vehicles had working radios that hand signals had to be utilized for communication and control once the battalion got under way.

The next morning, 25-year-old Captain James D. "Red" Berry, carrot-topped and full of pizzazz, shouted, "All right, let's move 'em out!" The untested young tankers of C Company rolled out in column in a ragtag gaggle of tanks and tank types and headed for Remouchamps, and thence to destiny in the Ambleve Valley.

Maj. Gen. Leland S. Hobbs, the 30th Infantry Division's commander, knew that things were bad and getting worse. Old Hickory was moving into the grinder. His 117th Infantry Regiment was headed for Stavelot, and his 120th for Malmedy. His 119th was to protect the U.S. First Army headquarters at Spa and move to block Kampfgruppe Peiper if the Germans came their way out of Stavelot.[8]

Still, Hobbs was unprepared for what he found in Spa on December 18 when he reported to Lt. Gen. Hodges, First Army commander. The situation was chaotic. Headquarters units were scrambling to pack files and equipment and preparing to fall back to Chaudfontaine, near Liege.

Peiper's armored columns, now no more than a dozen miles away, were loose behind the American lines and looking for bridges and gasoline. Moving quickly and bypassing resistance where he could, Peiper rumbled down into the Ambleve Valley that morning, broke through at Stavelot, quickly seized a bridge near Cheneaux, and then crossed the Ambleve. Beyond Trois Points, however, he was stymied as the bridge over Lienne Creek at Habiemont was blown. He had little choice but to backtrack to the north bank of the Ambleve, in the vicinity of La Gleize.

Already behind schedule, this would slow him even more. The road from La Gleize on through Stoumont twisted and turned along the river through the valley for at least ten miles before it broke out into the open at the Liege-Bastogne highway. The infantry would have to sweep the steep rise of the heavily forested hills on the other side of the road as the tanks moved forward. Dangerous work. Still, Peiper knew of a bridge beyond Stoumont —between the little village of Targnon and the railway stop at Stoumont Station. This would get him across the Ambleve and back on his way to Werbomont.[9]

Meanwhile, on orders from the 30th Infantry Division's General Hobbs, the 119th's commander, Colonel Edward M. Sutherland, diverted one of his battalions to Werbomont, to hold until the 82nd Airborne could get there, then plowed the rest of his regiment into the Ambleve Valley. They took up defensive positions at Stoumont and dug in.

That night, elements of the 119th began to probe in the direction of La Gleize. Patrols quickly spotted Germans out in the open one thousand yards away, with tanks in every direction near the Chateau de Froidcourt. Peiper had set up a command post in a nearby farmhouse, and it was here that the *Kampfgruppe* leader first learned about the massacre at the Baugnez crossroads near Malmedy. He also learned that the Americans were moving in behind him at Stavelot.[10]

He sent a panzer battalion to retake Stavelot, then turned his attention back to the job at hand—Stoumont. He wanted Stoumont and Targnon and the bridge beyond. He ordered a dawn attack.

Daylight came late that Tuesday morning, December 19, 1944. First light couldn't make its way into the dense forest until 7:00 a.m. A heavy mantle of frigid fog had infiltrated the whole of the Ambleve Valley.

At first, the 119th hung tough against the German onslaught. Their defensive tank support and a found bazooka stopped several tanks dead in their tracks, although the impenetrable fog made it difficult to distinguish friend from foe at any distance. The riflemen fought tenaciously against unremitting odds, and it appeared for the moment that they would throw the Germans back.

Peiper's heavy tanks, *SS Panzergrenadiers,* and paratroopers were only temporarily slowed by the stiff-backed American resistance. Peiper himself moved to the front to rally the full striking power of his force.

When the Germans began to pour into Stoumont, the completely overwhelmed elements of the 119th began to crack, then break—some in a hasty but ordered retreat, others in full flight. Entire companies were virtually wiped out.

The Americans pulled back in a fighting withdrawal, with German tank cannon and rifle fire kicking up dirt on their insides, and all around them. Their tanks were rapidly running out of ammunition.

Gradually, they fell back through Targnon, then down the hill to Stoumont Station. Near the station, a 90 mm anti-aircraft gun, with direct fire, blasted a German half-track and two tanks before the crew had to destroy their piece and abandon their position.

As reinforcements began to arrive and move forward, survivors of the front were withdrawing in long, battered lines on both sides of the road.

With significant elements of his 30th Infantry Division in a crisis, Maj. Gen. Hobbs asked Lt. Gen. Hodges for the 740th Tank Battalion, which he had learned was only a few miles away from Colonel Sutherland's 119th command post. General Hodges approved, and Hobbs immediately located the 740th's commander and personally assigned the 740th to the 119th Infantry Regiment.[11]

The 740th's Lt. Col. Rubel and his jeep driver, TEC 5 Larry C. Meyers, picked up sniper fire from the ridges as they raced along the Ambleve River to the 119th Infantry Regiment's CP. What Lt. Col. Rubel found was unnerving.

The enemy was almost upon them—only a few hundred yards away. The tank company from the 743rd Tank Battalion, which had been supporting the infantry, was pulling back, low on gas and ammunition. To add fuel to the fire, at least five German Panther tanks were reported to be on the road less than one thousand yards toward the front.

C Company's ragtag column of tanks clattered up to the Command Post, and Capt. Berry was briefed and ordered into the attack almost before the ground steadied under his feet. The 119th needed help now—before the infantry was completely overrun.

C Company's third platoon, commanded by 2nd Lt. (later 1st Lt.) Charles B. Powers, was to spearhead the attack up the road in column—with the first and second platoons following in order.

The commander of the 119th Infantry Regiment's First Battalion, Lieutenant Colonel Robert Herlong, was notified that the 740th Tank Battalion was coming in to help and was asked to attack abreast of the column of tanks as they came into position.

By this time, C Company was outfitted with a hodgepodge of M4 Sherman tanks, an assortment of M10 assault guns and Duplex-Drive (amphibious) Shermans, and at least one M36 tank destroyer with the big 90 mm gun. As the company rolled past the regimental command post where the staff was grinning out loud but shouting encouragement, Red Berry was heard saying, "They're bastard tanks, but we're shooting fools."[12]

Chapter 4

Into the Breach

A chilling, rain-drenched fog, and long lines of bedazzled, battle-scarred troops working their way wearily to the rear, slowed the column of tanks to a crawl as the 740th Tank Battalion moved toward the front.

"You're crazy to go up there!" a bandaged soldier cried out. Up and down the line: "They've broken through!" "It's a slaughter!" "It's a bloodbath!" "Those big bastard tanks are coming!"

Even as the 740th rolled forward, another company of American tanks was falling back, withdrawing from the fight. "We're low on ammo and fuel," one tanker shouted over the din. "It's holy hell up there, guys," called out another. "Good luck."

Gut check. This was it. The way it was going to be. It gnawed at their insides. And they began to sweat — in spite of the bitter cold.

Sergeant William H. Fagg's crew spotted the first enemy tank. The luck of the draw during that all-night fiasco at Sprimont had left them in an M10 tank, or "Gun Motor Carriage," as it was officially known. The only problem was that neither Fagg nor any of his crew had ever been in an M10 before. It had an open top turret, a short-barreled, three-inch howitzer cannon for high-angle firing at low velocity, and no hull machine gun.

Private First Class C.B. Seay[1] was designated bow gunner in Fagg's crew of five, but with no hull machine gun to man, Seay found himself odd man out, standing with Fagg that day in the open turret of that M10.

Seay spotted the German tank in the field to their right. "That's not one of ours!" he shouted. The crew struggled to bring their unfamiliar big gun around to fire when Fagg accidentally hung his hand in the breech of the cannon and was seriously injured.

Seay said the tragic thing about what happened is that it was all a false alarm. That enemy tank wasn't even manned. Abandoned in the field to die alone, he guessed. The wounded Fagg was evacuated and the crew sent to the rear to be reassigned.

Meanwhile, Second Lieutenant Charles B. Powers, C Company's Third Platoon leader, in an M4 Sherman tank, led his platoon around the stalled tank.

The column moved on, passing a second dead German tank just up the road to the right.

When the column reached the front and moved on line, the 119th Regiment's First Infantry Battalion began to filter into the forest abreast of the tanks, then spread out in a staggered line on both sides of the narrow, twisting road which paralleled the Ambleve River.

In the forest, dense with giant Christmas trees, the infantry would leapfrog forward as the tanks advanced slowly down the road. The infantrymen must have considered the ragtag column of tanks rather strange—so many different kinds of tanks, and no uniform markings. Still, all that armor buoyed their spirits and gave them new heart. Maybe they could turn this thing around.

Lt. Powers had great respect for the heavier armor and greater firepower of the enemy's tanks. His own 75 mm cannon was loaded with an armor piercing shell, and he figured a lucky first shot might give him a chance up close against a Panther. He knew they were in trouble if they ran head-on into one of the Tiger tanks, with its massive armor and powerful 88mm gun.

Dusk came early in the winter in the Ardennes. And the gloom and fog of late afternoon played tricks with his eyes. He had his driver work the cliff side of the road, and he prayed for the first shot.

Just short of Stoumont Station, both Powers and Technician Fifth Grade Harold L. Henry,[2] the loader, were standing, heads out of their turret hatches, eyes peeled for the first sign of trouble. Suddenly, the brush pile at the side of the road that Henry had been watching suspiciously materialized out of the fog. Gesturing excitedly, he shouted at Powers, "An enemy tank!"

Powers estimated the distance at 150 yards, put his gunner, Corporal Jack D. Ashby, on target, and called "Fire!" But Ashby's shot was already on the way. It struck the German's gun mantlet, ricocheted downward—a lucky strike considering the Panther's thick armor—and the German tank exploded and burst into flames. Henry dropped down to reload.

Within minutes, Powers spotted another tank deep in the fog, and again Ashby got off the first shot. The round struck the German's heavily armored front slope plate, ricocheted up, and spun crazily away in a shower of sparks. Ashby's gun jammed.

Frantically, Powers signaled his No. 2 tank, commanded by Staff Sergeant (later Second Lieutenant) Charlie W. Loopey, to move up.

Loopey and his crew were in an M36 tank destroyer with the 90 mm gun. Corporal William H. Beckham was his gunner.

Years later, when he was asked about that moment, Loopey said, "That German was moving forward trying to get into position to shoot. I called Beckham for an AP [armor piercing shell], HE [high-explosive shell]. Hell, anything! Whatever you've got in there!

5. Illustration from the files of Harry Miller

While on a train stopped at Stoumont Railway Station in the summer of 1946, a Belgian drew a depiction of what he saw as a result of the first action by the 740th Tank Battalion, in which three German tanks were knocked out in the Battle of the Bulge.

"Our first round hit him in the gun shield and kept him from getting down on us. We threw in several more rounds and blew a hole in his front left edge down low. Sparks flew, and flames shot up twenty-five feet in the air!"[3]

Back in Powers' tank, TEC 5 Henry had climbed out of the tank, screwing the two pieces of his rammer staff together as he ran to the front of the tank. Standing in front of the cannon, he pushed the wooden staff into the gun tube, then punched and shoved until the stuck round broke loose and backed out of the breech—a gut-check maneuver in the heat of battle.

With his cannon cleared, Powers then resumed the lead, only to face a third Panther tank on the opposite side of the road. Gunner Ashby's first shot miraculously blasted the muzzle brake of the German's cannon. He kept firing as the tank tried to back away, finally setting the German on fire.[4]

The 740th Tank Battalion was right smack dab in the middle of the war. Together with the 119th Infantry's First Battalion, they continued the attack into darkness and blunted the main thrust of Hitler's 1st SS Panzer Division's Kampfgruppe Peiper, gaining back over one thousand yards of bitterly contested front given up earlier that day. They held the line that night at Stoumont Station, most of them sleeping as best as they could in their tanks. This was the first good news to emerge from the Battle of the Ardennes up to that time, according to Col. Rubel.[5]

Part II

The 740th was born on March 1, 1943. The battalion took its basic training at Fort Knox, Kentucky. Six months later, the tankers were chosen to participate in a secret project in the Desert Training Center known as the Special Training Group, or "STG." They cleared the Arizona training camp in April 1944, and returned to Fort Knox en route to England, to coordinate their special project with the British.

After eleven days in convoy across the Atlantic Ocean, the battalion docked at Liverpool, England, on August 6, 1944. The tankers began to see the horrors of war and to appreciate the spirit and determination of the British people.

Inexplicably, it was learned that the special project might never be utilized, and the 740th was converted to a standard tank battalion. The tankers crossed the English Channel aboard two LSTs on October 30, 1944, but the passage was rough and two days in the making. It was not until November 1 that they emerged from the choppy seas and onto Utah Beach in their GI trucks.

Neither tanks nor orders awaited them in Normandy, so they set off for ETO headquarters in Paris in search of the war. There, they learned that the war was approaching the West Wall of Germany, and they began an arduous and emotional trek across France and into Belgium. It was November 6, 1944, and the war was at hand.

Chapter 5

The 740th Comes Alive

In his book, *Daredevil Tankers,* published in Germany just a few months after the end of the war in 1945, Lt. Col. Rubel says with pride, "Out in the great Southwest, in Texas and Oklahoma, the cry had gone out for volunteers for the Armored Force. The Army wanted men who could ride hard and shoot straight."[1]

He went on to say that "Young men in school laid down their books —on the farms marched the old gray mare into the barn and hung the harness up on the hook—from the cities sold their Model A's to their friends, and the trek to Fort Knox was on."[2]

Most of the proud, young men of the 740th who survived had to chuckle when they read that. Those were patriotic times. Still, not all of them remember their "trek to Fort Knox" in the same effusive terms Lt. Col. Rubel describes in his book.

America was in a terrible war on two fronts: in Europe and in the Pacific. There was no doubt about that, and there was no doubt about who the bad guys were and what they were trying to do.

A Gallup poll of Americans aged 16 to 24, published in the October 1940 Reader's Digest, found that America's youth was "loyal and hopeful," and believed that the country was "worth working and fighting for." Further, the survey found that young people had "faith in the future" and were "not radical," but were "surprisingly conservative in their views."[3]

Every American knew that there were sacrifices to be made. And most young men those days stood ready to do their duty. There were a lot of volunteers. Still, it was an awful war —a killing war, and a mostly unknown war to many young 18- and 19-year-olds. The fact was that most young men those days waited for the mail to bring "Greetings" before deciding when to go to war.

The draft became effective with the passage of the Burke-Wadsworth law, known as the Selective Service Act of 1940. Some fifty million men between the ages of 18 and 64 eventually registered with Selective Service before the war finally ended. Registration had been an intermittent process up until 1942, at which time all young men were required to register when they became 18. Very few failed to register, and those mostly because of pacifist beliefs. However, some interesting situations developed when some Indian tribes boycotted the registration process, saying that they were still technically at war with the U.S. and/or simply refusing to obey U.S. laws.[4]

Resistance to the Selective Service Act was rare and was turned over to the FBI. Penalties for violations ranged from a ten thousand dollar fine to five years in prison, and the general public firmly supported the government's stand on this. Sixty-five hundred local draft boards across the country decided who would be called up and who would not. Decisions were made depending on the various services' needs, individual physical and mental qualifications, and civilian occupation. Young men working in agriculture and defense plants were often deferred. Marriage and fatherhood were given special consideration. And although the armed services were segregated at the time, the number of African-Americans called each month could not be greater than 10.6% — their proportion of the overall population. Approximately one third of draft age men of all groups and distinctions were classified "IV-F," or unfit for military service.[5]

Typical of the young men going into the army at that time, a group came from the vicinity of Wichita Falls, Texas — a number of whom were to become future *Daredevil Tankers* of the 740th. They stood in line in the early morning darkness of a cold February morning in 1943, waiting to be transported by bus to the Armed Forces Induction Station in Abilene, Texas.

Induction into the U.S. Army was a one-day affair for them, and a thorough physical examination was the order of the day. It was a sobering experience. The men waited naked in line for everything. Sometimes they were standing upright, sometimes they were seated, and oftentimes, they were bent over. They were felt of, poked, prodded by cold hands and instruments, and seemingly embarrassed in every conceivable way. Many of the inductees were so intimidated by the process that doctors learned to accept rapid or irregular heartbeat as a sign of the times. Not to mention the unceremonious psychological screenings, with psychiatrists who long ago discovered the distinct advantages of interviewing men who stood naked before them.

Most of the men were determined to be both physically and mentally fit for "general service," although a number were not. Those who passed the examinations were proud and relieved. And not a little scared.

Their fingerprints were taken to be compared with the FBI files. Then they lined up for pre-assignment interviews, which gave them a chance to request a preference for type of service. Not many of them even knew what a tank was at the time, and the Air Force proved to be among the most popular choices. The infantry was not popular at all.

RECRUITING AND INDUCTION STATION,
Masonic Lodge Bldg.,
Abilene, Texas.

N O T I C E

You are now a soldier in the Army of the United States!
Congratulations! At your request you have been transferred to
the Enlisted Reserve Corps for seven days. You are directed to
report at the Reception Center in accordance with orders received
by you. If you have not received a notice from your Local Board
telling you of the hour and place of assembly at least forty eight
hours in advance of the date shown on your orders, contact your
Local Board immediately. Strict compliance with these instructions
is required.

B A G G A G E

After your arrival at the Reception Center you will be issued
a complete set of toilet articles, including shaving equipment,
tooth-brush and comb, and all necessary items of clothing. It is
essential that you refrain from taking extra civilian clothing,
hand luggage, trunks, radios, etc., to the Reception Center due to
the limited facilities for checking and safeguarding them. Cooperate
by taking with you only small articles which can be carried in your
pockets.

For the Recruiting and Induction Officer:

CLAUDE PARHAM,
1st Lt., A.G.D.
Adjutant.

6. Author's collection

Notice received in February 1943, by a Wichita Falls, Texas, inductee, who was assigned to the original organization of the 740th Tank Battalion at Fort Knox, Kentucky.

ARMED FORCES INDUCTION STATION
MASONIC LODGE BUILDING

SPECIAL ORDERS: Abilene, Texas.

NO.   43:   - E X T R A C T -   February 19, 1943.

X   X   X

3. Each of the following named enlisted men, inducted into the Army of the United States, this station, this date, is released from active duty this date, is transferred to the Enlisted Reserve Corps and will proceed to Wichita Falls, Texas. (Local Board No. 1.)

APPOINTED ACTING CORPORAL: Holman, Frank G.   38,371,458

Richison, James E.	38,371,404	Pratt, Kenneth N.	38,371,495
Morris, Willie F., Jr.,	38,371,428	Roberts, Warner J.	38,371,427
Morris, Calvin H.	38,371,425	Lanier, Essie N.	38,371,424
Kingsworthy, Mack C.	38,371,431	Jones, Tom P.	38,371,432
Hankins, Manuel P.	38,371,430	McLendon, Theodosus E.	38,371,434
Vandervort, Jack W.	38,371,435	Carver, Johnny E.	38,371,440
Greer, Joe B.	38,371,441	Hamilton, Garland W.	38,371,442
Davenport, Allie M., Jr.	38,371,443	Stout, Walter E.	38,371,429
Wilson, Lloyd T.	38,371,445	Pearson, Paul L.	38,371,446
Anderson, Henry L., Jr.	38,371,450	Sellers, Joseph B.	38,371,449
Clents, Don E.	38,371,448	Kirkpatrick, Jay D.	38,371,451
Cooper, Clarence D.	38,371,452	Scott, James C.	38,371,453
Schulz, Robert M.	38,371,457	Stonegol, Walter D.	38,371,456
Simons, Orion W.	38,371,455	Gillen, Carl F.	38,371,454
Derby, Lester E., Jr.,	38,371,459	Van Devonter, Floyd H.	38,371,460
Garrett, Walter T., Jr.	38,371,464	Moyer, Charles H.	38,371,463
Flowers, William E.	38,371,462	Roe, Clarence O.	38,371,461
Watson, Arvil A.	38,371,465	Lyles, Jack W.	38,371,466
Kilgore, Richard G.	38,371,467	Cox, Jack L.	38,371,471
High, John S.	38,371,474	Bassett, William C.	38,371,475
Roe, James W.	38,371,476	Smiley, George E.	38,371,478
Gibbons, Odis A.	38,371,479	Russell, Harry J.	38,371,480
Garrett, Walter E.	38,371,483	Ralch, Olen L.	38,371,497
Holcomb, Ira P., Jr.	38,371,498	Pink, John R.	38,371,507
Bumpers, Robert L.	38,371,512	Pearson, Jim B.	38,371,517
McCammon, Othe L.	38,371,516	Pratt, Aaron B.	38,371,515
Ritchie, Billie G.	38,371,514	Long, James R.	38,371,515
Basler, Cecill W.	38,371,519	Jobe, Wayne P.	38,371,521
Horry, Harold L.	38,371,522	Moore, Jack	38,371,523
Lynch, Thomas C.	38,371,520	Holt, Virgil F.	38,371,518
Voyles, Loyd M.	38,371,525	Woelder, Carl J., Jr.	38,371,524

Effective February 26, 1943, each of the above named enlisted men of the Enlisted Reserve Corps is called to active duty and will proceed from Wichita Falls, Texas to Camp Wolters, Texas, reporting upon arrival thereat to the Reception Center.

TC will furnish the necessary T & MX. TDN. FD 31 P 431-02 A 0425-23.

X   X   X

FLOYD S. WORTH,
Major, Cavalry,
Recruiting & Induction Officer.

Transportation furnished on this order to Frank G. Holman & 62 others from Abilene, Texas to Wichita Falls, Texas via SOUTHWEST COACHES on T/R WQ-8,388,459 and from Wichita Falls, Texas to Camp Wolters, Texas via BOWEN MOTOR COACHES on T/R WQ-8,368,670 and AMT No. 3068551 furnished for 1 meal each for 63 men. Chargeable to FD 31 P 431-02 A 0425-23.

ORBIN G. BOOTH,
1st. Lt., F. ...

7. Author's collection

Special Orders received in February 1943, by this group of inductees from Wichita Falls, Texas—a number of whom were assigned to and served together in the 740th Tank Battalion.

Ultimately, they put their names to their induction papers and were assigned army serial numbers, which they can still recite to this day. At the end, and with a certain amount of ceremony, they gathered together, and an officer of the army administered the oath.

With their official business done, the new soldiers boarded the bus for home and a seven-day leave before reporting to their respective reception centers. They were in the army now. They had the papers to prove it.

And so it was that these young *"Citizen Soldiers"* had a week's furlough to go home, get their affairs in order, and say their real good-byes. For the most part, it was a time of heartache, and rather frightening to leave behind family and friends, and more often than not, that special girl. They were unsure of their fate. Their very lives in the balance.

When the time came and their names were called, with only the clothes on their backs, they loaded onto the bus. The group from Wichita Falls, and most other Texans, were taken to the Reception Center at Camp Wolters, Texas, and the Oklahomans to Fort Sill, Oklahoma.

There, they learned the true meaning of "hurry up and wait." Again, they stood in line for more physicals—shots in the left arm, shots in the right arm, shots in the right buttocks, shots in the . . . . And they were square needles. They *had* to be. When a man fainted, they took him away, presumably to the end of the line so he would have sufficient time to recover before coming up again.

Then they stood in line to get their uniforms. Some of the uniforms fit, but whether they did or didn't, those young men were so proud in those new uniforms. They were soldiers now.

They stood in line for daily assignments. "Awright, you'se guys," cried the grizzled old sergeant, far too early in the morning. "Fall out chere! I wan yuh to line up like two rows of corn—a hoe handle apart!" Then later, "Awright, I wan all you'se college boys to take one step forward!" That was the last time anyone ever did that again. They stood in line for calisthenics. Stood in line for short-arm inspections. Stood in line for "chow." Stood in line to get a 3.2 beer at the Post Exchange—or "PX," as it was called.

They learned of the U.S. Army tradition, the Articles of War, military courtesy, and close-order drill. They had interviews and took aptitude tests and the Army General Classification Test—all of which were designed to help them find their logical places in the army, but which, in point of fact, seemed to have more to do with army needs than individual background, experience, or aptitude. Misplacements and wrong-minded assignments were legendary at the time. One notable example in army lore was the banker who became a baker, due to a typing error. And once posted in a slot, it was tough to get out. In his book, *G.I.: The American Soldier in World War II,* Lee Kennett found that the 4th Armored Division's quota of selectees in 1941 included a unique collection of future tankers:

"—five keypunch operators, seven airline pilots, two parachute mechanics, an optometrist, and an X-ray technician." Only the five keypunch operators were released.[6]

Still, the men from the Reception Centers at Camp Wolters, Texas, and Fort Sill, Oklahoma, who were selected for the 740th Tank Battalion, didn't know or care about all that. During the first week in March, they were on their way to the Armored Training Center at Fort Knox, Kentucky, just south of Louisville.

As their troop train chugged and whistled across the countryside, people waved and shouted encouragement. Although the ride was slow and long and tiring, it was strangely exhilarating. Whenever the train would stop at a crossing, or in a town, and the troops would unload for a break, a crowd would gather. They were immensely proud.

On February 27, 1943, an advance cadre of officers and non-commissioned officers from the 7th Armored Division, North Camp Polk, Louisiana, arrived at Fort Knox to organize the new tank battalion. Their commanding officer was Major Harry C. Anderson from the 9th Armored Division, Camp Campbell, Kentucky.

Battalion S1 was 1st Lt. Cecil J. Wright; S2-S3, Capt. Roy D. Vinson; S3-Air, Capt. Harry A. Greer; S4, Capt. L.A. Williams, Jr.; Personnel Officer, 1st Lt. Myron C. Prevatt; Motor officer, 1st Lt. Willis B. Chapman; HQ. Co. Commander, 1st Lt. Motte G. Sheppard; A Co. Commander, Capt. Graddy H. Floyd; B Co. Commander, 1st. Lt. Thomas V. Neidhamer; C Co. Commander, 2nd Lt. James D. Berry; and Sv. Co. Commander, 2nd Lt. William S. Palmer. Other officers added during the second week in March came from Classes 23, 24, and 26 of the Fort Knox Officers' Candidate School.[7]

The 740th Tank Battalion (Medium) was officially activated March 1, 1943. When the troop train arrived on March 7, the men were met and taken to their quarters just in time to see one of their barracks go up in flames. The area assigned to the battalion turned out to be the old obsolete wooden buildings located between 1st and 2nd Avenues and between 21st and 24th Streets. The barracks were two-story affairs, all the same handsome color: badly weathered gray. Latrines had coal stoves and rows of too few toilets, lavatories, and showerheads — all with zero privacy. This arrangement, along with a mess hall, supply and classrooms, and a headquarters unit, quickly became home away from home for them—with similar units for more than fifty thousand other troops. The huge armored training camp was to them like a city, with a fire department and police force and its own transportation, water, and sewerage systems. There were movie theaters, Post Exchanges, and 3.2 beer for the Sundays off. The only problem was that everything looked alike—from building to building, corner to corner, and street to street in all directions—and the new tankers often got lost if they wandered far from their own bailiwick.

On March 15, basic training began. Their working days were always crammed full and stretched from fourteen to sixteen hours. Physical training hardened their young bodies—calisthenics, drill, marches, obstacle courses, and bivouacs. Classroom subjects expanded their youthful horizons—the war and its purpose and progress, the organization of the army, as well as the usual military discipline and Articles of War. Of course, instruction included sanitation, first aid, and sex hygiene, of course, in such graphic detail it left them gagging at times.

It was quite a while before they even saw a tank. Soldiering in general always seemed to be the main topic of the day—guns and equipment, tent pitching, map reading, camouflage, chemical defense, mines, booby traps, and airplane identification, to name but a few. Inspections and guard duty usually rounded out the weekly routine, with a little KP here and there.

Mail call was a high point of every day, when the letters and packages from home were handed out. Although exhausted and falling asleep at the end of the day, most of the young men still regularly wrote home, or to their best girl or wife. However, only a minority was married. Soldiering took its toll on marriage. Not all letters were happy ones. There were always a few "Dear John" letters. And once in a while, "I'm sorry to tell you that your father has passed away." Still, mail call was always a high point, and it was a lonesome and homesick young man who turned away empty-handed.

There was time off, of course. A nearby Service Club offered indoor games and a lot of ping-pong, as well as a reading library and weekend dances, well-chaperoned of course. And after-hours poker and crap games were a wonder to behold, with piles of money stacked a foot high.

After a time, there were weekend passes to the world beyond the gates of the camp, into the nearby metropolis of Louisville, where the young tankers could let off steam. And they often did. There were some tumultuous times together in town.

Interestingly enough, they hung together. A 740th man was seldom found alone anymore. By now, most of them had formed a close friendship with a buddy or two—guys they believed in, could confide in, and trust. Real life, in the raw. They shared experiences. They were beginning to come together. They could cuss the army among themselves. But outsiders beware—these guys stood ready to defend their buddies and their outfit with their lives, their liberty, and their pursuit of happiness.

The days turned into weeks, and on May 3, the battalion began driving instruction. Two companies at a time moved into bivouac in Area 19, near West Point, Kentucky. Each man learned how to drive all of the different wheeled and tracked vehicles common to the tank battalion: the quarter-ton 4 x 4 utility truck (the Jeep, or "peep" as it was called in the Armored Force), the GMC two-and-one-half ton truck known as the "Deuce and a Half," the M3 half-track, and the General Sherman M4AI medium tank with a cast one-piece hull, a power-operated turret, and a 75 mm main gun.

"Weather was bad, being very cold and rainy, with some snow."[8] This left mud and slush in every direction, including the pyramidal tents in which the men lived. It was an exciting but miserable time. Meanwhile, the tankers were being placed in their "Table of Organization" jobs.

Until May 12, the 740th had been assigned to "Special Troops," Armored Force, but then the battalion was assigned to the 8th Tank Group, under command of Colonel Fay D. Smith.[9] For the next five weeks, "basic" training involved the organization of the battalion, some familiarization with the differing "jobs" in the battalion, the nomenclature and function of the various weapons to be utilized, and the several echelons of maintenance.

On June 14, "unit" training began, starting with a four-day period on the strategies of "maneuvering" tanks in the field, followed by tank "tactics" by companies. On July 5, the entire battalion was subjected to a simulated gas attack from the air. From July 12 to August 7, the battalion learned to shoot the .45 caliber Colt semi-automatic pistol and the Thompson sub-machine gun. Tank crews fired their 75 mm cannons and .30 caliber coaxial machine guns.

While the tankers were learning to shoot, however, big things were brewing for them in the nation's capital. By direct authority of the War Department, the 740th was to be furloughed from August 7 to August 30, half the battalion at a time, in preparation for some very specialized training.[10]

Unknown to the young tankers, their battalion had been selected to participate in one of the U.S. Army's most closely guarded war secrets.

Chapter 6

On the Home Front

As their furloughs came through and the young tankers packed their duffel bags for the long train ride home, they knew things would be different, but they were totally unprepared for what they found when they got there.

A number of homes in many of their cities and towns had gold stars in the windows. War was evident everywhere, as America's industrial might had turned from civilian to military production. There were shortages of all kinds and rationing of consumer goods such as gas, tires, bacon, butter, sugar, coffee, and canned food. People haunted the grocery stores, hoping a shipment of meat would come in, and there were often lines and long waits at restaurants for food of lesser quality and service. Almost everyone had a "Victory Garden." And, of course, daily home delivery of milk and dairy products was a thing of the past.

There were community and nationwide scrap drives for metal, rubber, and other scarce commodities. Natural rubber was in especially short supply as a result of Japanese conquests in the Far East a year earlier. Anything made of metal was scarce or impossible for the civilian population to get —new cars, refrigerators, stoves, lawn mowers, coffee pots, flashlights, batteries, and the like. Even phonographs and radios went out of production. And civilian clothing and shoes became harder to find, as more and more wool and leather were demanded by the military.

Still, most people had money jingling in their pockets. Because of the burgeoning defense industry, everyone who wanted to work had a job. Production for civilian use was generally so scarce, however, that the Office of Civilian Defense felt it necessary to appeal to Americans to not buy anything that wasn't absolutely necessary, stating that this would help to win the war. An advertisement in Time Magazine listed "Ways to put your home on a wartime basis," and said that "Thousands have signed the U.S. Government's Consumer Pledge to do these three things: (1) Buy carefully. (2) Take care of the things you have. (3) Waste nothing."[1]

Widespread patriotism was in the air. Being involved in Civil Defense (which had some 10,000,000 volunteers across the nation[2]), and buying War Bonds were the orders of the day. Signboards that said "Uncle Sam wants you!" and "Loose lips sink ships!" were on every corner. Even Hollywood got into the act. "Casablanca" won the academy award for best picture, and Paul Lucas was best actor for his performance in "Watch on the Rhine."

UNITED STATES OF AMERICA
OFFICE OF PRICE ADMINISTRATION

WAR RATION BOOK No. 3 Void if altered

NOT VALID WITHOUT STAMP

Identification of person to whom issued: PRINT IN FULL

(First name)   (Middle name)   (Last name)

Street number or rural route

City or post office _____ State _____

AGE	SEX	WEIGHT Lbs.	HEIGHT Ft. In.	OCCUPATION

SIGNATURE
(Person to whom book is issued. If such person is unable to sign because of age or incapacity, another may sign in his behalf.)

WARNING
This book is the property of the United States Government. It is unlawful to sell it to any other person, or to use it or permit anyone else to use it, except to obtain rationed goods in accordance with regulations of the Office of Price Administration. Any person who finds a lost War Ration Book must return it to the War Price and Rationing Board which issued it. Persons who violate rationing regulations are subject to $10,000 fine or imprisonment, or both.

OPA Form No. R-130

LOCAL BOARD ACTION

Issued by _____
(Local board number)   (Date)

Street address _____

City _____ State _____

(Signature of issuing officer)

8. Author's collection
War Ration Book issued to Texans in 1943

Newspapers, magazines, and books all did their part to inspire and bring the people together. Even some of the comic strip characters were in uniform by then.

Golf's U.S. Open was canceled that summer, and "Lucky Strike Green" went to war, as did silk and the new-fangled nylon.

Thus, the girls' legs were bare by the time the 740th's tankers got home on furlough in August of 1943. Of course, they didn't mind the bare legs that much. But Lucky Strike in a white package? Well, that was taking the war business a little too far.

Love and friends and family took on a whole new meaning in the short time they were home. Obviously, times had changed. They had changed. Now, they were soldiers. They had a job to do. Still, parting was not any easier than it had been before. It was, in fact, much harder now. But they were young, and there were enough hugs and kisses to go around, and suddenly they were on their way.

READ BEFORE USING 5-POUND
HOME CANNING SUGAR
COUPONS

Before the attached coupons are used for the purchase of sugar for home canning, you or any member of your "family unit" listed on the application must use each home canning coupon (OPA Form R-315). The person signing must enter the serial number of his War Ration Book Four thereon.

For the purpose of identification, it will be necessary for the signer to take his War Ration Book Four with him when he purchases the sugar.

These coupons are not transferable.

Applicant will print or type below his full name and complete mailing address

NAME Mrs Jerome K. Estes

ADDRESS 1909 Speedway

CITY, POSTAL ZONE, STATE Wichita Falls, Texas

(Do not detach)

WE MUST GET ALONG WITH LESS SUGAR THIS YEAR BECAUSE—

1. Military needs are high. Each soldier actually consumes twice as much sugar a year as the average civilian now receives.
2. Ships which otherwise might be bringing sugar into the United States are hauling supplies to the battle fronts.
3. Manpower is scarce at sugar refineries and shipping ports.
4. Beet sugar production last year was 500,000 tons short, making the stock of sugar smaller for this year.
5. Last year many people over-applied for canning sugar. We used so much sugar that stocks at the beginning of this year were abnormally low.

DO NOT APPLY FOR MORE SUGAR THAN YOU ACTUALLY NEED FOR HOME CANNING — HELP MAKE OUR WAR SHORT SUGAR SUPPLIES LAST ALL YEAR

9. Author's collection

Notice regarding sugar ration coupons

Chapter 7

Special Training Group

Everyone at Fort Knox knew that some kind of secret project was going on at "Area X." It had been the subject of countless rumors and a lot of speculation throughout the 740th ever since the men had returned from furlough. Until, on September 7, 1943, the battalion picked up stakes and moved there.

Three days later, the battalion was relieved from the 8th Tank Group and assigned to Special Training Group, Armored Command.[1] Area X was a bivouac site on the Reservation near Lebanon Junction and Hays School.

"In a hush-hush meeting, the Battalion learned that [its] name had been changed to 740th Tank Battalion [Medium] [Special], and right there everyone held up [his] right hand, took the oath of secrecy, signed a book, and then heard the details of the project."[2]

They learned that they were part of a secret project called the Special Training Group, or "STG." The instructors outlined plans for the project and stressed the importance of utter secrecy. There were demonstrations in the use of the special equipment to be utilized, and technical classes began almost immediately.

There was to be ironclad security, and nobody from then on was allowed to leave Area X for any reason. This order was a shocker for most of the men — especially those who were married and had families living nearby.

They had their own PX and an open-air theater. Such amenities somewhat eased their healthy desire to go into Louisville. But there was to be no female companionship.

However, the strategy behind STG was unique. Theoretically, it could revolutionize tank warfare, and the men generally were excited about being involved and about the potential of the project. They studied, practiced, and worked morning, noon, and night. But it was all technical. They could hardly wait to get into the field to test the theory.

All the while, big things were awaiting the 740th Tank Battalion in the Arizona Desert. Preparations were being made to put the secret project's theories into practice.

In early 1942, Maj. Gen. George S. Patton was ordered by the War Department to organize a Desert Training Center to prepare American troops for the invasion of North Africa. The huge installation began to take shape in southeastern California's Mojave Desert—a remote expanse of blistering sand and cactus scrub, where the temperatures were always extreme, from below freezing in the dead of winter to 120 degrees in the shade in the summer. Still, from Patton's point of view, it was perfect. It would toughen the troops for what lay ahead.

Patton commanded the training center in its first few months, then left to help General Eisenhower with "Operation Torch," the allied invasion of German-held North Africa later that year.

The training center quickly expanded into Arizona and eventually covered an area from Pomona, California, to Phoenix, Arizona, and from Yuma, Arizona, to Boulder City, Nevada—87,500 square miles. In time, it became the world's largest military installation and was known as the California-Arizona Maneuver Area, or CAMA.[3]

Camps with such names as Iron Mountain, Granite, Essex, Ibis, Hyder, Horn, Laguna, Pilot Knob, and Bouse trained nearly a million American servicemen and women in massive tent cities, complete with tanks, maintenance, hospitals, aviation complexes, anti-aircraft and field artillery units, scorpions, tarantulas, and rattlesnakes.

Sand was everywhere. The tankers could taste it in their food, watch it settle to the bottom of their mess cups, feel it on their oily weapons and in their underwear and bedrolls, and wipe it from their tear-stained eyes and gritty mouths. All the while, the wind blew.

In early July 1943, Colonel Joseph G. Gilbreth, Lt. Col. George K. Rubel, and Major James R. Hughes, under blanket orders from the War Department, set out from Camp Campbell, Kentucky, to go to the Desert Training Center. Their job was to locate and build a special camp for the 740th and the Special Training Group—a place for them to put the theories of the secret project into practice. The place ultimately chosen was called Butler Valley, a waterless expanse of about three hundred square miles of desert, between the Buckskin and Harcuvar Mountains. The campsite was twenty miles east of Bouse, Arizona.

Forty-five miles of highway were built, a well dug and water lines laid out, water pumping equipment brought in, shower buildings and latrines constructed, and frames erected for kitchen, supply, and company headquarters' tents. A large wooden building with several thousand feet of floor space and a concrete floor served as group headquarters.

Since no one in the secret project could be separated from that point on, a hospital was built on-site to accommodate those who would be injured or become ill. Around September 1, the 150th Station Hospital, with a full complement of medical officers, nurses, and assistants, under the command of Major Mueller, was transferred in from a camp in Mississippi.

By September 10, the camp was gradually beginning to take shape and began to look like something more than a huge bramble in a dust storm. It was just about this time that a massive thunderstorm, with uniquely strong gusts of wind, virtually blew the camp away. Even the chaplain's tent went down, and most of the personal goods of those on site were washed in a raging torrent hundreds of yards down through the camp. It was a disaster and took a week to repair the damage.

As a result, the 740th Tank Battalion, scheduled to leave Fort Knox for Camp Bouse on October 3, was delayed. Eventually, the desert training camp was ready, and the battalion moved from Area X to the railroad station at Fort Knox — only to learn that there was no train available.

They moved out to a bivouac area near the government's gold vault, and as might be expected, small groups of tankers began to lay elaborate schemes to sneak onto the grounds in the dark of night, maneuver into the depths of the massive vault, and liberate some of the gold being held captive by the natives. However, it was not to be. They had no tanks with which to stage a frontal assault, nor any trenching equipment with which to dig a deep underground tunnel. And besides that, their sergeants wouldn't let them out at night.

Eventually, even the boldest of the would-be conspirators gave up their dreams of gold and riches and harem girls, and on October 12 they climbed aboard two trains and headed for the desert — and whatever fate might have in store for them there.

The first train chugged into Bouse, Arizona, in the middle of the night on Sunday, October 15. The second arrived about 11:00 a.m. It had been a pleasant, almost enjoyable trip, with people stopping and waving along the way.

GI trucks were waiting to take the battalion to its new home. The sun was shining brightly in a cloudless sky, and the tankers could not help but notice that everything was covered with a fine layer of golden dust. They were completely surrounded by mountains and not much vegetation — mostly sagebrush, mesquite trees, and cactuses. They'd heard about the jackrabbits, coyotes, bobcats, lynx, mountain lions, bighorn sheep, deer, and antelope, but saw none of them that morning.

They had yet to learn about the rattlesnakes, sidewinders, Gila monsters, tarantulas, and scorpions that ran wild — mostly away, Praise the Lord — in vast numbers across the desert. What eventually became evident to each and every one of them, however, was that nearly everything in the valley had a sting to it or a thorn on it.[4]

Camp Bouse, Arizona, 1943

10. Photo credits: 740th Tank Battalion Association Archives
Rattlesnakes, lizards, and dust storms.

After a twenty-three mile trip over rough, rocky, dusty roads, the tankers got their first look at Camp Bouse when the trucks rolled through the entrance gate at the mountain pass. The huge tent city in that particular part of the desert failed to inspire them with enthusiasm. Nor was their ardor sparked when the trucks pulled up to a high dust halt in front of the rows of pyramidal tents that were to be home for the foreseeable future. Nor did dinner that night cheer them up a whole lot as the wind blew the sand all around their "C" rations.

The 740th had become part of the 9th Tank Group, commanded by Colonel Joseph G. Gilbreth,[5] who, along with Lt. Col. Rubel and Major Hughes, had located and developed the camp. The days were hot, the nights were cold, and there was no hot water until the battalion hauled in coal for themselves and the rest of the camp. It was difficult to understand the hot-to-fizzling beer and cokes handed out in the PX, until they learned that ice had been ruled out of all camps in the Desert Training Center as a "personnel hardening" process.

A number of battalions had arrived at Camp Bouse in advance of the 740th, and it had apparently been decided by the high command that the order would be first in, first out. So, while the others were training, the 740th ended up with most of the work details to organize and keep the camp up to snuff. All the while, morale took a beating, and the men were barely scratching on the various training tests given the battalion by the 9th Armored Group.

Tanks and equipment were provided, but the battalion had been so engulfed with work details that they had not even had the opportunity to get their tanks fully operational.

Lieutenant Colonel George K. Rubel assumed command of the 740th on November 12, 1943.[6] Captain Graddy H. Floyd was appointed executive officer, and things began to turn around for the battalion. The work details were cut by two-thirds, and the battalion immediately became involved in the training process. The basic principles of driving, firing, and working together as teams were reassessed by the crews. They hovered over their tanks, learned how to make them battle ready, and drove them day and night, with and without lights, and over the roughest terrain.

11. Photo credit: 740th Battalion Archives

Lt. Colonel Rubel

They fired the Individual Tank Crew Test without any prior training, and found themselves sadly lacking. They trained intensively for the tests. On the second trial, they passed with a battalion average score of 83.73%, the highest record in the Armored Force at that time.[7]

The tankers then rolled successfully through the Individual Training Tests, and the battalion moved into platoon training. A series of training positions was established across the desert, and platoons of five tanks each moved from point to point on schedule. Platoons were graded, and scores were posted in the combat training area for competitive effect.

"During this training, considerable money changed hands, as one platoon would bet against the other on their scores. The officers of the battalion put up a pot that totaled a little over $80.00, which was to go to the tank crew with the highest score in the individual crew tests. This caused quite a bit of speculation — a helluva lot of gun polishing and careful sight adjusting. In addition, the ten highest scoring individuals were to be granted short leaves."[8]

In the Platoon Combat Firing Tests conducted in early January 1944, the battalion average was 88.2%, which was believed to be unequaled as of that date.[9]

"We adopted a motto that we would do everything first and do it better than anyone else," Rubel said.[10]

The battalion built a minefield over eight hundred yards in length that contained fourteen hundred practice mines, then filled it with booby traps, in addition to the practice detonators. One company would lay a strip of mines and another company would have to go out at night and dig them up. What with all the trip wires secreted throughout the field, it often sounded like a real war going on out there in the dark.

On January 15, 1944, the battalion was relieved from the 9th Armored Group and attached to the 10th Armored Group, which was under the command of Colonel Walter Burnside.[11]

As the 740th moved into the Special Training Group Program, the men found the concept exciting, and plunged into the work.

Specially designed armored searchlights were installed in the turrets of tanks. In a surprise attack, a group of such tanks moving forward in line at night could literally dazzle and temporarily blind the defense, utilizing high-intensity, carbon arc lamp projectors, positioned in sealed-off sections of the tanks. At one thousand yards, the powerful beams of light were thirty-four yards high and three hundred forty yards wide.[12] As the tanks moved forward, the infantry could infiltrate the enemy lines in the forward shadows between the lights of the tanks.

The blinding lights enabled the attacker to see the enemy clearly in the dark, while making it virtually impossible for the enemy to see the attacker. Night fighting would become commonplace—a revolution in tactical warfare.

Searchlights in warfare had been used as early as 1863, and at brief interludes throughout the years, but the British experiments with searchlights in tanks came to naught in World War I.

Now, the British had two operational "CDL" (Canal Defense Light) brigades—the 1st, with three battalions, and the 35th, with two battalions. Approximately six thousand soldiers passed through the British schools.

America, although an active participant, was playing catch-up. The 9th and 10th Armored Groups, each with three battalions, were training in the Desert Training Center's Special Training Group. Ultimately, some eight thousand Americans were involved in the program.[13]

The STG training was interesting and involved, and the battalion progressed rapidly under simulated conditions. The catch was that the necessary equipment was quite limited. There were too few of the specially designed tanks for far too many people. All too often, the practice turrets were on the deck rather than in the tanks. Therefore, standard tank battalion training and techniques were stressed, except for commands and terminology. The battalion did use what they called "precision commands," developed in coordination with the British. "Right turn. March!" became "Prepare to Clock 3—Clock 3 NOW!" The "Line of departure" became the "Start line," and so on. These terms became so entrenched into the tankers' vocabulary that they continued to use them later in combat in preference to the traditional commands.

"Every man in the battalion learned to drive a tank. Every man in the battalion fired every weapon. During our training period we worked on the theory that if we learned to be better drivers and better gunners than the enemy, we would beat him. Our tankers were taught that everyone looked for targets, and if they didn't see the enemy first, they didn't live. Our tanks never 'buttoned up' [closed hatches] in training nor in combat. This practice, although it resulted in a few minor head wounds, never caused a fatality, and paid for itself thousands of times. In nearly every instance, some member of the tank crew saw the enemy tank or anti-tank gun first, and the gunner knocked it out before it had a chance to fire," said Lt. Col. Rubel.[14]

Due to the special nature of the project, ammunition was plentiful, and the battalion fired literally thousands of shells in the desert. They were called on to fire at different types of targets at a variety of ranges, even "surprise" close-up targets.

A tank commander and his gunner became highly proficient in estimating the range of targets. The driver braked immediately, and the cannoneer (loader) literally slung the called-for shell—usually armor piercing or high explosive, and sometimes white phosphorus—into the cannon's breech. The bow gunner positioned himself to blow away anything in front of his .30 caliber machine gun. And the sleek 75 mm cannon shell was on its deadly way in a matter of seconds.

Meanwhile, unless another cannon shot was called for, the gunner was able to lay down a blanket of machine gun fire from his coaxially mounted .30 caliber at, or on either side of, the target. All said and done, the M4A1 Sherman tank was a deadly fighting machine. The 740th didn't know its weaknesses yet.

The one time they all remember "buttoning up" was when one platoon fought another with their .30 caliber machine guns in simulated combat. Other platoons would fire their 75s over the area, and in between the tanks to "add realism" to their training.

Later, the mortar platoons and the recovery vehicle tankers practiced lobbing mortars right in the tank park. The mechanics would be repairing a tank, then suddenly drop everything and race for their mortars to repel a fictitious enemy attack. Cast iron practice rounds were used in most of the practice firing, but it didn't seem to lessen the impact when a round plopped down in the sand near an unsuspecting tanker who happened to be in range.

The maintenance officers placed an empty fifty-gallon barrel about five hundred yards out, and the bet was on to see who would be sharp enough to drop one in the bucket. The only problem was that the "bucket" was almost too close to the refueling area when the tankers came rolling in to gas up. They quickly learned, however, to keep a sharp eye out and make a "strategic withdrawal" when the maintenance guys scrambled and headed for their mortars. It was apparent to all but the uninitiated, that not all of the maintenance people could hit the can, as it were.

"We did quite a bit of night firing, which proved of great value (later on) as much of our fighting occurred at night," said Rubel. "We practiced with star shells in the desert, using the illumination of the shell and flash shooting to hit the target before the light went out. Many members of the Wehrmacht, if alive today, could testify to the effectiveness of this type of fire."[15]

The training program included crawling through an "infiltration course," dragging their equipment, while live machine gun bullets were flying less than three feet over their heads. Tank guns were firing as well. There was scrub brush, barbed wire, and ditches, and just to liven things up, firecrackers added to the melee. It had all the violence of combat and was an electrifying experience — like Hades all lit up. Still, they were excited about it and knew that the training had "purpose." Only one tanker didn't make it. Even with a jagged hole in his leg, he was not released from the Top Secret project.

The battalion also underwent a phase called "Combat in Cities." Having no cities in the desert, they had to build their own. They gathered all the unused and unattached buildings in the area and constructed a mock Nazi village, with five buildings on each side of the street. They laboriously dug trenches and blew up simulated shell holes, laid out barbed wire, installed pop-up targets in doors and windows, and booby-trapped it all. The tankers went through the village on foot by tank crews, two crews at a time, one on either side of the street. Working as teams, crews fired their weapons at anything that moved, threw grenades at anything that didn't, and generally shot up everything in sight.

Tanks were set up at the starting point, and during each attack they fired their 75 mm cannons and .30 caliber machine guns down the street and over the tankers' heads. All the while, mortars were flying overhead and dynamite charges blew gaping holes in the street.

By the time the last building was cleared and the last pop-up Nazi was overpowered, the tankers were worn to a frazzle. The exhilaration of the day remained with them for a long time to come. This was what war was all about.

Precision in map reading and compass bearing was vital. Service Company's "ration" section would lay out rations by company, then transport each company's food allotment to a designated point several miles out in the desert. Each company was then furnished with map coordinates or compass bearing and distance, and it was left to the company to locate dinner. It all became rather serious business from that point on, since a company that couldn't find its rations didn't eat.

Although the 740th never had a full complement of equipment for the special project in which they were involved, they knew how to use the special tanks and assumed they would eventually fight with them. The time to put the theory into practice came when General Henry from the War Department made an unexpected visit to Camp Bouse; he wanted to see a demonstration. Lt. Col. Rubel volunteered.

And the 740th got the job. Enough of the special tanks and equipment for three platoons from the 740th was assembled to put on a show. A daytime demonstration showed how the special project worked, and a nighttime attack showed why it worked. Most of the men never knew whether General Henry went away pleased and excited about what he saw that day, but they certainly knew that they themselves were. It had been good. They'd learned their lessons well and did themselves proud.

However, they began to more fully understand some of the very real problems inherent in the project. Having a "searchlight" in a tank certainly did blind the enemy directly ahead. And friendly infantry, hidden in the shadows between and ahead of the advancing line of tanks, could certainly create consternation and confusion as they moved into the enemy lines. That was true. But that little group of Germans positioned up on the hill with their 88mm could be a problem for the tankers, down there in the dark with their lights shining brightly. *Verstehen Sie?*

The Desert Training Center had served its purpose. The commanding general announced its closing as March 15, 1944. The men of the 740th had been in the U.S. Army for a little more than a year now. And as their training drew to a close, these citizen-soldiers came to realize that they were soldiers now — that they were good soldiers. They had already set some records in the Armored Force, and they were proud of themselves and of their battalion. They knew what lay ahead and believed they were ready for it.

Since they had been one of the last two battalions to arrive at Camp Bouse, they were scheduled to be the last to leave. The 740th and the 739th caught the detail of closing up the camp. Their orders were to "police the area, salvage as much of the camp as possible, then go to Fort Knox where they could draw clothing and equipment in preparation for Europe."[16]

On April 24, 1944, the battalion boarded the train in Bouse, Arizona, in two serials. It was to be a slow and tedious trip. Heavy rain and flooding along the way had washed out the some of the tracks. But they were on their way.

Coded cables were flying back and forth from Washington, London, and Moscow. The Allies were quarreling among themselves again. They simply could not agree on the interpretation of "unconditional surrender" demanded of the Germans and flashed around the world following the Big Three conference at Teheran just five months earlier. President Roosevelt was adamant, but Prime Minister Churchill and Marshal Stalin were concerned that the phrase might cause the enemy to fight on to the death, prolonging an Allied victory. General Eisenhower, now appointed Supreme Commander of Operation Overlord, was uneasy about the phrase.[17] Grinning broadly, Hitler undoubtedly smacked his left fist in his right palm, and stamped his right foot in a little jig of joy, as was his wont when excited and happy.[18] He knew this was going to happen. There was just no way that the allies, with their totally different philosophies, would hang together when the going got tough.

12. Author's collection, World War II[19]

Adolf Hitler, **a personalized photograph album from 1936.**

Chapter 8

Return to Fort Knox

The rain was pouring down when the 740th's already waterlogged train pulled into the Fort Knox station on April 28. By the time they unloaded and got to their quarters, the men were soaked through to the skin. Their quarters seemed familiar. They were the exact same old, outdated buildings they had left behind six months before.

No matter, they were only going to be there a couple of weeks, long enough to draw equipment and clothing, and then be on their way. But the quartermaster had different ideas, telling them they should have drawn equipment in the desert before they left, not at Fort Knox. Hopefully, some equipment would be available in about a month.

"The Armored Command staff set to work on the problem, and by begging, pleading, and demanding, finally raked up enough stuff to make us fairly presentable. They were given the same line that we had been given in the desert: 'Everything is being shipped overseas, and we could get it there,'" said Colonel Rubel.[1]

The 740th's "shipping out" date was postponed by at least a month. The battalion drew ten to fifteen tanks from the "boneyard," along with a goodly supply of 75 mm ammunition, and went to work improving their maintenance and shooting skills. The tanks were in rather sad condition, having been scrapped by the Armored Center and the Armored School and cannibalized for parts. However, battalion maintenance did a great job in getting most of them running, and the battalion then got in a lot of shooting.

A new training circular was just out; the battalion was asked to fire the course, take a hard look at the results, and recommend changes. This they did, one company at a time, firing the course, while another company built and repaired targets and operated the range. Meanwhile, the third company practiced range estimation and trained in infantry/tank tactics, camouflage, and concealment.

The 740th qualified every man except one, according to the War Department's history of the battalion. Qualifying percentages were "Expert," 41.4%; "First Class Gunner," 55.0%; and "Second Class Gunner," 3.3%.[2] Outstanding scores.

The waiting time at Fort Knox was generally well spent in practice and procedure, if boring at times. Still, things were always happening to enliven the proceedings. Colonel Rubel, in his book, *Daredevil Tankers,* relates a couple of interesting anecdotes.[3]

In the desert, the tankers had fired at anything that moved or was big enough to shoot at, so it was of little consequence to Colonel Rubel when he was asked about firing bazookas at some chunks of concrete in the Wilcox Lake training area. "Yes, go ahead," he said.

Well, when these chunks of concrete turned out to be a rather important launching site for anti-aircraft balloons, they were given a choice of court-martial or repairing the site forthwith. As a result, in very short order, the battalion got a lot of experience in concrete construction.

To further complicate matters, several hundred Italian prisoners of war were billeted just next to the battalion. The tankers could live with this, no problem, until the POWs were given permission to visit the PX and imbibe the local brew. Then things began to pop. After a few beers, there was always someone who would take offense when a POW would temporarily grow foggy, forget where he was, and start bragging about the American tanks they had shot up in North Africa and elsewhere. This inevitably led to some pretty fair brawls, usually ending up with a number of Italians laid out flat. And this, of course, always required investigation.

The weeks turned into months. The battalion was still locked into the Special Training Group. The men had to go on passes into Louisville — three, four, and five in a group. Top secret stuff, you know.

June 6, D-Day, came and went, and the 740th was still four thousand miles from the front.

June 12, 1944. Six days after the invasion of France, General Eisenhower and the Joint Chiefs of Staff left Portsmouth, England, aboard a destroyer, the *U.S.S. Thompson,* for a tour of the Normandy beachhead. The English Channel was peaceful at the time, and the horrors of war seemed far away until they got close enough to see the barrage balloons looming over the ships that were anchored along the shoreline. When the *Thompson* docked at the Mulberry Harbor on Omaha Beach, the scene took on an entirely different complexion. Although much of the carnage and debris of D-Day had been cleared away, the offloading of men and equipment continued at an unbelievable pace.[4]

The Americans had taken a beating at Omaha Beach, and the beachhead was still anything but secure. In fact, both the Mulberry and Omaha were still under occasional artillery fire. Boatloads of dead and wounded were continuously being loaded for their return to England.

General George C. Marshall, U.S. Army Chief of Staff and Ike's boss, was one of the visiting chiefs. Of course, he had been there before—in 1918 as General John J. "Blackjack" Pershing's operations officer at the Meuse-Argonne and Saint-Mihiel in World War I. The fact was, President Roosevelt appointed Eisenhower, not Marshall, as Supreme Commander because he believed that the Army Chief of Staff was personally indispensable to him in pursuing the war.

The VIP group ate K-rations for lunch at First Army Headquarters near Point du Hoc, while General Bradley and his subordinates brought them up-to-date on the strategic situation.[5]

Although the Allies had complete control of the air, the German reaction to the invasion was bitter and intense. The legendary and respected, but aging, Field Marshal Gerd von Runstedt, was nominally in charge of the German armies in the west, and Field Marshal Erwin Rommel, the Desert Fox, was in tactical charge of the coastal defense. Both were Old Guard, tough, experienced generals. Even though the Allies now had a lodgment in France ten miles deep by sixty miles wide, neither Montgomery nor Bradley had been able to break out.

What none of the western leaders knew, of course, was that Hitler was running the show. He had come to believe that Normandy was a feint, with the main thrust still to come at the Pas de Calais. He held powerful reserves in place there, a hundred twenty miles away. At the same time, von Runstedt's panzer divisions of armored reserve were uncommitted, all waiting for George Patton's mythical First Army Group to come pouring into France at the Pas de Calais.[6]

Chapter 9

"We're going over . . ."

The excitement began to build among the men of the 740th when word came down on July 16, 1944, that their time had come. Orders were for the main body of the battalion to pack up and head for Camp Kilmer, New Jersey, so as to arrive July 20 to 21.

A section of the battalion, including some two dozen tankers from A Company, headed for Rock Island, Illinois, to guard the special CDL "Gizmo" tanks (as they were called). They were to be "reconditioned" before going overseas, according to Technician Fifth Grade C. O. "Chigger" Webster, who was with this group all the way. These special tanks and tankers then moved to Fort Hamilton in the Brooklyn Army Port area of New York, and later followed the main body of the battalion to England.[1]

By and large, there was a general eagerness to get the show on the road. And spirits rose. Few of them had ever seen the Statue of Liberty, let alone travel overseas. England, France, Belgium, Germany —these were just places on a map, studied perhaps in high school or college. But this was different. They were going over there. There wasn't that much thought of war.

Still, the idea of leaving home and family —and leaving the United States— troubled most of them.

It was not until they boarded the long troop train on July 19 and began the cross-country trek for Camp Kilmer that a lot of the excited chatter began to wane, and the tankers began to seriously consider what was really happening in their lives. It was one thing to go overseas as a civilian —those guys almost always came back. But in uniform . . . well, it was much different.

Their train pulled into Camp Kilmer on Thursday, July 20, 1944. The battalion arrived at the Port of Embarkation in a state of breathless expectation. The men were soon busy processing, drawing supplies, packing and crating, completing their inoculations, and hauling baggage and equipment to the port.

Nearly 1,000,000 Allied troops were already in Normandy, France by July 1, as were 500,000 tons of supplies and 177,000 vehicles.[2] Still, the situation was extremely tenuous. The Allies were jammed into the beachhead and surrounded on all sides. Trench warfare was a frightening possibility, reminiscent of World War I.

To the north, Montgomery was still stymied at Caan, where the Germans had massed the bulk of their armor. To the south, Bradley was inching toward St. Lo and plotting a massive attack to break out of the hedgerows and into the open.

Although the dead and wounded were carefully removed, each day new bodies lay rotting on the ground, and the bloated carcasses of dead farm animals dotted the fields of Normandy. The stench of decaying flesh was everywhere.

In Germany, on July 20, the attempted coup to assassinate the Führer was quickly broken, and some fifteen thousand suspected conspirators were rounded up and executed or sent to concentration camps as a result. Hitler ordered the V-1 attack on London doubled.

The main body of the 740th Tank Battalion left Camp Kilmer on July 24 for the four-hour train ride to Hoboken, New Jersey. From there, they were ferried to Pier 84, Grace Line Docks, in New York City. By midday, they were aboard the U.S.S. General William Mitchell and learned that Col. Rubel had arranged for them to "sort of work their way over" by serving as ship's staff—that is, to help operate the kitchen and provide the guard details.

"I did this for two reasons..." said Rubel, "... first, that the time aboard ship would pass more quickly if we kept busy, and second, it would entitle us to three meals per day. I had made the trip before with the First Armored Division in 1942, and I knew that time hung heavy when the only work to be done was to sit in a cabin and watch other men become seasick."[3]

As a matter of fact, the ship's food was very good. The duty was not all that arduous and did keep a number of the men busy part of the time. It did not, however, involve all of the battalion, and it failed to keep all too many of them from getting desperately seasick on the way over.

They sailed out of New York Harbor on July 26 and joined a large convoy of ships a few miles out to sea. The weather was hot and sultry.

The tankers guarding the CDL "Gizmos" set sail about a week later on the U.S.S. J.G. Blaine in a similar convoy of over one hundred ships.[4]

The U.S.S. General William Mitchell was relatively new, on only her fifth trip. With no portholes and no ventilation system, the compartments below were almost unbearable, and the troops generally stayed in a sweat, relishing their assigned duties and time on deck. Even though the salt-water showers stung like fire, they were a welcome relief from the heat.

Five days out, the weather turned quite cool, and on August 3, eight days out, there was enough excitement to cool everyone down. As the Mitchell moved into an area known as "Hell's Corner" off the northern coast of Ireland, the ship's radar picked up a blip that looked suspiciously like a German submarine. "General

Quarters" sounded. All troops were ordered below, and the ship's guns manned. The ship changed course.

The tankers hoped and prayed the sailors knew how to do their jobs. Those they had met certainly seemed confident and well trained. Still, they were moody and quiet until the all-clear sounded sometime later. Word filtered down that the "blip" on the radar had been merely a school of fish.

13. Photo credit: From the files of Harry Miller

The U.S.S. General William Mitchell. Launched October 31, 1943, and commissioned January 19, 1944. Length: 622'7" Width: 75'6" Speed: 20.6 knots Troop capacity: 5,289 Ship's crew: 452 Original armament: four 5-inch guns, sixteen 1.1 guns, and twenty 20 mm guns.

The *Mitchell* slipped quietly through the fog-shrouded North Channel into the Irish Sea on the morning of August 4. Had the tankers been able to see, they would have seen Ireland on their right and Scotland on their left. On August 5, the ship moved ghostlike past the Isle of Man and anchored in the river below Liverpool, then docked the next morning. They were in England.

By 3:00 a.m. on August 7, the tankers had loaded onto GI trucks and were on the train to Camp Rosebush in Glynderwen, Wales. They were attached to the 9th Armored Group. Tent Camp Rosebush was lashed somehow to the wind-swept side of a very rocky hill. Cold, rain, and fog were the orders of the day. It was still daylight at 11:00 p.m.

Col. Rubel was able to secure some of the special equipment and several tanks, but there was no way to work out in that type of terrain. The tanks were road-bound. It was not until the battalion moved on August 20 to Castle Martin — a British tank training center in southwest Wales, near Pembroke — that any kind of training program could begin.

"It was a good camp," said the colonel. "A good location right on the sea, and we got in some good training—for the first time with our special equipment. We also did some anti-aircraft firing."[5]

It was not all work, however, and the tankers found time to hit the roads to Cardiff, Pembroke, Tenby, and other nearby points of interest in the area, for a little R&R and a taste of that warm Welsh beer. "Drink up, lads, before it gets cold."

The 740th moved once again to Warminster, England, on September 24. The camp at Longbridge Deverill provided good housing, recreational facilities, coffee and doughnuts every night, a battalion orchestra, and dances with the English girls. When Camp Sutton "B" Camp was evacuated on October 6, the battalion moved to Wiltshire, England, with its brick buildings, movies, and hot showers. Gloucester, Bath, Weymouth, Salisbury, and Stonehenge were at hand during their free time, as well as a number of other places.

It was in Wiltshire that the rumor began that the 740th Tank Battalion might not be utilized in the secret project for which they had long and stressfully been trained. Instead, the talk was that they were to be converted into a standard tank battalion.

As push came to shove, the process of reorganization began. A standard tank battalion required a whole new table of organization, and the three medium tank companies that were already formed needed the addition of a light tank company, a mortar platoon, and an assault gun platoon. Men in the regular tank companies were transferred to different platoon formations in the new company and given new duties.

The 740th tankers shepherding the CDL "Gizmos" across the ocean, including the U.S.S. J. G. Blaine convoy, made it to England pretty well on schedule, although one of their ships was sunk off the coast of North Ireland, creating quite a stir. The Blaine lay at anchor in the Clyde River in Scotland for nearly a month while the authorities decided where to unload its still-secret cargo. Eventually, the ship was sent to unload in Barry Docks, Wales. After unloading, each "Gizmo" was driven into a Quonset hut and carefully locked up.

"Our group stayed in Wales until mid-November, when we moved to Southampton, loaded on an LST, and crossed the channel to Le Havre, France," Webster said. "We did not catch up with the battalion until the latter part of November. They were already in Neufchateau, Belgium. Believe me, we didn't have long to wait then until the battalion went into combat in the Ardennes."[6]

Some three million American military personnel disembarked in England from early 1942 through the end of 1945.[7] For many, it was merely a waypoint, or a train ride, or the back of a GI truck on their way to France.

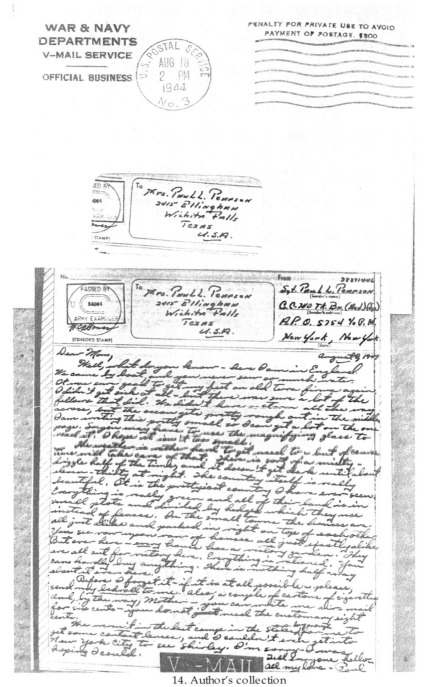

14. Author's collection

Official WWII US V-Mail letter, 1944.

Others came to know and understand the people and saw much of the countryside—sometimes for a year or two. Some viewed the country only through a hospital window while recovering from wounds received on the continent.

The English people were easy to like. They were, in the main, patient and understanding with the Americans crowded into their small country. It seemed that most of them had all too little left in the way of worldly goods, having suffered the trials and tribulations of war beyond the tankers' beliefs. The threat of German invasion and the heavy bombings had passed because of the Allied dominance in the sea and air. But the V-bombs were still sputtering in and creating terror and havoc.

As the tankers spread out on leaves and passes, they found that towns and cities were decimated. Families torn asunder.

Not all, but most of the English children were back with their families now. At the height of the bombing, some two million of them had been evacuated from the major cities to the safety of foster homes in rural and suburban areas. Many of the pregnant women, invalids, and the elderly were relocated as well.[8]

During their three-month stay, the men of the 740th came to appreciate the courage and determination of the British, especially the kindness shown to them personally. Of course, there was a lot of homesickness, and the dreary weather of England was oftentimes depressing. For the most part, it was an experience of a lifetime.

Weekend passes provided plenty of opportunities to raise their spirits. The capital city of London, even with all the damage, was a lesson in history to these young men. In the land of Shakespeare and Charles Dickens, there was so much to see: Big Ben, the London Bobbies, the River Thames, Westminster Abby, the Tower of London, the Houses of Parliament, the grand palaces, Hyde Park, Trafalgar Square, Haymarket, and Piccadilly Circus.

But the war was closer than they knew.

There'll always be an England / And England shall be free
If England means as much to you / As England means to me.
Words and music by Parker and Charles © Unknown

15. Photo credit: Truman Library Photographs U.S. Army Signal Corps
Winston Churchill

It was said: "He's a pugnacious looking bastard."

"We shall not flag or fail. We shall go on to the end. We shall fight in France, we shall fight on the seas and oceans, we shall fight with growing confidence and growing strength in the air, we shall defend our island, whatever the cost may be. We shall fight on the beaches, we shall fight on the landing grounds, we shall fight in the fields and in the streets, we shall fight in the hills. We shall never surrender."

–Winston S. Churchill

Chapter 10

Marching as to War

The battalion was ordered to the port of Weymouth, England, on Oct. 27, loaded into GI trucks on two LSTs the next day, and crossed the English Channel on Monday, Oct. 30, 1944.

It was a rough and emotional passage. They reached Utah Beach the same day, but the waters were so choppy that an immediate landing was out of the question, so they stood off the beach until Wednesday, November 1.

With no orders awaiting, no place to camp but in the mud and slush, and the battle clear across France and into Belgium, the 740th's commander, Col. Rubel, asked for and received permission to head for ETO Headquarters in Paris for rations and fuel. After arranging to meet at a designated crossroad just west of Paris on November 3, he sent an advance party on ahead to let them know that the 740th had arrived and was ready to go to work.

Staying off the beaten path and away from the "Red Ball Express," the battalion began the slow trek toward Paris. The advance party met them on November 3 just north of Maintenon. Orders assigned the 740th, as a standard tank battalion, to the First U.S. Army, destination Aubel, Belgium.

The European Theater of Operations, United States Army (ETOUSA) was apparently chagrined that the battalion had moved across France without written orders, but went ahead with arrangements for fuel and rations and a motorcycle escort through Paris. The battalion bivouacked for the night at Maintenon, went through the outskirts of Paris the next day, and bivouacked that night at Clichy-sous-Bois, on the eastern edge of Paris.

The column of trucks, along with a few half-tracks and peeps, plowed through mud and rain all the next day. Packed in and worn to a frazzle, and still without any tanks, their spirits could not have been much lower when, suddenly, the area began to take on the look of a war zone with bombed out villages and towns and shot up vehicles along the way. Cold and miserable, but with hearts picking up a beat, the battalion rumbled into Aubel, then Neufchateau, Belgium, on November 6, 1944.

As the tankers settled into an apple orchard for the night with the vestiges of war all around them, they didn't know that their commander in chief had just been elected to an unprecedented fourth term. Franklin D. Roosevelt defeated Thomas E. Dewey by winning thirty-six states and 53% of the vote. Harry S. Truman, an obscure but decisive and well-thought-of senator from Missouri, was elected to be the new vice president.

Back home, the stirrings of war and the tremendous expansion of the defense industry into almost all phases of the American way, had ended the worst economic depression in the history of America. Everyone who wanted a job had one. Times were good for all practical purposes. Still, there was a thriving black market in ration stamps, oil and gasoline, retread tires, butter, sugar, and other scarce commodities.

There were other problems as well. That past summer, the Philadelphia Transit System had gone on strike when several black employees were promoted as "motormen." The system served nearly one million war plant and shipyard workers every day. President Roosevelt concluded that the war effort came first and ordered the army to seize control of the system. The workers were given forty-eight hours to get back on the job; their leaders were threatened with arrest; the strikers were warned that they could face a change in their draft deferments to A-1.[1]

America must have heard the front lines of fighting troops all over the world cheering at the tough stance taken by their Commander-in-Chief regarding labor strikes on the home front. It is interesting to note that the black motormen got to keep their promotions.

The sights and sounds of war kept the 740th's tankers awake and abuzz most of their first night in Belgium. That night alone they counted about fifty of Hitler's hellish V-1 buzz bombs passing directly overhead, headed for important targets behind the American lines—Antwerp or even London, they guessed. Later, they would count scores of these juggernauts a day.

Although only a few exploded in the immediate vicinity in the time they were in the Neufchateau area, the tankers never knew for sure what the next rocket would do. Occasionally, one of the terrifying monsters would pass over safely, then suddenly cut out, turn, and come back in a wild dive, exploding with an earsplitting *KA-BLOOM!*, leaving a huge hole in the ground. It was enough to make an otherwise reasonably brave fellow shiver in his boots.

Luckily, none of the tankers was wounded by the vicious weapons, but the battalion medics often had to tend to civilians who were caught in the middle in and around Neufchateau.

The tankers' steel helmets took on a whole new meaning as the anti-aircraft guns in the area began to open up every time one of the fiery devils flashed by, and shell fragments came zizzing down from above with great regularity.

On November 8, the battalion moved into billets in the towns of Neufchateau and Mortroux. They were just a mile and a half from the Meuse River, between

Liege, Belgium, and Maastricht, Holland. And there, in and among the people, the 740th made lasting friendships—friendships that blossomed and thrived through the years and abound to this very day.[2]

The battalion was in army reserve, assigned to Lt. Gen. Courtney Hodges' First U.S. Army, in Bradley's 12th Army Group. The tankers were issued a handful of tanks on "loan" and told that they would have to be returned on call.

Hopefully, there would be tanks available "after the first of the year." No major assignment for the battalion was expected until then. Tentatively, they were attached to the 99th Infantry Division. Their code name was "Daredevil." They were just north of the Ardennes—where all hell was about to break loose.

Enemy activity increased over the next few weeks. The First U.S. Army Headquarters at the Grand Hotel Britannique in Spa was edgy, expecting an air attack. The 740th's job was to use all available weapons to help counter any such attack and then round up any enemy paratroopers who might have been dropped behind the lines. No one seemed to know for sure what the 740th was going to use for weapons, and no one seemed overly concerned.

By mid-December, the Allies were basically at a halt along the German border, although they continued to press ahead in the Saar and Roer regions. They were concentrating their strength for the main attack in the north and had taken a calculated risk in thinning their defense of the Ardennes. It was evident to SHAEF that the Germans were in no shape to come out from behind the vaunted West Wall and launch any kind of a major attack anyway.

How totally wrong they were. Hitler's long-planned *Wacht am Rhein* (Watch on the Rhine) caught the Allies flat-footed and surprised. In the Schnee Eifel, just across from the Ardennes, the wily German leader concentrated his forces in the west so secretly and in such numbers, that he totally astounded the Allies. His plan: break through the thinly held American sector of the Ardennes, isolate Montgomery's British-Canadian 21st Army Group to the north, and retake the Allied supply port of Antwerp. This would set the western Allies back for months, if not altogether destroy their will to fight. None of his generals approved of the plan nor thought it even feasible, instead proposing a "smaller solution" of their own. But the Führer was unyielding and stamped his foot.

And so they came.

Part III

The Germans came by the hundreds of thousands, through the fog and snow of the Ardennes — around, over, and through the thin line of American forces. The Americans, outnumbered ten to one, were demoralized. With the 30th Infantry, the 740th Tank Battalion was thrown into the breach at the Battle of Stoumont - La Gleize.

In this first action, elements of the "Daredevil" Battalion would be awarded the Presidential Unit Citation. Then came their breakthrough on the Siegfried Line at Udenbreth with the 82nd Airborne Division. The drive to Duren at the Ruhr and Cologne at the Rhine, all took a heavy toll on both tanks and tankers.

Almost without respite, they were called to load their tanks on railway flatcars and race 350 miles to the south, into Rhineland-Palatinate, where the 63rd and the 70th Infantry Divisions were waiting for them to crack the Siegfried Line again, in the vicinity of Ensheim.

Back on the flatcars, they headed north to Siegen to help the 8th Infantry Division split the Ruhr Pocket.

Finally, after crossing the Elbe and making the incredible race to the Baltic Sea with the 8th Infantry and the 82nd Airborne, the *Daredevil Tankers* ended up at Schwerin, the British on one side and the Russians on the other.

Men Spricht Deutsch
Ich hab'n allig.
Iph habb'n allig.
I am in a hurry.

THE STARS AND STRIPES

Daily Newspaper of U.S. Armed Forces   in the European Theater of Operations

Ici On Parle Français
Y'a-t-il des droits de douane?
Yatest-day drunk dah du-ANY
Does it pay duty?

Vol. No. 147   1 Fr.   New York—PARIS—London   1 Fr.   Thursday, Dec. 21, 1944

Biggest Battle Since D-Day

Reich Hurls Its Best Men Into Attack

By Dan Regan
Stars and Stripes Staff Writer

WITH FIRST U.S. ARMY, Dec. 20.—It is apparent to observers at the front that the war might be won if the Allies can smash the current German counter-offensive—an assault designed to snatch victory or at least a favorable peace from what the Germans felt was an Allied steamroller.

The Nazis are using the best troops they have on the Western Front.

German officers are promising their men that they will spend New Year's Eve in Paris, that they will have Antwerp in five days, that Aachen will be given to Hitler for a Christmas present, and other such promises to hype the Nazi soldiers into fanatical action.

The military commentators say that this offensive was planned and is being directed by "a soldier"—which means that apparently Von Runstedt, and not Hitler's intuition, is at the helm.

Aim for Supply Dumps

One present aim of the Nazi spearhead will be to grab American supply dumps for the hoped-for German drive through Belgium and France.

Their present German drives are salients composed of armored columns, tanks, trucks and armored infantry. The Germans are using the same technique we used in our recent armored spearheads across France with armored units dashing in several directions.

The aim of these spearheads appears to be to cut off our communications and harass our troops.

First Army forces are holding strongly along neighboring sectors of the drive, but the center still is fluid. It is difficult to map the columns exactly since they are in

(Continued on Page 2)

Zizzi Finds Zizzi, Seeks Other Zizzis

Cosmo Zizzi, a sergeant in a PA battalion, got a Christmas package addressed to Cosmo Zizzi. "Well" said Cosmo, "I ate contents of same."

"Later I look at the address," he continued. "It's meant for Cosmo Zizzi all right, but another one."

Cosmo wrote Cosmo explaining what had happened, and now, he says, "all is forgiven." The two Cosmo Zizzis are a couple of pals, happy to share the name of Zizz.

But why they want to know now is, are there any more Cosmo Zizzis in the ETO? If so, maybe they could start a Cosmo Zizzi Club.

Nazis Try Comeback Trail

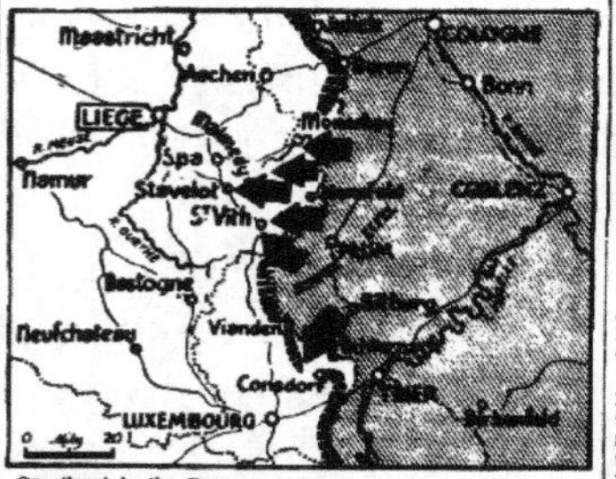

[MAP: Maastricht, Aachen, Köln, Liège, Namur, Born, Spa, Stavelot, St. Vith, Bastogne, Neufchâteau, Vianden, Consdorf, Luxembourg]

One thrust in the German counter-offensive has been halted at Monschau, but in Belgium and Luxembourg Panzer Divisions spear in the areas of Malmedy, Stavelot, St. Vith and Consdorf.

Headlines Grim Reminder To U.S. War Far from Over

By Carl Larsen
Stars and Stripes U.S. Bureau

NEW YORK, Dec. 20.—Germany's sudden shift to the offensive in Belgium, mounting American casualties on the Western Front and stepped-up draft requirements brought the nation a grim reminder today that the war in Europe is far from over.

The nation's newspapers used their boldest headline type to report the German threat. Editorial writers checked history books to draw parallels between the current Nazi drive and the Germans' final 1918 offensives under Ludendorff. However, no attempt was made to dismiss the threat lightly, although Washington officials said there were still enemy elements to be mopped up.

Meanwhile, the War Department announced that the ground forces in western Europe suffered 57,775 casualties during November, including 9,250 dead, 43,330 wounded and 6,186 missing. The Western Front toll since D-Day is 256,124.

The War Department also dis-

(Continued on Page 2)

British Armada Is Under Nimitz

PEARL HARBOR, Dec 20 (ANS).—Conferences between Adm. Chester W. Nimitz and the British Pacific fleet commander, Adm. Bruce Fraser, who arrived here with his staff yesterday from Australia, were begun today and their first act was to aid Adm Nimitz' command of Fraser's British armada.

As the naval experts conferred, possibly on plans to increase British co-operation in the war against Japan, B29s, based on Saipan, were bombing Tokyo. It was the third superfort raid in the last three days on the Jap mainland.

In the Philippines, Yanks on Leyte seized a Jap airfield practically intact and captured Valencia, Jap headquarters on the island, then drove northward in an effort to engage the Japs fleeing into the dense mountains.

British Report Gains Along Faenza Front

ROME, Dec 20 (UP).—British troops of the Eighth Army made limited gains today near a land northeast of Faenza against strong resistance. Polish and Indian troops of the same army virtually cleared all organized enemy resistance west of the Senio River and west of the main Bologna-Rimini highway.

Germans' Assault On 60-Mile Front Is Halted in North

The security veil over the German counter-offensive was lifted partially yesterday to reveal the bloodiest battles since D-Day raging through eastern Belgium and Luxembourg where masses of men and armor were locked in one of the war's decisive struggles.

German armor smashed more than 20 miles into Belgium in the first 48 hours of the Nazi blitz, the like of which has not been seen in Belgium since 1940. Exploding Saturday on a 60-mile front from the Monschau Forest to the German-Luxembourg frontier, the offensive penetrated U.S. First Army positions at four points by noon Monday.

Nazi armored strength in the drive was estimated at between five and six Panzer divisions, including an unstated number of SS Panzer divisions. Eight or nine infantry divisions were thrown into the assault, which obviously was planned to kick-off when murky weather would handicap superior Allied air power.

Panzer divisions encountered by Lt. Gen. Courtney H. Hodges' battling First Army men included units met and smashed at Caen. These had been re-fitted for battle.

It was predicted the Germans probably will continue to make progress. Counter-measures, it was said, cannot be prepared in a day and it was warned that immediate results cannot be expected.

Only in the north, in the Monschau Forest, has the drive been reported as brought to a halt. There, First Army men smashed enemy forces which entered the town of Monschau. Americans also managed to regain a portion of their old line east of the town where there were still enemy elements to be mopped up.

Feverish German activity was spotted behind the U.S. Ninth and Third Army lines, according to front reports.

Stars and Stripes Correspondent Jules Grad with Ninth Army reported that Ninth Air Force tactical commands Monday blasted the greatest concentration of German military transport seen since the Falaise Gap. He said trucks camouflaged with brown and green

(Continued on Page 2)

Foe Employing Tricks Aplenty

WITH THE FIRST U.S. ARMY, Dec. 20.—The counter-attacking Nazis were pulling every rabbit they had out of their helmets yesterday, using old and new tricks in an attempt to bewilder U.S. troops and infiltrate into American positions.

German vehicles were painted to look like those of U.S. units, and some were even emblazoned with white and yellow stars similar to those which distinguish Allied combat vehicles.

Captured U.S. tanks and equipment were being used by the Nazis. In one instance, Germans in an American tank pulled close to U.S. infantrymen and yelled in English.

"Come on over here."

When the GIs came over they were mowed down by the Nazis. Germans in civilian clothes or wearing civilian garments over Wehrmacht uniforms were captured filtering into the U.S. lines in instances of sabotage and espionage reminiscent of 1940.

B17s Bomb Nantes Again— This Time With Toys, Gifts

LONDON, Dec. 20.—Some 2,000 children will be guests of the 384th Bombardment Group, veteran Flying Fortress unit of the England-based Eighth AF, at a Christmas party in the war-blighted French city of Nantes.

Several B17s will take off with a cargo of presents for the children. The party will be held on New Year's Eve. France's traditional day for exchanging gifts and the presents include candy, toys, toilet articles and clothing.

The gifts have come from the group's rations, from PX purchases, and from parcels requested from home. In addition, officers and EM contributed £180 to purchase more gifts for orphanages in Nantes.

Lt. Oscar Picard, of Linwood, Mass., said a party will be held for 300 children in one of Nantes' few undamaged orphanages, and another celebration will be held in the city's window manufactured hall for 2,800 schoolchildren.

The 384th, commanded by Lt. Col. Theodore R. Milton, of Washington, D.C., in carrying out 245 operations over Europe, has hit targets at Nantes on several occasions.

---

16. Photo credit: Hugh Lauter Levin Associates, Inc., Publisher

The Stars and Stripes: World War II Front Pages

Chapter 11

Breakthrough in the Ardennes

Saturday, December 16, 1944. The Germans came out of the mist and fog and snow of the Ardennes—two hundred thousand strong in the first assault alone, against some 83,000 Americans. A superiority of six to one in troops and two to one in tanks at various points of concentration.[1] With nearly one thousand tanks and armored assault weapons and two thousand big guns, it was a massive attack against the weakest sector in the American lines. It literally crushed everything in its wake. When the entire sixty-mile "Ghost Front" of the Ardennes suddenly came alive with fire and flame at 5:30 a.m., the surprise was total; the devastation and fear up and down the American lines was rampant.

From Monschau in the north, to Echternach in the south, the heavy German artillery blasted the American positions for the better part of an hour, cutting down American soldiers and German villagers alike. People were screaming, running, and diving headfirst into any kind of cover. Outposts, entire frontline encampments, even small villages shattered into broken little pieces.

Telephone lines splintered. Battalions, companies, platoons, even foxhole buddies split wide apart, and if still alive, were totally out of communication. Trees, shelters, foxholes, now nothing more than black splotches in the snow. Bodies and pieces of bodies were here, there, everywhere. The experience was beyond belief—even combat-hardened veterans had never seen anything like it. Just as the awful pounding lifted, and those who survived began to move about and gather their wits about them, the German infantry emerged from out of the mist and fog. White-clad, charging forward with guns blazing, thousands upon thousands of them. Racing forward, shouting *"Heil, Hitler!"* Total mayhem. The Americans' world had gone completely crazy.

Spotlights beamed back and forth across the low-hanging clouds, reflecting back down, casting an eerie light on the surreal scene that faced the American soldiers.

Finally, the German tanks began to move from out of the forest, crunching the fir trees and showering snow in their wake, machine guns chattering, and cannons spewing death and destruction.

The thin line of Americans was completely overwhelmed. They fell back, hundreds, thousands, wounded or in shock. Individual and small group acts of heroism took place up and down the line. A single soldier would turn to make a stand and fire hopelessly into the oncoming hordes, only to be shot to pieces and trampled underfoot. Others would group together and lay out enough fire power to slow the enemy mass, but it was only temporary. There was no stopping the terrible onslaught. Many just fled in the panic that ensued. It was a fearful sight.

The German juggernaut quickly broke through in dozens of places, and the First U.S. Army began to bulge inward. With all the shelling and confusion, the Nazi *Skorzeny's* English-speaking spy teams, in American uniforms, were busy cutting telephone lines, spreading rumors, and causing havoc behind the lines. One team, disguised as MP's, took over at a strategic crossroads, switched road signs, and misdirected entire American columns coming and going.

When the breakthrough came, the 740th was in army reserve and living with the people in Neufchateau and Mortroux, just north of the Ardennes. The battalion had only a handful of borrowed tanks and didn't expect to see action until the first of the year.

Out of the blue, Lt. Col. Rubel received orders to turn over the battalion's nine "borrowed" tanks to the 745th Tank Battalion in the vicinity of Aachen. With this done, the next day he headed for First U.S. Army headquarters in Spa.

The news was not good. He learned that the Germans were coming in strength and that the 740th might have to fight as infantry, utilizing only what vehicles they had.

Cooks, clerks, truck drivers, every available man was given a gun and sent forward into the line to try and stop the powerful German counteroffensive. Entire divisions were routed and in full retreat. Two full regiments of the 106th Infantry Division were surrounded, surrendered, and began to make their tortured way slowly to the east as prisoners of war. The weather was so bad that Allied fighter bombers were of no help in stemming the tide.

On December 18, the battalion was ordered to move by truck to an ordnance vehicle depot at Sprimont, Belgium, and there equip themselves with whatever combat vehicles were available. They were then to proceed to the vicinity of Aywaille, Belgium, and hold at all costs.

What happened there is recounted in some detail in Chapter 2, but briefly: the depot turned out to be an ill-equipped "way station" for the salvage and repair of tanks that had been given up for dead in combat. There were probably twenty-five tanks of various kinds in the depot, and all of them had been cannibalized in one way or another. Generators and starters gone, breech parts missing, radios and transmitters on the blink or AWOL, tools and rammer-staffs hard to find, and not a single tank had a combat load of ammunition.

The battalion command post was established, and the 740th's Service Company took over the depot. A tank crew was assigned to every vehicle that even remotely looked as if it could be made serviceable. The tankers worked frantically through the night, stripping the remaining tanks and vehicles of any piece or part that could possibly be used.

Sergeant (later Staff Sergeant) Billie C. Ritchie said C Company had been out searching for enemy paratroopers the night before they learned they were moving up to the front within the hour. Already beat, they rolled out and arrived at the Ordnance Depot around 8:00 p.m. By the time his platoon got in to draw tanks, it was 1:00 a.m. "We got three old beat-up Wrights [and] one Ford [engine], and my crew got a TD," Richie said. "It was nearly eight in the morning before we were ready to move out."[2]

Sergeant John A. Thompson and his crew ended up with "a damned duck," a Sherman tank fitted with a duplex drive and a waterproof canvas flotation screen for amphibious operations. And it was "half gone," Thompson said. Too many other tankers had used it for spare parts. He had a "very nice" 75 mm gun "but no breechblock." No ammunition or machine guns. And "My crew consisted of one other man besides myself," he said. "If anybody has a darker moment than that, I'd sure like to hear about it."[3]

By noon the next day, Captain James D. "Red" Berry's C Company had two five-tank platoons in defensive positions at Remouchamps. He told Thompson to fall in at the rear of the attacking tanks with his "damn duck."

Chapter 12

Into the Breach

Tuesday, December 19. The Sixth SS Panzer Army's main spearhead, *Kampfgruppe Peiper,* smashed through one tiny village after another, taking no prisoners. Peiper's armored columns rumbled down the Ambleve Valley through Stavelot, heading for Stoumont and Targnon and the bridge beyond, which would provide a direct route to Liege and Antwerp.

The American 30th "Old Hickory" Division's 119th Infantry Regiment stood in the way and was in a desperate fight for its very life. One battalion was completely overrun and destroyed. Two others battered and at half-strength.

By the time Peiper's powerful *Kampfgruppe* had slashed its way into Stoumont, the American lines were fighting in a full-scale retreat. The 740th was ordered into the breach.

Having worked frantically through the night at the ordnance depot in Sprimont, the battalion moved into position with a handful of makeshift tanks. Capt. "Red" Berry's C Company moved out first, picking up elements of the 30th Infantry Division's 119th Regiment on the way. With the Tanks leading down the narrow, twisting road in the rain-chilled fog, they smashed headlong into *Kampfgruppe Peiper's* lead columns.

C Company's Third Platoon was leading. En route to the front, Sgt. William H. Fagg accidentally smashed his hand in the breech block of his tank's cannon. He was quickly evacuated and his crew pulled back.

Second Lieutenant Charles B. Powers, the platoon leader, moved into the lead in his M4 Sherman tank. As the column of tanks came on line, Powers' gunner, Corporal Jack D. Ashby, opened up with a torrent of machine gun fire on both sides of the road, which paralleled the Ambleve River. The infantry spread wide through the forest on both flanks, rifle fire blasting away at anything that moved or looked suspicious.

Powers respected the firepower of the heavier German tanks. He had his driver work the cliff side of the road and prayed for the first shot. Just short of the Stoumont Station, an enemy tank materialized out of what had at first appeared to be a pile of brush. Powers quickly estimated the distance for his gunner and shouted, "Fire!" Ashby's shot was already on the way, and Powers and his crew watched the German tank explode and burst into flames.

Vue panoramique de la Vallée de l'Amblève à **Stoumont** (vers l'aval) et Targnon.

17. From the author's collection of postcards by Luma, circa 1944

Valley of the Ambleve at Stoumont

18. Photo credit: Monsieur Freddie Lemaire and the La Gleize Museum in Belgium and After the Battle, publishers of Battle of the Bulge: Then and Now, by Jean-Paul Pallud.

German tank No. 211 was the third Panther set ablaze by the 740th at Stoumont Station. Note the split muzzle brake on the cannon.

What happened then was recounted in detail in Chapter 3, but briefly, this is what happened in those next few nerve-shattering minutes.

Luckily, in this ragtag group of tanks, Loopey and his crew were in an M36 tank destroyer, which had a big 90 mm gun. Loopey put his gunner, Corporal William H. Beckham, on target and shouted, "Fire! Fire!" That first shot kept the German from bringing his gun down on them, according to Loopey. He then had Beckham throw two or three more rounds into the Panther until flames surged high in the air.

Powers had his cannon cleared and resumed the lead, only to face a third Panther tank at a slight twist in the road. His alert gunner's first shot luckily blasted the muzzle brake of the German's cannon, and he kept firing as the German tried to back away, ultimately setting the third enemy tank on fire.

The 740th was now teeth-chattering deep in the war. With elements of the 30th "Old Hickory" Infantry Division, they continued the attack to Stoumont Station, blunting the advance of the famed 1st SS Panzer Division's Kampfgruppe Peiper and gaining back one thousand yards of bitterly contested front given up earlier that day. It was the first good news to come out of the Ardennes since the massive Nazi breakthrough.

In the gloom of the forest darkness, the tankers pulled off the road in sheltered positions to secure for the night. Powers' loader, TEC 5 Harold Henry, said most of the Third Platoon stayed in their tanks that night, but some tankers farther back in the column bailed out of their tanks and chopped and dug large rectangular holes through the ice and snow. When they were knee-deep, they drove their tanks up over the holes, unlimbered their big bedrolls from the back of the tanks, and bedded down under all that armor for the night. They took turns at watch, keeping at least one crew member awake at all times.

It wasn't exactly the Waldorf that first night of combat, but they had their cold K-Rations, and if they were down deep enough through the snow, a measure of warmth.

The infantry, glad for the security provided by the tanks, dug in all around them. It was bitterly cold. There would be sleet and snow before morning, and the tankers didn't envy the doughboys in their mostly unsheltered foxholes. A great affinity would develop between these infantrymen and the tankers as they fought side by side in the bitter Battle of the Bulge in the days ahead.

Col. Rubel noted that in this battle, on through Stoumont and La Gleize, the 740th Tank Battalion would either stop the German breakthrough, or be annihilated as other units had been before them.[1]

Communication was increasingly disrupted throughout the "bulge" as the Germans viciously hammered the American lines. On December 20, General Eisenhower decided to shift the American forces to the north of the breakthrough from Lt. Gen. Bradley's 12th Army Group, to Field Marshall Montgomery's 21st Army Group. The Supreme Commander believed that this would also encourage Monty to bring in the British reserves to help stem the Nazi tide.

This action placed both Lt. Gen. Hodges' First and Lt. Gen. Simpson's Ninth U.S. Armies in the 21st Army Group. The American generals—and as soon as they realized what happened, The American Press and thence the public—found this hard to swallow and were profoundly disturbed by the change in command, even though it was temporary. By this time, the American forces on the continent outnumbered the British by more than three to one.[2]

These changes left Bradley's 12th Army Group south of the breakthrough with only one army, Patton's Third. Both Bradley and Patton were fit to be tied at Eisenhower's decision to hand off two American armies to the British field marshal's command, believing that he had succumbed to British pressure rather than military necessity. The U.S. First and Ninth Army generals, Hodges and Simpson, were deeply frustrated by the change in command, but there was little they could do about it, except fight on. The First Army's V Corps was under siege and in fear of being overrun in the Ardennes.

The 740th Tank Battalion, in the thick of it with the V Corps' 30th Infantry Division, temporarily came under British command.

The 740th's action in turning back *Kampfgruppe Peiper's* grinding attack along the Ambleve River gave new heart to the infantry. The battalion held the line at Stoumont Station the night of December 19 and prepared for a 4:00 a.m. attack with as many tanks as they could bring on line. This meant C Company again for the moment, although Lt. Col. Rubel was hoping to field at least one platoon from both A and B Companies by mid-day on the 20th.

Rumors ran rampant that night. The tankers knew the heavily forested valley was packed with enemy troops on the prowl. And there was little doubt that the panzer column they had hit that afternoon would regroup and be spoiling for a fight by morning.

In the meantime, the SHAEF reserve—the two airborne divisions, the 82nd and the 101st, that made up the XVIII Airborne Corps—had been ordered in to help stem the Nazi tide. Word came down that the 82nd Airborne had moved into position in the vicinity of Werbomont on the tankers' right flank, which was comforting. And rumor had it that the 101st Airborne was committed just south of them, at Bastogne.

It was finger-numbing cold that night as the tankers hacked at the ice and snow to dig holes deep enough for their five-man crews to sleep in. With the job done, their tanks drawn up overhead, and the doughboys dug in all around them, they felt relatively secure for the moment.

They stripped open their small, waxy boxes of K-rations, and tried to eat.

The breakfast ration with the little tin of scrambled eggs was generally the most popular. The four cigarettes that came in the ration were always welcome, but the tankers were extremely careful with the flare of the match and the glow of the cigarette because of enemy snipers.

They unbuckled their combat boots for a change of socks. They peeled off wet socks, rubbed their cold feet, and then searched for dry socks inside their undershirts where the heat from their bodies prepared yesterday's socks for yet another day. They pulled their boots back on and climbed into their makeshift bedrolls, trying not to think too much about tomorrow. As they shivered from the cold and the emotions of the day, they knew that the road ahead—toward Targnon, Stoumont, and La Gleize—would challenge the best that was in them.

Wednesday, December 20. A slight drizzle and light snow brought a ghostly quality to the forest in the pre-dawn darkness. Time to go. Word spread quickly from one tank to the other. The doughboys were already out of their foxholes, moving cautiously about, taking care of those things that simply had to be done before the jump off at daybreak.

Although the ground was frozen, the Ambleve River was not, so heavy fog permeated the valley. The tanks were to spearhead the attack, with the infantry clearing the forest on both sides of the road as the attack moved forward. The attack was to be so fierce as to sweep aside the opposition and take Targnon by noon.

By daybreak, the tanks had roared to life and formed a column on the narrow winding road. C Company's Second Platoon led the way this second day out. The attack was barely underway when a German Panther tank that was covering the road opened up on them. The lead 740th tank, commanded by 1st Lt. John E. Callaway, quickly got off an armor-piercing round that split the muzzle of the Panther's cannon, and the column continued to clank slowly forward. The column engaged and knocked out two enemy half-tracks on their way into Targnon, and they began to believe that the Germans were pulling back.

Staff Sergeant (later 2nd Lieutenant) Homer B. Tompkins' tank took over the lead. The 30th infantrymen stretched out in line through the dense forest on both sides of the road, although there was a rather steep incline to the left. Machine guns blazed left and right across the icy road and into the woods. Cannons blasted anything big enough to shoot at or that seemed to move in the shadows on the road. Surely, nothing could withstand such a withering blanket of fire.

Suddenly, about one thousand yards east of Targnon, Tompkins' tank hit a minefield in a bone-shattering explosion. German Teller mines exploded under both tracks. Then the Germans opened up with rifle and machine gun fire from dug-in positions on the high ground to the left. Thinking, "This is it!" the tank's crew came scrambling out, surprised to be alive.

Although his eyeglasses were smashed and gone from his bloody face, Tompkins' gunner remembers seeing everything with great clarity when he hit the ground. A dead infantryman, apparently caught in the explosion, lay sprawled at the foot of the tank, his rifle at his side. The tanker remembers stopping only long enough to grab the infantryman's rifle before zigzagging down the right slope to the safety of a concrete culvert, the *brrrrrrp* of German machine gun fire digging up the ground around him.

As quickly as the infantry cleared the hill, the engineers moved in with sweepers to clear the mines. The tank had not caught fire, and the crew was still gathered near the culvert, congratulating themselves on their good fortune when one of those wicked shoe mines blew. An American engineer screamed and dropped, writhing to the ground. His right shoe plopped down in front of the tankers. His foot still in it.

Later, the crew learned just how lucky they really were. Twin 88mm anti-tank guns were zeroed in on the next curve in the road. Had they been "lucky" enough to negotiate the minefield on the road without mishap?

Yes, Lord, miracles really do happen.

The wounded gunner was evacuated. Service Company was eventually able to move the blown tank to clear the road, and as darkness fell, C Company pushed on to within a few hundred yards of Stoumont. It had been a slugfest all the way. While the infantry managed to beat back several counterattacks through the woods, the tankers engaged and destroyed another German tank, a half-track, and an enemy-held Sherman.

St. Edouard's Sanatorium, a large multi-storied brick chateau just northwest of the village, was a convalescent home for children and the elderly in the care of a Catholic order. On a steep hill overlooking the road, the sanatorium became a strategic location for both the Germans and the Americans. As a result, it became a hotbed of fierce fighting, and changed hands several times that day and night. From a road at the top of the hill, Peiper's tanks moved up close enough to fire directly into the building. The SS Panzergrenadiers charged, screaming *"Heil, Hitler!"* and the fighting erupted room to room and hand to hand. At one point, the Germans controlled all but one small area of the building. In that annex, a handful of men from the B and C Companies of 1/119 hung in there and fought tenaciously. A stone retaining wall and the steep slope of the hill kept the 740th tankers locked on the road below, unable to help, and in an untenable position. German tanks from above knocked out two of their Shermans, and a Panzerfaust set another on fire.[3]

In one of the unique ironies of war, the priests and sisters, the children, and the scores of other terror-stricken civilians caught in the sanatorium huddled in semi-security below ground in the basement and somehow survived. To add to the confusion, wounded soldiers from both sides were shepherded down the stairs, while both a German and American medic worked together to assist those in most need of help.[4]

In a gesture of compassion, a German soldier fired up a cigarette and put it between the lips of a badly wounded American who had just been given the last rites of the church by one of the priests. The bloodied GI inhaled a puff and pulled himself together enough to tug a piece of chocolate from his pocket and hand it to the German. The German thanked the young American, then turned away. "I can't eat it," the German soldier said to the priest. "It's covered with blood."[5]

19. Photo credit: Konecky and Konecky, publishers of The Ardennes: The Battle of the Bulge by Hugh Cole.

Stoumont Station, St. Edouard's Sanatorium

In the meantime, the star-crossed future of the 740th Tank Battalion had already begun to take shape. C Company was engaged near Stoumont, along with one platoon from A Company and another from B Company. The bulk of A Company was still getting equipment at Sprimont, while the rest of B Company was moved into division reserve just north of Malmedy. D Company was on-call from a holding position back near Remouchamps, and the battalion assault guns were attached to 30th Division artillery. The battalion forward command post was with the 119th Regiment command post at Lorce-Chevron, while the battalion rear command post was still at Sprimont. From one outfit to another, the splitting up of the battalion and its assignments — where the going was toughest — was to become a way of life.

Ammunition was consumed so rapidly that both ammunition and fuel had to be brought forward several times a day. Service Company trucked new supplies up as close as possible, then transferred into M20 armored utility cars to make the final run to the front, often under sniper fire.

Just across the Ambleve River, the 82nd Airborne Division's 504th Parachute Infantry was probing toward Cheneaux. Peiper's troops were there in force as well, and the only access to the town was across open fields crisscrossed with barbed wire fences. Both sides desperately needed the nearby bridge. The paratroopers' attack on Cheneaux would be costly, and as it so happened, heroic. Unknown to the 740th tankers, they would join the 82nd paratroopers in a matter of days.

Thursday, December 21. The 740th's C Company moved out in the predawn hours, and had barely traversed the length of a football field before the First Platoon's lead tank was clobbered by an anti-tank gun. The platoon leader, 1st Lt. David Oglensky, believing that the enemy was beginning a tank attack, struggled to turn his tank enough to block the road. Then, another explosion rocked his tank. He and the crew came tumbling out, and he commandeered the next tank just as it was blasted by a Panzerfaust. At the same time, two more tanks were blasted by *Panzerfausts,* leaving three 740th tanks in flames on the road.[6]

"We were about the sixth or seventh tank back when all hell broke loose," said TEC 4 Robert Russo. "Looking out my [driver's] periscope I saw that three tanks in front of me were burning fiercely. Through my mind ran the thought of my trapped buddies. Everything seemed a madhouse. I could see figures running back and forth, silhouetted by the flames of the burning tanks. A mortar hit [our tank] and blew our gunner's helmet off. I remember our loader, Corporal [William] Waddell, feeding rounds into the gun as quickly as the gunner fired. Keeping all the guns firing, he jerked the co-ax [.30 caliber machine gun] from its mount when it was too hot to fire any more. I noticed his hands were bleeding. Flares [lighting the darkness] right over our tank. I don't know to this day what actually kept us from getting hit. Maybe it was the wonderful coordination of our tank commander, gunner, and loader. They fired everything in the books at the Jerries, and when we were out of ammunition Sergeant [later Staff Sergeant] Willie Morris finally told me to back up and take cover behind a house. That was music to my ears."[7]

During the counterattack, the infantry stood tough and held their ground, even though the casualties were high—nearly two hundred men. The sanatorium on the hill at Stoumont was extremely costly to both sides.

A smoke screen was laid down for cover, and Capt. Walter Williams and his maintenance section moved in with their recovery vehicles. They attached lines and retrieved the three burned-out tanks. Oglenski's original tank had not burned, and TEC 5 James E. Flowers volunteered to go for it, although movement anywhere drew enemy fire. Flowers made it through the forest and up to the road, then crawled up under the tank. He entered through the escape hatch in the floor of the tank, managed to bring the tank to life, and drove it safely to the rear. The road was clear.[8]

During the day, Lt. Col. Rubel commandeered a 155 mm self-propelled gun and laid down some fifty rounds of direct fire from a position in Targnon. That night, Capt. Berry infiltrated enemy lines to reconnoiter the area around the sanatorium, searching for a way for his tanks to move up. Recruiting infantry to work with his tankers, and using cropped and shot-up trees and shell casings, he succeeded in devising a rough corduroy road over which his tanks could roll.

It was almost midnight, and the snow began to fall as four of Berry's tanks clambered up over the embankment and pulled up close enough to the sanatorium to fire point blank through the windows. Berry, on foot, ran from tank to tank directing fire. The Germans began to fall back.[9]

By morning, C Company armor had taken out two defending German tanks, and the final infantry assault took the sanatorium in hand. First Lt. Powers and S/Sgt. Loopey led that small group of tanks in ferocious fighting against heavy hostile fire that night, and they and a number of others were cited for their actions.[10]

Peiper's SS troops slipped away during the siege and fled to La Gleize, where the *Kampfgruppe* leader was concentrating his entire force. Two hundred and fifty Catholics, children, and others who had taken refuge in the sanatorium during the battle, were shocked at the scene as they emerged from the cellar. The building was nothing but a shell with fallen beams and shattered walls. Soldiers from both sides lay dead amid the gore and the rubble. As the Americans entered, they picked up children where they could and carried them to safety. One GI pulled a pair of dirty socks from his pocket and tugged them over the freezing feet of a little barefoot girl.[11]

Friday, December 22. As Jochen Peiper backtracked out of Stoumont, vacating his command post at a nearby castle, the Chateau de Froidcourt, the 740th's strength and confidence was beginning to grow. In addition to C Company, the 1st Platoon of A Company and the 2nd Platoon of D Company joined the attack at daybreak. It was reassuring to learn that a task force of the Third Armored Division was moving in their direction, out from Spa.

Still in support of the 30th Infantry, the 740th led the attack on Stoumont. The tanks slowly moved in column down the road as machine guns blazed away into the forest, and cannons belched fire at anything big enough to hide behind. On both flanks, and with marching fire, the infantry pushed through the snow-blanketed forest. With devastating firepower, the tanks rolled into the town. A unit of the Third Armored Division, believed to be Task Force Lovelady, moved in to secure the area shortly after the 740th passed through.

20. Drawing from Ardennes: 17 Decembre 1944 by Gerd, Cuppens, Belgium. Translation courtesy of Sylviane Finck. Author's collection.

The Americans succeeded in taking the sanatorium, but Peiper's men counter-attacked. Four 740th tanks moved up to the fight, but three of them were eventually destroyed. Depicted here is a burning Sherman, left, as two Panthers and a Flakpanzer IV close in.

Elements of *Kampfgruppe Peiper* were known to have established a bridgehead across the Ambleve nearby at Cheneaux. That afternoon, D Company came up to protect the rear and south flanks as the tankers began to move on La Gleize. Two German Panthers, and yet another enemy-held Sherman, were destroyed as the attack roared forward, but resistance was fierce, and two 740th tanks were lost in the skirmish. With the First Platoon of A Company out front, Staff Sergeant Frank M. Quick's tank had just taken the lead. Quick's gunner, Corporal M.W. Chism, traversed the turret left, and raked that side of the road with his coaxial .30 caliber machine gun, his 75mm cannon still hot and ready for larger targets. Down below, TEC 5 Lloyd P. Wright, the bow gunner, sprayed the right side of the road with his .30 caliber. The total effect was devastating to enemy ground troops.

Suddenly, Wright spotted an anti-tank gun dug in to the left. Yelling over the radio with his throat mic, he scrambled to alert Chism and Quick. By then, the intense fire from the column of tanks had driven the Germans from their gun, and

Quick was on it. As their tank rolled by, Chism traversed backwards and shot it to pieces.

W right settled back behind his bow gun and got his eyes in the scope just in time to see two Germans with Panzerfausts off to his right. He braced himself as the first one aimed and fired. The round struck the tank and blew him backwards but somehow failed to penetrate the tank. He recovered quickly, got back on his machine gun, and let go with a burst just as the second Panzerfaust erupted. Both he and the German missed, but as the Germans scattered, Wright slowly began to breathe again.

21.Photo credit: From the files of Chauncey Lester, taken in April 1945
The embattled St. Edouard Sanatorium, Stoumont, Belgium

Just as Wright's jangled nerves were finally settling down, they were confronted by an enemy tank that whacked them head-on. A huge thud sounded low and to the front. The round came into the tank and hung in the gear box. After safely bailing out of that one, they all promised to be preachers and spread the Good Word, if only they lived through this.

Later, off by himself near the Chateau de Froidcourt, Wright came upon another unimaginable scene from an unforgettable war; it must have happened during the fanatical infantry battle. The enemy dead were piled high to one side. On top of the pile was a fellow human who had perhaps been shot through with the armor-piercing round of a cannon. The body had a ragged hole in the center of the chest, and you could see right through him.[12]

Battalion Command Posts were set up in the vacated Chateau de Froidcourt, and an air strike on La Gleize was requested. However, visibility was so poor across the valley that the request was denied. Even so, German transport planes roared over that night dropping ammunition, fuel, and food to Peiper's forces—along with some paratroopers behind the lines. This kept the tankers who were back in the Assault Gun Platoon on edge, since they had no infantry dug in around them for protection.

A task force from the Third Armored Division rolled into Stoumont just behind the 740th, and the 504th Parachute Infantry Regiment of the 82nd Airborne Division fought a bloody battle across open fields and barbed wire fences into Cheneaux, just across the river. To the south, Stavelot had been retaken by the Americans. The noose was tightening around Kampfgruppe Peiper, and although much colder, the weather was beginning to clear.

The situation to the south was critical. Two vital road junctions, St. Vith and Bastogne, were fraught with danger for the Allies. St. Vith was lost. The 101st Airborne Division, the "Battered Bastards of Bastogne," was gamely hanging in there, even though completely surrounded. Brigadier General Anthony McAuliffe, the 101st acting commander, was faced with an ultimatum to surrender or suffer the consequences.

At the end of the first week of the massive German offensive, the situation was grim. President Roosevelt said in his Washington press conference that this was a critical time, and that those on the home front must work harder than ever to support our fighting men overseas. General Eisenhower was a virtual prisoner of his own guards at SHAEF Headquarters in Versailles, just outside Paris. Parachutists had been seen in the area, and it was believed that the German *Skorzeny's* saboteurs were out to assassinate the Supreme Commander.

Fussing and fuming at the restrictions being placed on him, Ike said to hell with it and walked past his stunned guards for a breath of fresh air and a stroll in the gardens. He told his secretary, "If anyone wants to shoot me, he can go right ahead. I've got to get out."[13]

Ike was in a dark mood. He knew that the American forces in the Ardennes were fighting for their lives, and he was scrambling to reinforce them with every man jack at his disposal—clerks, cooks, anyone who could carry a rifle. The forward supply dumps in the area were prime enemy targets. If any of them were captured, the enemy would have what he needed to overrun the Meuse River. The Americans simply had to stand and fight.

He felt better after his walk—more optimistic, more confident in the rightness of his cause and the opportunity provided by Hitler's desperate gamble. He seldom wrote "Orders of the Day," but on this day he was compelled to write, in part:

By rushing out from his fixed defenses the enemy may give us the chance to turn his great gamble into his worst defeat. So I call upon every man, of all the Allies, to rise now to new heights of courage, of resolution and of effort. Let everyone hold before him a single thought—to destroy the enemy on the ground, in the air, everywhere—destroy him! United in this determination and with unshakable faith in the cause for which we fight, we will, with God's help, go forward to our greatest victory.[14]

Grand'Route de l'Amblève près du Château de Froidecourt à Stoumont.
22. From the author's collection of postcards by Luma, circa 1944
Grand'Route de l'Amblève près du Château de Froidcourt à Stoumont

La Vallée à Targnon au confluent de l'Amblève et de la Lienne (Stoumont).

23. From the author's collection of postcards by Luma, circa 1944
The Valley of Targnon at the confluence of the Ambleve River at Stoumont

German anti-tank fire knocked out two more of the 740th's tanks that day, but the tankers reciprocated by taking out two Panther tanks, and yet another Sherman tank, which was being utilized by the enemy. A D Company tanker had actually bagged a plane.

Enemy transports, often accompanied by fighter-bombers, began filtering into the area, dumping ammunition, fuel, and rations for Peiper's task force. The tankers occasionally fired off a few wild shots at them. This was generally not a problem, but the situation turned grim rather quickly when out of the blue, one of the German fighters swooped down to strafe a "sitting duck" D Company tank that was temporarily out of action on the side of the road. With the rest of the crew out for a quick break, TEC 5 Joseph W. Hatchel Jr., was alone in the tank. He made a mad scramble for the .50 caliber mounted on the top of the turret and blasted away, only to see the stream of tracers arc down well short of the plane as it sped away.

Hatchel watched with some trepidation as the German plane went into a slow roll and turned back for another pass. By this time, his crew was shouting encouragement. "Get him, Hatchel. Get him!"

As the plane completed its loop and swooped back down the road, Hatchel let loose with a steady barrage of those big 50s, his heart pounded wildly above the awful clatter of the gun. The place suddenly exploded into a fiery ball then crashed to the ground and burned. "You got him, Hatchel—you got him!"

The pilot was dead, of course, and both he and the plane were burned to a crisp by the time the tankers reached the wreckage. They buried the charred remains of the pilot in his parachute, and some members of the crew cut off pieces of his parachute for scarves. But Hatchel became physically ill at the scene; it was gut-wrenching for him. The remembrance of the horror of that day never left him.[15]

Saturday, December 23. Fierce flanking fire from the Germans on the high ground northwest of La Gleize beat back the daybreak attack, and infantry casualties were heavy.

The huge 155 mm self-propelled artillery piece that Lt. Col. Rubel had commandeered was brought up onto the grounds of the Chateau de Froidcourt, and 1st Lt. George W. Merritt's Assault Gun Platoon set up their 105 mm guns nearby. The colonel stood on top of the castle wall and directed fire on the town, which was in clear view. Further back, division artillery laid down a blanket of fire. Then the 740th's 105s opened up, and Rubel finally had his personal crew blasting away with huge ninety-five pound shells over the open sights of his 155 mm gun.

When darkness finally called a halt to the intense shelling, La Gleize lay in ruins and came to be called The Cauldron (Der Kessel), by the Germans who survived.[16]

In the cellar of the little schoolhouse in La Gleize, Jochen Peiper and his staff shuddered every time that big gun thundered in. The pounding had left the village smoldering and cellars cramped with hundreds of German casualties, along with scores of American prisoners. Peiper's food and ammunition were low. Reinforcements were impossible. And fuel for his tanks was almost nonexistent.

His drive into the Ardennes had failed to capture the huge American gas dumps, which were necessary for his ultimate success. Supplies dropped by parachute filtered mostly into the American lines. Permission to withdraw was repeatedly denied, although requests went all the way to Hitler's headquarters.

When the long-range artillery and Lt. Col. Rubel's big gun finally let up for the day, Peiper sent for Maj. Hal McCown, his senior American prisoner. McCown had commanded the 30th Infantry's 2nd Battalion of the 119th until his capture a day earlier while on reconnaissance. Peiper spoke English well and wanted to talk. Their conversation went on into the night.

McCown was wary at first and knew that elements of three U.S. divisions surrounded the battered village. But Peiper wasn't after military information. In the course of their conversations, Peiper went from cold and impersonal, to warm and friendly, displaying an obvious culture and intellect, along with a strong sense of humor. McCown found Peiper to be fanatical regarding the Nazi cause and the *Führer's* dream of a unified Europe, but a very experienced and professional soldier. Peiper admitted to certain wrongdoing on Germany's part, but argued that they were fighting to "eliminate the communist menace" and were actually "fighting your fight" against the Bolshevics.[17]

McCown, a graduate of West Point who later became a general, was admittedly taken by the wit and charm of the man. Still, he was certain that Peiper's troops had committed the atrocity at the Baugnez crossroads, and he feared for the safety of his fellow prisoners of war—at least one hundred fifty of whom were crammed into the cellars and basements of the village. He appealed to Peiper's sense of honor, and the German gave his word.[18]

Sunday, December 24. In the freezing cold of the early morning hours, with McCown in tow and under guard, Peiper, on foot and without his tanks, led the remnants of his once mighty *Kampfgruppe* out the back door of La Gleize, down a rough track to the river, and out through the Ambleve Valley. The numbers vary, but probably no more than eight hundred escaped from an original force of well over five thousand. These few kept watchful eyes over their shoulders as they slipped and slid, ghostlike, through the ice and snow of the Ardennes Forest that Christmas Eve morning.

Just before dawn, a powerful explosion up ahead in La Gleize startled the Americans at their outposts on the front lines. Then another, and another, until the village seemed on fire. Counterattack? Not this time. Unknown to the Americans, it was just Peiper's rearguard blowing up his remaining Royal Tiger, Panther, and

Mark IV tanks, along with the other heavy equipment—half-tracks, cannons, flak weapons, mortars, other weapons, and vehicles—left behind in the frantic German exodus.

24. Photo by Chigger Webster

During this traumatic action, Technician Fifth Grade C.O. "Chigger" Webster was awe-struck with this embedded drawing of Christ on the wall in the depths of the Chateau. To his amazement, on a visit with the Battalion Association in 1999, he discovered it was still decipherable.

The American attack that morning went forward as planned. Artillery plastered the village as the tanks of the 740th began to roll. Moving cautiously through the woods, the infantry cleared the flanks. When the artillery lifted, Capt. Red Berry's C Company roared into the village with guns blazing.

As the tankers pulled to a halt and the infantry infiltrated the town, they were shocked at what they saw. Scores of dead and wounded Germans were everywhere. Knocked out tanks, half-tracks, anti-tank guns, and smoldering vehicles of every description—over a hundred seventy-five by Lt. Col. Rubel's count, including a number of captured American tanks and trucks.

In La Gleize, it was confirmed that Peiper had kept his word to McCown. The American prisoners were safe; those who could walk helped those who could not. Some two hundred infantrymen were rescued that day—men from the 119th who had been overrun and captured just days earlier when *Kampfgruppe Peiper* exploded through the American lines.

Technician Fourth Grade Jay D. Kirkpatrick remembered La Gleize quite well. He was driving for 2nd Lt. John E. Calloway when a German 88 clipped a bogie and damaged the suspension system. Not too bad, everything considered. They all got out alive, and finally got the tank into La Gleize several days later, hooked it onto a wrecker, and headed for battalion maintenance in Spa. While en route, they ran over some German mines stacked on the side of the road. *Kabloom!* Kirkpatrick knew they'd been hit by another 88.

When he came to, he had his arm over the gun tube that he credits for saving his life. His eyes were blistered, his was face burnt, and he had to feel his way around the turret to the back of the tank to see who else was hurt. No one seemed to be there. Suddenly, he realized his clothes were on fire. He jumped off the tank and rolled around in the dirt and mud until he got the fire out. As best as he could, he breathed a sigh of relief when he learned from the lead peep that the others were already on the way to the hospital in Spa, and that he was next.[19]

25. Photo credit: A/P Images

Outside La Gleize, infantrymen eased cautiously past a German King Tiger tank, which had been knocked out by the 740th Tank Battalion, its crew simmering inside.

The tank recovery guys were among the unsung heroes of the battalion. Technician Fourth Grade Joseph B. Early of Service Company was cited for his devotion to duty during this battle. He shepherded his recovery vehicle to the most forward elements of the 740th on the 23rd, and cleared the road of two knocked-out enemy vehicles. The next day, on Christmas Eve, they went back to the front lines to evacuate two of the disabled tanks.[20]

The maintenance people did remarkable, even heroic, work. First Lieutenant

Gerard C. Lange, A Company's maintenance officer, "went to the fighting elements of his company's tanks under the most adverse conditions to repair and evacuate vehicles which had been knocked out by enemy action."[21] Technical Sergeant Joseph J. Salvestrini of C Company "advanced to the foremost elements of the fighting tanks time after time to evacuate tanks or make necessary repairs on knocked out vehicles. A large measure of the success C Company had in repulsing the enemy's strong and constant counterattacks at this time was due to his outstanding performance."[22]

Christmas Eve was an all-around incredible day. Service Company's Staff Sergeant Francis W. Rebel, still headquartered behind the lines at Sprimont, watched as American bombers flew overhead in a wedge formation, sixteen planes in a group. The sun was shining, making the silver planes truly beautiful against the blue background of a cloudless sky, Sgt. Rebel said.

Later, the first formation was on its way back, then the second and the third. As the third formation came directly overhead, three German fighters attacked from the rear. Smoke began to roll back from the bombers; they appeared to be almost helpless against the smaller, faster enemy fighters.

The bombers were obviously trying to hold their positions, but the fighters dove and came up underneath the bombers with all the firepower they had. The last bomber broke out in flames. Two more bombers, along with a German fighter, fluttered down, trailing a black cloud of smoke. The Service Company guys were out and watching now, running around, some in tears.

26. Photo credit: 740th Tank Battalion Association Archives

A dead German Panther stands amid the ruins of La Gleize. Artillery fire caused much of the damage.

Captain Willis B. Chapman, the company commander, considered that the crippled planes might fall near the ammunition dump. He hollered at Rebel to get the peep. He could see some of the Germans coming down in parachutes. Then, about four hundred yards away, the first plane hit the ground.

Rebel and Chapman tore off in the direction of the first bomber that hit the ground, Rebel said. As they approached the burning plane—thinking they somehow might be able to help—the plane exploded. A baseball-sized piece of shrapnel struck Capt. Chapman in the arm, knocked him out of the jeep, and onto the ground. Rebel ducked, slammed on the brakes, and jumped for safety. He landed right on the captain just as the second explosion blew the plane to pieces. The two pulled themselves together, piled back into the jeep, and headed for the first aid station.[23]

The temperature dropped into the teens that night on Christmas Eve 1944, and the snow crunched underfoot as Peiper's troops struggled desperately to escape the American noose tightening around them. Bright moonlight cast eerie shadows behind every tree as the column moved cautiously through the forest. Exhausted, Peiper was everywhere—up and down the column, pushing hard, allowing his burned out and hungry men only the briefest intervals of rest and relief along the way.

The pounding of La Gleize had been mind-numbing, and there was little food. Finally, the weary column of enemy troopers reached the Salm River and crossed the icy waters toward the German lines at Wanne.

As luck would have it, an element of the 82nd US Airborne Division was withdrawing through the area to set up a new defensive position, and a vicious firefight broke out. Rifles cracked, mortars thumped, shrapnel whizzed, machine guns flashed and tracers zipped back and forth through the fir trees. As quickly as it had begun, it was over, but men had been ripped apart on both sides.

Peiper's American prisoner, Maj. McCown, and his German guards, scrambled for cover in the darkness. He dropped to the ground and crawled belly-down at right angles in the snow, away from the fighting. Finding himself alone at last, McCown got up and cautiously made his way on foot. He believed he was near the area from which friendly fire had come. Moving slowly and uneasily, he whistled "Yankee Doodle Dandy" with as much braggadocio as he could muster.[24] McCown was later quoted as saying that he really couldn't remember the tune.

McCown was wet, shivering cold, and his face slashed and torn when he stumbled into an American outpost. Still, when an angry GI voice rang out, "Halt, goddamn it!" he knew he was home free.[25] Lt. Col. Rubel said, "Major McGowan [sic] escaped on the night of the 23rd and we found him on the 24th, badly shaken but still on his feet."[26]

On Christmas Day, as the 82nd Airborne troops finally completed their withdrawal, Peiper and his *Kampfgruppe* survivors made it back to the safety of the German lines at Wanne. Having been slightly wounded in the firefight and by then totally spent, Peiper collapsed at the last and had to be carried into the aid station at Wanne. His return, however, brought a hero's welcome. His superiors had already recommended him for the Third Reich's most prestigious award: the Swords to his Knight's Cross. He was only 29.

In their crucial role of blunting the spearhead column of Jochen Peiper's *Leibstandarte Adolf Hitler* panzers, the 740th had been both unflinching and lucky. Although the battalion lost six tanks and ten men were wounded, not a tanker had been killed.

Monday, December 25, 1944. Heavy German artillery, along with rifle and machine gun fire, rained down on the 740th's C Company and the Third Platoon of D Company as the American attack ground forward again on Christmas Day. Still in support of the Second Battalion of the 30th Infantry's 119th Regiment, their job was to rescue a small force cut off at a road junction just south of Petit Coo. They achieved their mission, but hellfire broke loose in the process, when, without warning, their column of tanks came under attack by American fighter planes.

Mass confusion erupted on the ground as the P-47s swooped down, bombarding and machine-gunning the column up and down the road. When their bombs were gone, they circled and came back, their .50 calibers chipping away at the tanks. The tankers hauled out their orange identification panels, but nothing would deter the American pilots. They were having a field day.

In short order, one of the tanks was blown and three men were wounded in the attack. Road-bound and stalled in column, the tankers were sitting ducks. They couldn't even shoot back. With the machine gun slugs clanging off their tanks and chopping up the road around them, they piled out of their steel death traps and scrambled for cover across the snow-encrusted field.

They dove headfirst into the cover of one of the far-flung hedgerows, and one of the 2nd Platoon's gunners lay on his back in the freezing water, watching in horror as his own planes dived, screaming and blazing away at his column of tanks. Again and again, they circled and came back. He could only pray that they would run out of ammunition.

Between the fright and the freezing cold, it was a nerve-shattering experience. At last, someone finally got through to a spotter plane, and the American fighters were called off.

Funny how things work out.

The sky finally darkened as the planes left. The lucky tankers who escaped unscathed began to regroup, chattering excitedly, each with his own vivid recollection of what personally happened to him.

Angry and shivering from the freezing wet and cold, they fired up the tanks and gathered behind the huge exhausts, drying out and hoping to warm up just a little before moving out. And wouldn't you know, God bless 'em, the company mess trucks came skidding up with cold turkey sandwiches all around. Merry Christmas.

Word came down that the battalion had done its job well and was due a few days' rest. The tankers spent the next couple of days in division reserve on roadblocks, with the promise of a little R&R to come. On December 27, one of C Company's tanks and a Service Company ten-ton wrecker were blown up by mines. Five were wounded, but none were killed.

With the battalion still scattered over the area, and widespread concern about the massacre of American troops at Malmedy, Lt. Col. Rubel sent two jeeps to Malmedy to investigate the massacre.

Robert Frank Cole, then a staff sergeant in the Mortar Platoon (later technical sergeant), became profoundly emotional when he recently spoke of his memory of that incident. "It must have been about December 27," he says, "shortly after Christmas." Cole shuddered, then with considerable effort, continued. "I remember that there were eight of us in two peeps. I think the colonel wanted us to see what the enemy was really like—what we were fighting for." Tears welled up in his eyes. "We'd heard some things. The massacre of our guys, and all that. But there was no way we were ready for the carnage spread out across that field."

He tried to contain himself but stopped to cover his eyes with both hands. Still, he managed to continue. "Eighteen- and nineteen-year-old boys frozen in the snow. In grotesque positions. What you'd see—" he shook his head in disbelief, remembering. "A face half-covered with black, frozen blood, and white snow, and the rest of him . . .

"Bodies twisted and contorted sticking up out of the snow and ice. The thing that haunts me the most was a body frozen in the snow with uplifted arms like he was reaching out for help—and I couldn't help him! I grew deathly sick and threw up.

"A grave registration crew moved here and there among the bodies, stacking them up in piles—" Cole reached for his handkerchief and could not go on.[27]

Dwight R. Davis, Jr., then a TEC 4 payroll sergeant and records keeper in Headquarters Company, was also with the investigating team, and to this day finds it gut-wrenching to talk about the experience. Hesitantly, and with a catch in his voice, he remembers. "With the battalion as widely dispersed as it was, Lt. Col. Rubel wasn't entirely sure if any of our troops had been involved, so off we went.

"It was awful. Our guys were shot-up and littering the field everywhere, scattered across the open area. The total effect was unbelievable. You really couldn't comprehend it. You just went kind of numb.

"It turned out that there were no tankers involved. We checked with the grave registration people, and that's what we reported to Lt. Col. Rubel—no record of any dead tankers. The slaughtered Americans were all infantry artillery personnel." Davis shakes his head tragically. "It all seems like a horrible nightmare, even after all these years."[28]

27. Photo credit: Konecky and Konecky, publishers of The Ardennes:
The Battle of the Bulge, by Hugh Cole.

Victims of Kampfgruppe Peiper, frozen in the snow, were from the 285th Field Artillery Observation Battalion.

Finally, the battalion, minus the Assault Gun Platoon and the First Platoon of A Company, was withdrawn from action and pulled back for a hot bath, hot meal, and a little R&R in a couple of hotels in Spa, Belgium. A welcome relief.

Still, the tankers were not allowed to bask in any such glory for long. They did get warm, and well fed, and they got a change of clothes for the first time in weeks. But they were hardly dry from that incredible hot bath and had barely begun to partake of the R&R in Spa, when word came down to "Crank 'em up" and roll out again. They were relieved from the 30th Infantry Division and ordered to join the 82nd Airborne Division on December 29 in the area of Werbomont, Belgium, a crossroads some twenty-five miles north of Bastogne. The 82nd was fighting as part of the First U.S. Army's XVIII Airborne Corps, Maj. Gen. Matthew B. Ridgway commanding.

Presidential Unit Citation

The 740th's C Company, the First Platoon of A Company, the Second Platoon of B Company, several members of Service Company, and the Battalion Reconnaissance Platoon, were awarded the Distinguished Unit Citation for "outstanding performance of duty in action against the enemy from 19 December to 21 December in Belgium." The First Battalion, and other elements of the 30th Infantry's 119th Regiment, also received the prestigious award.

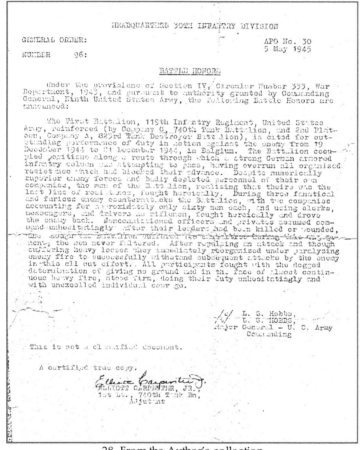

28. From the Author's collection

Battle Honors

Chapter 13

Christmas at Home

Back home, Christmas had been a reflective and a lonely time for most American families. Of course, there was no invading army ravaging the country. The U.S. mainland was way out of reach and return of even the longest flying land-based enemy planes. And the risk was too great for aircraft carriers that close to American shores.

The Japanese did get one flight into the States, however, early on in the war. A Japanese Zero was launched from a submarine off the West Coast, and the pontoon-equipped plane dropped incendiary bombs on an Oregon forest. The firestorm that was supposed to sweep down the coast and blacken the region never developed, so the sub reluctantly headed for home.

The Japanese also launched thousands of frightening, high-altitude, balloon-borne bombs across the Pacific, but only a scattered three hundred or so made it to America. A few floated as far in as Iowa and Kansas, but most fizzled out. Other than a few fires, the only real casualties came when one of the deadly missiles exploded on Mount Gearhart in Oregon, killing a woman and five children on what appeared to be a church outing.[1]

Still, every man, woman, and child knew there was a war going on. Most had loved ones deeply involved in the war in one way or another, if not in the fighting itself. Although air raid drills were less common now, American families continued to buy war bonds and collect old tires and scrap metal "for the boys over there." As for whatever happened to be available at the time, trying to buy almost anything for themselves was still somewhat of a scramble.[2]

A person really could not eat, nor dress, nor shop, nor travel without being somehow affected by the shortages. It was undoubtedly the greatest undertaking and "pulling together of the people" in American history.

In one of his "fireside chats" on the radio, President Roosevelt challenged the American people to help make the United States the "great arsenal of democracy," noting that the U.S. must provide for its allies, as well as itself. Slowly but surely, American industry shifted from civilian to war production. The world had never seen anything like it––more than 296,000 airplanes, 102,000 tanks and self-propelled guns, 372,000 artillery pieces, 47 million tons of artillery ammunition,

87,000 warships, and 44 billion rounds of small arms ammunition before the war came to an end.[3]

It is difficult to imagine the difficulties involved in such an incredible undertaking in a democratic society. All the government intervention in priorities and allocation of materials was an anathema to American businessmen — all the dictates from Washington, all the regulations, all the paper work. Still, when the no-risk, "cost plus" contracts were ultimately worked out, there was money to be made. And in the American way, big business went to work.

Old Henry Ford was all pacifist in both world wars, but he was all-American when his country became involved. By the time the U.S. entered World War II, he had built a mammoth new Ford Motor Company building at Willow Run, just outside Detroit, vowing to produce a bomber an hour. At the time, it was the largest aircraft assembly plant in the world. By 1944, at the age of eighty-two, the pioneer automaker had a B-24 Liberator rolling off his newfangled production line every 63 minutes — 8,685 in all by war's end.[4]

For the duration, the great assembly lines of mass production in Detroit, and across the country, turned to the propellers, wheels, and tracks of war. Every day, there was a trainload of tanks — two-and-a-half million trucks: the incredible new four-wheel drive General Purpose vehicle, or "Jeep" as it came to be called; and the DUK-W, or "Duck," was part truck and part boat. And there were weapons of every description.

Then there were the shipbuilders. An organizational and technical genius, Henry J. Kaiser built the bulk of the nation's merchant vessels. These "Liberty Ships" — then later, "Victory Ships" — carried much of the war materials to foreign shores. Kaiser was a big, dynamic man from the construction industry, but he was new to the shipyard. He forever called the ship's bow the "front end."

Andrew Jackson Higgins was a rough-hewn Irishman with uncanny abilities. In September 1943, the American navy had just over 14,000 vessels, nearly 13,000 of which were designed by Higgins Industries, mostly built at the Higgins plants in New Orleans. "Higgins boats" included not only the high-speed PT boats, but also the various landing crafts capable of carrying troops, mechanized equipment, and supplies.[5]

The entire world marveled at the industrial might of the United States of America. By 1944, the industrial and manpower resources of the United States were greater than that of Germany, Japan, Great Britain, and Russia combined.[6] When Stalin, Churchill, and Roosevelt had their first face-to-face encounter a year earlier at Teheran and made the decision to invade western Europe, the Russian premier proposed a toast "to American production, without which this war would have been lost."[7]

In the movies at home, the Allies always won, of course. And singing the *Star-Spangled Banner* before baseball games became a tradition. Next to the American flag, "V is for Victory" became the most highly regarded symbol of the war effort.[8] The knock on the door bringing word that a loved one was wounded, or dead, or missing in action in some faraway land, was the thing that haunted most folks back home.

Chapter 14

And to the South: Bastogne

The Battered Bastards of Bastogne. While the 740th tankers were up to their hip pockets in alligators in the area of Stoumont and La Gleize, the "Screaming Eagles" of the 101st Airborne were surrounded and under siege at Bastogne, just twenty-five miles to the south. Attacking in force on December 22, the Germans halted the fighting long enough to send in a four-man party under a white flag to demand "the honorable surrender of the town," threatening the Americans with "annihilation." When the demand reached the acting division commander, Brig. Gen. Anthony C. McAuliffe, the first words out of his mouth were "Aw, nuts!" At the urging of his staff, the American general's famously memorable reply to the confused German commander was just that, "Nuts!"[1]

Dawn broke cold and clear the next day, unleashing the American Air Force for the first time in days. The planes came over Bastogne by the hundreds. C-47 transports roared in to parachute ammunition, food, and supplies. Some were shot down, and many of the parachute packs fell outside the American lines, but enough help found its way inside to bolster the spirit of the embattled garrison.

Then came the fighter escorts. The paratroopers cheered as the P-47s blasted the enemy with high explosives and fragmentation bombs, napalm, and machine gun fire. The Germans were staggered but undeterred. In white snow camouflage, they counterattacked in force.

By Christmas Eve, Hitler had become aware of the situation at the vital road hub and demanded that Bastogne be taken the very next day. He was still intent on breaking through to the Meuse River and was angered that such a small, stubborn American force could stand in the way. An all-out attack was ordered for Christmas morning.[2]

Still, in the command posts and cellars of the beleaguered town, hope had come alive. Earlier in the day, the battered Americans received a succinct message from Lt. Gen. George Patton: *Xmas Eve present coming* up. *Hold on.*[3]

Patton, under Bradley's command, had been ordered by General Eisenhower to disengage his Third Army in the region of the Saar and launch a major counterattack from the south to relieve Bastogne, then slug his way north toward Houffalize. Meanwhile, Hodges was to turn elements of the First Army south to meet Patton at Houffalize as soon as the battle in the Ardennes stabilized, thus effectively cutting off the German salient.

In a remarkable turnaround on December 22, Patton broke off his operation in the Saar and swung north with three divisions, never doubting his ability to gain Bastogne by Christmas Eve. However, it was not to be. The rain, the snow, the mud, and the determined German resistance frustrated the Third Army's march to the north. The 101st troopers on the perimeter of Bastogne were still freezing in their foxholes on Christmas Eve, hoping against hope that relief would come soon. Amid thoughts of home and time running out, they shook hands and wished one another a Merry Christmas.

Christmas Day came and went. The 101st troopers were grimly hanging on, having withstood everything the Germans could throw at them. On December 26, elements of Patton's Third Army ultimately broke through the German gauntlet to the "Battered Bastards of Bastogne." Just a few days later, the Americans were in complete control of the city.

With *Kampfgruppe Peiper* and other major forces in the north blunted or in retreat, with the relief of Bastogne to the south, and with the heroic stand of the American forces at St. Vith to the east, the devastating blitzkrieg in the Ardennes was brought to a halt. Hitler's bold gamble was thwarted, and the Americans were ready to go back on the offensive.

Chapter 15

With the 82nd Airborne Division

A deep blanket of snow spread out ahead of the 740th as the awkward column of tanks rumbled from their brief respite in Spa to join the 82nd Airborne Division in the area of Werbomont, Belgium.

At division headquarters, plans were underway to launch an attack south toward Lierneux at daybreak on January 1. The paratroopers' experience with tanks apparently had not been all to the good, according to the 740th's commander. Lt. Col. Rubel's reception at the 82nd headquarters was subdued, to say the least. They were afraid the tankers could not keep up with them and thus be of little value. The crusty colonel let it be known that *his* only concern was that the 82nd troopers would be able to keep up with his tanks. As it turned out, the paratroopers' hard-nosed attitude would change dramatically during the coming campaign.

The tankers rolled into a heavily wooded assembly area just northeast of Werbomont on December 29. The snow was at least two feet deep, and the mercury dipped down below zero at night. Miserable conditions, but according to the locals, it was typical weather for this time of year.

Experience had taught Rubel that rubber tracks would be a necessity in this weather and on these hills, and he sent battalion maintenance out scrounging for rubber tracks to replace the steel tracks on the tanks, for better maneuverability. It wasn't easy, but persistence gradually paid off. Maintenance salvaged what they could from knocked-out tanks and TD's in the area, and then searched far and wide for the rest, lugging some of the tracks over two hundred miles. By the first of the year, most of the tanks were fairly well equipped.

With the frigid weather and heavy equipment coming in, the roads had become almost impassable as the buildup for the American push continued. The jump-off date was postponed to January 3. Supplies and heavy equipment supporting the attack could not get set up in time. Moving into position, the artillery's big guns would often slide across the icy road and crash wildly down a hill. Infantry transport found it impossible to move about, and the poor doughboys on foot found themselves slogging and cursing through the mush and waist-deep snow to get to where they were supposed to be.

The waiting was tense, since both sides were patrolling actively. The tankers were constantly on the alert. Sporadic small arms fire erupted regularly on both sides of the lines, but mostly between patrols blundering into one another. As the American artillery gradually drew into position, it boomed steadily, the shells screaming overhead toward suspected troop concentrations and enemy-held villages. In turn, the Germans laid down "harassing" fire on the American lines by shuffling self-propelled guns about, lobbing in a few rounds, and then shifting to another position before the Americans could zero in on them. A real battle of nerves.

In preparation for the impending attack, A Company was attached first to the 551st Parachute Infantry Battalion and then to the 505th, while B Company went to the 325th Glider Infantry Regiment. The Assault Gun Platoon was attached to the 456th Glider Field Artillery and moved into firing position in the vicinity of Rahier, just west of Cheneaux and Trois-Ponts. C and D Companies assembled in a wooded area nearby, awaiting assignment.

On New Year's Eve, a platoon of tanks from D Company, 1st Lt. Thomas T. Munford in command, was sent on a recon mission from nearby Basse-Bodeux toward Fosse to see what they could find. Two peeps full of paratroopers from the 82nd were attached. The group ran into an enemy hotbed just north of Fosse, and in a brief firefight, knocked out a German half-track, killed a number of their troops, and made it safely back with nine prisoners on the backs of their tanks. Gathered around the campfires in the snow that night, stories were told.

First Lieutenant Warren M. Halverson led a patrol out from Les Sevrailles with orders to check resistance to the southeast, a euphemism that meant, "Move out down that road until fired upon." It was an exciting tank maneuver that definitely got the old adrenaline pumping. This patrol was soon withdrawn, however, due to the proliferation of enemy mine fields in the area. Still, it was by a long shot, the loneliest, coldest New Year's Eve these young tankers had ever spent. Happy New Year.

New Year's Day, 1945. The German *Luftwaffe* attacked in force that New Year's Day, throwing their reserve of more than eight hundred planes at Allied airfields in Belgium, Holland, and northern France, particularly in and around the "Bulge." It was yet another surprise by the Nazis, and the Allies lost a multitude of aircraft on the ground. Although more than three hundred Allied planes were destroyed, the enemy's own losses were irreplaceable at this stage of the war—especially with the loss of their pilots.[1]

Excitement buzzed through the ranks as the 740th received twelve new tanks. These brought the battalion combat vehicle strength up to thirty-four M4 Tanks with 75 mm guns, fifteen M4 Tanks with 76 mm guns, six M4 Tanks with 105 mm howitzers, five M5A1 Light Tanks with 37 mm guns, six M8 Assault tanks with 75 mm howitzers, two M24 Light Tanks with 75 mm guns, and four M32 Tank Recovery Vehicles.[2]

It was near dark as Lt. Col. Rubel stood watching enemy gun flashes from a small rise near Werbomont. Suddenly, the ground exploded under his feet. The concussion sent him tumbling down the embankment onto the icy road below, where he ended up skidding downhill on his backside. Fortunately, he was not seriously wounded. But, for a time, the incident played havoc with his disposition and his ability to sit at ease in front of the staff.

As the war moved into 1945, the Allied forces began to grind forward on the offense again, ever closer to Germany's western border. General Eisenhower had hoped to be farther along by then. In fact, he lost a five-pound bet (about twenty dollars at the time) to Field Marshall Montgomery that the war would be over by Christmas.

Since landing on the continent in June, the Allies had liberated France and Belgium and captured, wounded, or killed hundreds of thousands of Germans. However, the all-out surprise German counteroffensive in the Ardennes set the Allies back on their heels, and clearly upset their timetable. The *Siegfried Line* stretched out dead ahead.

The GIs dug in at the front were cold, hungry, and exhausted, but as the Battle of the Bulge began to turn their way, the smell of victory was in the air. Help was on the way.

With the once deadly German submarines now only an occasional threat, the Allied supply lines, which stretched clear across the Atlantic Ocean, were jammed with replacements and equipment. The huge transports and freighters were dumping their magnificent payloads not only in Great Britain, but also at Cherbourg and Le Havre in France, and now, even closer to the front at the Belgian port of Antwerp.

Long lines of GI trucks began their bumper-to-bumper scramble toward the front lines. Mountains of food, clothing, ammunition, fuel, and the vehicles of war filled supply dumps. At the same time, forward motor repair depots and tent city hospitals were being constructed where they would be most valuable.[3]

Five hundred thousand Belgian, Polish, and French troops were equipped to guard lines of communication. General Eisenhower requested the transfer of troops from Italy and initiated a plan for volunteers from the segregated American Negro support units to join the infantry. He asked for General Marshall's help in getting the Soviets' long-awaited winter offensive underway. Stalin continued to claim bad weather but now promised to attack in force by mid-January.

The powerful Soviet offensive from the east had ground to a halt near

Warsaw, Poland, some months before, and it had been at least two months since Marshal Stalin had promised the "last, final mission —in the near future."

In truth, the Red Army had serious problems of supply. Their front line varied from twelve hundred to fifteen hundred miles from primary production facilities. The shortage of truck transportation was forever. And the rail system in war-torn eastern Poland had to be completely rebuilt.[4]

However, the massive German attack on New Year's Day had been a virtual last hurrah for the *Luftwaffe,* and Allied planes dominated the air. Both the British and American heavy-bomber forces played havoc over Germany —British by day, and American by night. Along the Rhine and in the region of the Ruhr Valley, important industrial areas and city after city was in flames or long ago in ruins. Oil and rail centers and V-weapon sites were all heavily hit.

With Allied fighter-bombers continually on the prowl, German supply trains and trucks had dwindled to camouflage or oblivion, traveling only at night. Shot-up and abandoned vehicles and equipment were strewn up and down bombed-out roads.

Hitler's desperate gamble in the Ardennes had failed, just as his generals knew it would. Still, none dared incur the Führer's wrath by telling him so. His health was failing. The assassination attempt had taken its toll, as had the stress and occasional weird medication he received from his personal physician. But he was undeterred, ordering a reorganization in preparation for an attack in the south. He knew that Lieutenant General Jacob L. Dever's U.S. Sixth Army Group was considerably overextended in the south now that Patton's Third Army was moving northward.

The German Führer still ruled with a dictator's hand, but that hand was weakened now, and it trembled. His back was bent, his face was haggard, his hair was gray, his left shoulder drooped. He could hardly write. At times, an aide had to forge his signature on important documents.[5]

The battle in the Ardennes surged as Allied counterattacks began. Hitler had rejected his generals' pleas to pull back and defend at the vaunted *Siegfried Line.* Instead, he ordered a war of attrition in the area of the breakthrough to keep the Allies out of Germany as long as possible.

In spite of the miserable weather, an impatient General Eisenhower was prodding Field Marshal Montgomery to counterattack south out of the Ardennes by January 1 with Hodges' U.S. First Army, which was still temporarily under British command. Eisenhower and Bradley hoped to cut the German bulge in half by linking up the U.S. First Army at Houffalize with the Patton's U.S. Third Army, which was slugging its way northward from Bastogne.

Monty, however, saw things differently. He believed the Germans had another full-blown attack left in the making and wanted to absorb and control that before counterattacking. And, he still pressed hard for a single major thrust to the north, while placing Patton in a "holding role" in the south. He imperiously wrote to Ike demanding full control of the land battle, since Ike's "broad front" strategy had been "tried and failed." He then presented a "directive" to that effect for Ike's signature.

Ike was so furious with Monty's intransigence that he wrote the British Field Marshal an "I do not agree" letter, and told Monty that he would not further debate the subject of command. He was so angry that he set about to present their differences to the Combined Joint Chiefs of Staff and let them choose between him and Monty, if necessary. Fortunately, the matter never got quite that far. Ike had General Marshall's clear support, and when Monty got word of Ike's toughened attitude, he quickly backed away and wrote that he was merely giving his best advice—that Ike could count on him one hundred percent, and to please "tear up" his previous letter.

Hitler had always believed that when push came to shove, the deep-rooted political and philosophical differences among the Allies would eventually split the grand alliance. This was about as close as the Allies had ever come to proving him right.

With the crisis of command temporarily at ease, the U.S. First Army turned south in a pincer movement to meet the U.S. Third Army coming north, and on January 3, the big Allied counteroffensive got under way.

The two armies were only about twenty-five miles apart, but trouble with a capital "T" lay between them. The terrain was rugged, with deep gorges, frozen rivers, slick ice-hardened roads, and a forest full of snow. And according to Stephen Ambrose in his book *Citizen Soldiers,* filled with "tens of thousands of battle-hardened German troops who were highly skilled in utilizing terrain features and villages as fortified positions."[6]

The U.S. First Army's XVIII Airborne Corps, commanded by Major General Matthew B. Ridgway, consisted of two fighting divisions for this particular counteroffensive: the 30th Infantry, with which the 740th had fought up to this point; and the 82nd Airborne, to which the 740th was now assigned. Major General James M. Gavin commanded the 82nd Airborne Division, and this division was to carry the main weight of the offensive. The 7th Armored and the single-regiment 106th Infantry Divisions were in reserve.

Now with the 82nd Airborne, the 740th Tank Battalion was again being thrown into the breach.

The first days of 1945 in the Ardennes were bitterly cold, snowy, and heavily overcast. When the 740th jumped off on the morning of January 3, A Company was in support of the 505th Parachute Infantry. The objective was to capture Reharmont and Fosse and then take the high ground overlooking Abrefontaine.

The First Platoon advanced down the road in column, spearheading the attack, with the infantry spread out and clearing the forest. Small arms fire cracked, occasionally zinging off the tanks. Some mines were encountered, but no real damage was done. Staff Sergeant (later Second Lieutenant) Dexter B. Ledbetter and Sergeant Jim B. Duke's tanks each shot up an anti-tank gun and a bazooka team.

Suddenly, the column ran into a buzz saw. First Lieutenant George W. Merritt, the platoon leader, was hit and evacuated when shrapnel from a shell or tree burst ricocheted off the turret of his tank. Ledbetter was charged with command of the platoon, and the fight was quickly rejoined.

Another enemy anti-tank gun slammed into Sergeant Frank M. Quick's tank, throwing it out of action. Ledbetter called for artillery fire, but the infantry's battalion commander ordered him to attack the hotbed straight on. Although the platoon laid down enough fire to claim its objective, the direct frontal attack had been costly. Merritt's tank had continued in the advance, but both it and Sergeant Howard J. Cluck's tanks were eventually destroyed by AT fire.[7]

When A Company's Second and Third Platoons were stopped in their tracks by a blown bridge, the troopers decided to make a frontal attack on Reharmont without the tanks and suffered extremely heavy losses. After the bridge was repaired, the tanks led the infantry into the town from two different directions, guns blazing, forcing the Germans to withdraw.

Sergeants Nello Fasoli, Jack McPherson, and Herman Beard's tanks engaged several machine gun nests, and Staff Sergeant Hendrix's tank flushed out other dug-in positions and enemy CP's. The 740th tankers and the 82nd Airborne troopers were a good team.

A section of the Third Platoon was then ordered on to Fosse. The tankers shelled the town for several minutes, then thundered forward with infantry on the backs of their tanks. First Lieutenant Allen C. Christi commanded the section, and his tank led the column, dodging Panzerfaust fire all the way. Sergeants Harrell and J. S. Montgomery's tanks shot up a bazooka team, an AT gun, and a number of dug-in machine gun positions as they blasted their way in. The troopers let loose with everything they had. About seventy of the enemy were killed, and the infantry took nearly two hundred prisoners.[8]

B Company attacked in support of the 325th Glider Infantry Regiment towards Noirfontaine. Only small arms fire slowed their advance to Heid-de-Heirlot, their first objective. The attack continued toward Odrimont.

Each of B Company's platoons was now attached to a separate infantry battalion. The First Platoon was attached to the Second Infantry Battalion, the

Second Platoon to the First Infantry Battalion, and the Third Platoon to the Third Battalion.[9] This was typical of the way in which the 740th was split up and utilized throughout the war—as a battering ram for the various infantry units to which it was assigned. At full strength, each platoon had five tanks. However, replacements were often slow in coming, and platoons were only occasionally at full strength.

With their .30 caliber machine guns chattering and 75 mm cannons booming at anything moving or large enough to shoot at, B Company clanked forward against small arms fire for the first couple of miles. Suddenly, the First and Third Platoons drew anti-tank fire, and both First Lieutenant Charles S. Walker's and Sergeant Russell L. Lucas' tanks were knocked out. Private Noah Davis was wounded.

Corporal (later Sergeant) Joseph C. Schooley (Walker's gunner at the time) remembered exactly what happened when his tank was hit.[10] "First, the mind-numbing blast of the armor-piercing shell exploding into the tank center front. The horror as the tank shuddered and died. The incredible screech of jagged metal crashing through, as the shell ricocheted off the drive shaft, burst up through the steel floor, and bored a hole through the back wall of the tank near the radio. The shock and smell of white-hot sparks, like fireworks from hell," said Schooley.

When the order to "Abandon tank!" came down, those still able to do so clawed their way up and out. Their greatest fear: the dreaded explosion within, and scorching fire sure to come. The tank was filled with ammunition.

By some miracle, there was no further explosion, and the tank did not catch fire. Schooley's initial shock gradually gave way to anger. He came out of the tank fighting mad, clutching the little .30 caliber Carbine always at his side, his pockets full of extra clips. He doggedly took off across open ground toward the forest and that damnable German anti-tank gun, small arms fire zinging past and kicking up the ground around him. Ejecting one clip and slapping in another, he fired back helter-skelter as he zigzagged across the field and dived into the woods.

The German gun crew, secure down amid their sandbags, screamed with alarm when Schooley suddenly appeared like an apparition behind them, not twenty feet away. As they grappled for their rifles, Schooley opened up with his Carbine. When the smoke cleared, four of the enemy gun crew lay sprawled on the ground, and the fifth raised his hands in surrender.

Meanwhile, Lieutenant Walker managed to get back to Staff Sergeant Wilson's tank, climb up, and continue to direct the fight from there. However, the attack was soon halted when Sergeant Gilford W. Crowell's tank was also hit.

Private Noel C. Causey was killed in the fight. Sergeant Crowell and Private Arthur C. McBrayer were wounded. "A mortar shell exploded near our tank," McBrayer said. "This did some damage to our tracks which we repaired ourselves after we moved back—we immediately joined our platoon. As luck would have it, we had not been back very long when [we got a] direct hit from an AT gun. I was knocked out, for how long I don't know, but as soon as I came to, I could hardly move. I finally got strength from somewhere and managed to get out, and with the help of an infantryman, got to an aid station."[11]

Sergeant (later Staff Sergeant) Mayford L. Perkey's tank blasted the big gun that had been firing on the Third Platoon tanks, and the First Platoon destroyed a German Mark III tank and three AT guns during the day.

Staff Sergeant George E. Wright was doling out hot coffee during a brief respite the next morning when mortar fire came slamming in. One round hit the tree under which he had parked his 3/4-ton truck and blew the canvas top down over him. As Wright dug himself out, he saw his comrades-in-arms scrambling for their very lives, diving under their tanks, or any other cover to be found.[12] At least a dozen tankers lay dead or wounded on the bloody ground around him.

TEC 4 Winifred E. Hayden, TEC 5 Carl W. Krempin, and Private First Class Eugene H. Pollard were killed, and nine others were wounded in the melee.

B Company, still in support of the 325th Glider Infantry, captured Hierlot and Odrimont that day, but the toll in men and machines still mounted. By late afternoon, the Third Platoon had regrouped and stormed on through Amcômont. The Second Platoon rumbled down the road to attack and capture Chapelle. The First Platoon moved on to Odrimont, heavily shelling the town as they neared, taking out a Mark IV tank and an AT gun.

An 88mm AT gun blasted Second Lieutenant William H. Hamilton's tank, killing him and his loader, Private First Class Curtis R. Maxey, and wounding Corporal Robert J. Bell and TEC 4 James C. Sonntag.

With the infantry mopping up, B Company forged its way through Odrimont and set up a defensive perimeter for the night. Following the loss of Lieutenant Hamilton, Staff Sergeant Kenneth Nettles temporarily took command of the Second Platoon until First Lieutenant Raymond E. Davies took over.

Meanwhile, A Company, with the 505th Parachute Infantry, resumed their attack early that morning, January 4. Sergeant Howard J. Cluck's tank spearheaded the First Platoon's attack, with the other tanks in the platoon alternating the lead, as the column advanced on Abrefontaine. Cluck's tank blasted two AT guns, captured two others, and is believed to have shot up a half-track before being hit itself. This was Cluck's second tank in two days, and this time his luck played out. Although his tank did not burn, Cluck, his gunner, loader, and bow gunner, all were wounded and evacuated. Only the driver escaped injury.

The driver, Technician Carl D. Miller, bailed out of the tank and crawled about thirty yards when he realized he was by himself, not a crew member in sight. Small arms and mortar fire were still coming in, thick and fast, but Miller quickly made his way back to the tank to help. He found the bow gunner with his arm paralyzed, and another seriously wounded crew member. He helped them out of the tank and to a safe spot out of the line of fire, and then returned to the tank for blankets and to search for the others. He found a badly wounded Sgt. Cluck, got him back to the aid station, guided the medics to his wounded crew members, and helped evacuate them.[13]

It was a mean and ugly day for A Company's Third Platoon. Still, Ledbetter's and Quick's tanks destroyed at least three anti-tank guns and emplacements, and they accounted for a German half-track, an enemy held American jeep, and an enemy tank destroyer that was knocked out and burned. This sort of evened things up. Finally, the platoon was pulled out of the line, sent back to Reharmont in reserve, with time to reorganize.

The tankers remained alert. It seemed as if they could never relax completely, even with the infantry strung out around them. A German sniper was killed in Reharmont during the day.

Late that afternoon, First Lieutenant Charles H. Tribby decided to reconnoiter south of the town in a single tank advance. However, he quickly ran into heavy fire and had to fall back. When word came down that a battalion strength counterattack was forming in that area, he called on Sergeant Fasoli and Sergeant Charles D. Kilgore to fire up their tanks and join him.

Under intense small arms, mortar, and bazooka fire, they roared up the hill, blasted away, and completely overran the enemy troops. They killed and wounded upwards of one hundred fifty of the enemy, and took nearly two hundred prisoners. Both Fasoli's and Kilgore's tanks were hit by bazooka fire during the charge, evacuated, then found operable, re-entered, and pushed forward in the attack.[14]

The 740th's C and D Companies were held in reserve for the time, and Service Company stayed at the railroad station in Aywaille. Captain Walter H. Williams moved the Battalion Maintenance Platoon to Basse-Bodeux, and these guys were doing a "land office business, retrieving and repairing knocked out tanks," according to Lt. Col. Rubel. Although some "replacement" tanks rolled in, it was a tough order. The ordnance depot at Huy was a two hundred mile round trip.

The division's 504th Parachute Infantry Regiment moved to take the high ground southeast of Fosse on January 4. It was midnight before they accomplished their mission, but the 82nd Airborne now dominated all the crossings of the Salm River in the vicinity of Grand-Halleux. Enemy resistance had been relatively light and consisted primarily of small, isolated units. Having been up against the SS Panzer Grenadiers earlier in the Bulge, some of the 504th troopers reported that the soldiers they were now up against were of a lesser quality — "raw, ill-trained recruits — even drafted Russians."[15]

Was the tide really beginning to turn? The tankers hadn't felt the pressure slackening one little bit. They were still losing tanks every day. Jerry was out there with his powerful anti-tank guns and his monster tanks, stubborn as hell as far as the tankers were concerned. He was hurling those terrifying 88mm armor-piercing shells in their direction at every move. Those hell shells went in one side of their little olive drab Shermans and out the other — if the crew was lucky.

The tankers of A Company rolled south through the little Belgian town of Abrefontaine the afternoon of January 5. Where the road was wide enough, they moved forward in two columns, doubling their firepower, blasting away at everything forward of their tanks. The Second Platoon on the right of the road, the Third Platoon on the left. A section of the Third Platoon shadowed the main columns to the rear in reserve.

They engaged and destroyed an AT gun and several machine gun nests and shot up an enemy-held U.S. armored car, a German supply truck, and a number of enemy dugouts. Opposition was light, however, as they rolled through town and organized defensive positions for the night, setting up roadblocks leading to Menil and Geronne.

Just before sundown, Sergeant (later Staff Sergeant) Herman R. Beard's tank got in the first shots at two attacking Mark IV tanks and knocked them both out. That was close. Both tankers and infantry suffered through the night from heavy enemy mortar and artillery fire. Sadly, during the attack, Sergeant Jack D. McPherson was killed from the freakish ricochet of an incoming round off the turret of his tank.

The next day, B Company took the high ground out of Abrefontaine toward Lierneux against small arms and high velocity anti-tank gunfire. Lieutenant Walker lost his second tank in three days to AT fire, but Sergeant (later Staff Sergeant) Mayford L. Perkey's tank blasted the gun that got him. As darkness fell, the Third Platoon set up defenses on the hill, while the First and Second Platoons pulled back to Odrimont for the night.

Although it was another long night of scattered incoming artillery and mortar fire, Corporal (later Staff Sergeant) O.B. Wood caught the trail of and managed to capture a four-man bazooka team to the rear of the company's position. Since the company had lost several tanks and a number of tankers, a tank and crew from D Company was sent over to help.

In the meantime, D Company's First Platoon, under First Lieutenant Lloyd P. Mick, was with the 504th Parachute Infantry Regiment in the Fosse area, while First Lieutenant Thomas T. Munford's Second Platoon was hooked up with the 517th Parachute Infantry at Basse-Bodeux.

On January 6, B Company set up defenses in the area of Odrimont, while A Company settled in near Abrefontaine. The Battalion's rear command post was at Chevron at the time, so the forward CP moved on up to Abrefontaine, barely five hundred yards from enemy lines.

Recon Platoon Private First Class John C. Tullier remembers Abrefontaine very well. He was one of those unsung messenger heroes who roughed it day and night in an open peep throughout the war. By day, he drove the Battalion Exec, Major Graddy H. Floyd, from company to company, assessing needs. At night, he jeeped reports between the forward and rear CPs. It was touch and go on the open road, which regularly came under mortar or self-propelled anti-tank gun fire, especially on moonlit nights. So Tullier often had to make his own roads through the shadows of the forest, always playing a treacherous game of "hide and seek" with the enemy guns.[16]

The miserable weather and the tenacity of the Germans had taken their toll on the whole of the 82nd Airborne. Total casualties were high—138 killed, 647 wounded, and 44 missing in just the first four days of the attack.[17] Day after day, it seemed, the fog got thicker, the snow deeper, the temperature lower, and the icy winds worse. When the troopers weren't slogging through knee-deep snow in the dense forest, they were faced with cutting flurries of sleet and snow in the open marshland.

It was grimly cold in the tanks as well. Of course, there were no heaters, and the tank commanders really couldn't see all buttoned up, so they seldom closed their hatches when their tanks were on the move. The cold came right up through the steel floor of the tank, through their damp feet, and infiltrated their whole bodies. When they began to tremble and shake uncontrollably, they were never quite sure whether it was just the cold, or the fear of what would happen next.

For the most part, the tanks were road-bound, and the few roads available were usually slippery with ice and a blanket of snow. With mine fields laid out ahead of the Americans, and anti-tank guns zeroed in on the sharp turns, the dug-in Germans could stall a tank advance until the infantry managed to fight through to the enemy strong points.

In addition, tanks stalled easily in such frigid conditions, and without warning, could slide terrifyingly out of control down a hillside, taking out whatever was in their wake. Individual survival depended not only on clashes with a stubborn enemy, but also on the freezing cold and icy conditions.

Trench foot and frozen fingers, noses, and ears, took a heavy toll on the men. "If you touched a tank with your bare hands—the skin remained there when you pulled your hand away," noted Lt. Col. Rubel at the time.

The miserable weather contributed to the German surrender rate as well, Rubel said. By this time, the 740th had counted over seventeen hundred prisoners, mostly from the 62nd *Volksgrenadiers*.[18]

By now, German air attacks at the front were negligible, no more than a handful a day. The Allies controlled the air. Still, the fearsome V-1 and V-2 rockets continued to hurtle toward Liege and Antwerp and Brussels in Belgium. It was London, however, that forever bore the brunt of the rocket attacks, and as a result, suffered the greatest number of casualties.

The V-1s rumbled through the air in plain sight of those on the ground. When the rumbling stopped, everyone for miles around frantically dashed for cover, with barely a minute to wonder if their time had come. The V-2s were even more nerve-wracking. They came down, without warning, and blew away a block full of buildings and people, killing and wounding hundreds. The Allies had nothing with which to stop them.

The 740th was in column and ready to roll by 6:30 a.m. on January 7, waiting for enough light to move out. The final phase of the attack with the 82nd Airborne was underway. Company A was still with the 505th Parachute Infantry. Company B attacked with the 325th Glider Infantry, and Company C, with the 508th Parachute Infantry.

29. Photo credit: A/P Images

German prisoners file past a column of tanks in the icy conditions of the Battle of the Bulge.

Company A moved out south of Abrefontaine. Objective: Garonne. First Lieutenant Allen C. Christie's Third Platoon, reinforced with elements of the Second Platoon, encountered only sporadic opposition, but did destroy a number of machine gun nests, mortar positions, and enemy vehicles, including a motorcycle and rider. Sergeant (later Staff Sergeant) Herman R. Beard's tank came upon three towed anti-tank guns, shot them up, then spotted three more guns dead ahead and zeroed in on them, along with a couple of ammunition carriers. The advance hardly slowed until the platoon hit the bridge into town, which had to be cleared of mines by the engineers. This done, the tanks blasted their way on in.

Coordinating their assault on the town, the Second Platoon ran into a buzz saw. They spotted a Mark VI Tiger Tank, and Sergeant Nello J. Fasoli's tank got off five quick rounds, while Staff Sergeant Jesse M. Hendrix covered them. All five of Fasoli's rounds were direct hits, temporarily jamming the German's turret, but failing to knock the tank out.

With his tanks vulnerable, Lt. Tribby called for two nearby tank destroyers with 90-mm guns to maneuver into position. Unfortunately, the German panzer came to life long enough to get its powerful 88mm gun on them and left both TD's dead and burning.

Another TD, along with a towed 57 mm anti-tank gun, was called up, and Tribby and Fasoli dismounted and carefully placed them in position for sure, and more secure, shots. The TD unloaded fifteen rounds into the flank side of the huge German tank at hardly more than one hundred fifty yards but couldn't penetrate the 125,000-pound behemoth's armor. The tank did eventually burst into flames, and the crew bailed out.

The assault continued with Fasoli in the lead. As his tank rumbled into town, machine guns chattering, he ran head-on into another Mark VI. His gunner got off two quick shots at fifty yards and scored direct hits, but the effort was hopeless against the Tiger's heavy armor. With his good humor gone and his good health at stake, Fasoli, still firing, quickly determined that withdrawal was the better part of valor, and hastily backed into the cover of a building. Those shots merely ricocheted away as well. Still, the pounding must have left the Jerry crew inside with a painful headache, since they missed all three of their return volleys. By the time the cavalry arrived, in the form of an American bazooka team loaded with captured Panzerfausts, the Germans had decided to pull up stakes and run. Much to the relief of Fasoli and crew.

Meanwhile, B Company, still in support of the 325th Glider Infantry, was supposed to take the high ground overlooking Grand Sart, then roll on to Thier del Preux and Gernechamps. The company made steady progress but was constantly slowed by vicious small arms fire.

Each of the three platoons had its own problems, but the Second Platoon, commanded by 1st Lt. Davies, got into a unique situation. The platoon was ordered to attack down a road known to be mined. Davis protested the order, as did Lt. Col. Rubel. But reason failed to prevail, and Davies moved out as ordered. His tank rolled over a mine and was destroyed. Fortunately, there was only one casualty. Private First Class Donald B. Peterson, the gunner, was wounded around the eyes and face and evacuated. Still, the mission was accomplished by mid-afternoon.

C Company's tanks moved through the 325th to join the 508th Parachute Infantry Regiment. While the Second Platoon was held in regimental reserve, the First Platoon was attached to the First Battalion of infantry, and the Third Platoon was attached to the Third Battalion. Story of their lives.

The deadly Teller mine nightmare continued as C Company's First Platoon lost Sergeant (later Staff Sergeant) Alton M. Fleming's tank in a minefield. There were no casualties, but the platoon had to give up on its assignment as the anti-tank fire grew entirely too hot.

The Third Platoon slammed through to its objective and geared down to set up defenses for the night. The Second Platoon was still in reserve.

D Company's First Platoon of "light" tanks was assigned to the 551st Parachute Infantry Battalion in an attack on the heavily defended village of Rochelinval that evening. First Lieutenant Lloyd P. Mick was in command of two M5A1 tanks with 37 mm cannons, and one M24 tank with a 75 mm cannon. According to the 740th's After Action Report, the tanks were held in battalion reserve due to woods and narrow trails, while the infantry jumped off.[19] Heavy automatic, mortar, and artillery fire poured down, and the infantry's commanding officer, Lieutenant Colonel Wood Joerg, ordered the M24 to move up and fire into the town and pull back again. By the time the tank got into position, Col. Joerg had been killed, and Staff Sergeant Roy Parks, commanding the M24, fired his entire combat load of 75 mm shells and most of his .30-calibre ammunition into the town. As mortar fire began to zero in on his position, Parks withdrew to reload.

The situation was confused when D Company's commander, Captain Raymond R. Smith, arrived. Although small arms fire was heavy, there had been no anti-tank fire, so the two M5 light tanks were called up. Smith then had Parks' M24 set up in a defiladed position to provide a base of fire while the M5s made flanking attacks from left and right with infantry.[20]

As the tanks sprayed the hedgerows and foxholes with their .30 caliber machine guns and blasted other defensive positions with their 37s, the Germans came out of their holes and shelters with their hands held high, shouting "Kamerad!"

The two tanks were about one hundred yards apart as they moved into the town, shooting into basements and anything else big enough for their cannons. But with friendly 82nd troopers all over the place, the tank commanders had to go to their top-of-the-turret machine guns to avoid hitting their own people. The enemy began to surrender in mass. Ultimately, about two hundred prisoners were taken and escorted to the rear.[21]

The entire division was on its objectives by the evening of January 7. Precision firing by the 740th's Assault Gun Platoon drew a lot of praise from the 456th Parachute Field Artillery Battalion, to which it was attached for the operation, according to Lt. Col. Rubel.[22] The "platoon," a six-gun battery of Sherman tanks with 105 mm guns and supporting vehicles, fired twenty-four hours a day—more than four thousand rounds in a hundred sixty-nine missions. Lt. Col. Rubel noted that a lot of tankers owed their lives to the "counterattack busting" ability of the assault gun battery, with their big guns and indirect fire: Captain Ross Kirwan, First Lieutenant Starr T. Whitley, the "heroic" efforts of Sergeant Gilbow, and the fifty-five other "unsung heroes" of the platoon who "fought doggedly, constantly, willingly, and effectively."

The Assault Gun Platoon was always attached to an artillery battalion throughout the Ardennes Campaign. The platoon operated as an "extra battery," big guns booming from foxholes of steel.

Mad as hell at the top. *By this time, the British press was championing Field Marshall Sir Bernard Montgomery's role in the Allied turnaround of the German blitz into the Ardennes, at the expense of General Eisenhower. As the word leaked to the world press, both the American people and the American generals were outraged, since the American soldiers were obviously carrying the brunt of the battle.*

On January 7, Montgomery called a press conference, ostensibly to help bring about Allied solidarity. In fairness, he probably tried to do just that. Most of what he said was complimentary: to Eisenhower, as "Captain of the team," to whom he "was absolutely devoted"; and to the Americans, saying he would "never want to fight alongside better soldiers." But then he went on to say that the GIs made great fighting men when given proper leadership, and in the end his remarks became so overbearing and self-serving as to infuriate the Americans.

The Germans had driven a "deep wedge into the center of the United States First Army, and the split might have become awkward," Montgomery said. "As soon as I saw what was happening I took certain steps myself to ensure that if the Germans got to the Meuse they would certainly not get over that river."

Montgomery said he "took precautions" and was "thinking ahead." Nevertheless, he said, "The situation began to deteriorate" and "General Eisenhower placed me in command of the whole Northern front . . . I employed the whole available power of the British Group of Armies."

"Strategically," he said, the British were brought "into battle with a bang" and are now fighting alongside "American forces who have suffered a hard blow. This is a fine Allied picture."[23]

Montgomery went on to claim that the battle had been possibly one of the most interesting and tricky he had ever handled, rather like El Alamein.

And that blew it. The Americans had brought the bitter Ardennes offensive to a standstill on their own, and British forces had hardly been engaged. The political stakes were high among the allies at the time. Ruffled feathers had to be smoothed at home and in the field. The brouhaha must certainly have confirmed Hitler's suspicions about an Allied split, and *der Führer* undoubtedly did a little jig right there on the spot.

It was left for that grand old British orator, Winston Churchill, rising before the House of Commons, to set the record straight. He said that the Ardennes was "the greatest American battle of the war and will, I believe, be regarded as an ever famous American victory."[24]

The ruckus finally glazed over.

None of it mattered much to the tankers of the 740th, nor the troopers of the 82nd Airborne, who were fighting for their lives in the freezing cold and snow. The closest most of them ever got to a general was the 82nd's "Slim Jim" Gavin, who occasionally came rushing up into their midst to see what was going on at the front. At 37, Gavin was the youngest division commander in the army: reed thin, hard as a rail, and every bit as cold as his shivering men in that snow-clad forest.

Half a world away in the Philippines, the biggest battle of the Pacific War was unfolding with U.S. landings on Luzon. Only on such a huge island, easily the size of Great Britain, could battles of the size and complexity of those being fought in Europe be undertaken in the Pacific Theater of Operations. American land and sea forces committed there were second only to the Allied drive through France. More Japanese died on Luzon than on any other island in the Pacific war.[25]

The deadly experience on Luzon forewarned America of the cruelty and fanaticism of the Japanese, and the unimaginable consequences of the eventual invasion of the Japanese homeland. How many young American lives would it take? The considered estimate at the time: up to 1,000,000.

When the 75th Infantry Division began its relief of the 82nd Airborne on January 10, the 740th withdrew to a quiet area near Winamplanche, just west of Spa, Belgium. But even *that* was an experience. The frigid wind kept the snow swirling and piling up waist-high on the roads. Bulldozers had to be brought in order to get through.

Still, the tankers were happy. They had earned a respite. The townspeople welcomed them, and they had good billets. They were safe from snipers and mortar fire for a while, and except for the gun flashes at night and the faint booming of heavy artillery in the distance, it was almost eerily quiet. Of course, there was that weird ME 109 German jet flashing low through the sky every evening, pursued incessantly by American tracers never quite able to catch up.

The huge Russian bear finally broke loose from its long winter quietus on January 12, and attacked with its greatest offensive of the war, all up and down the Eastern Front. The Germans were heavily outmanned and outgunned in the battle, but Hitler would allow no withdrawal. With pockets of resistance fighting stubbornly to the death, some two hundred thousand Germans were killed within a matter of days, as the Russians gave no quarter and seldom took prisoners. By the end of the month, the Red Tide had swept into Germany and was within one hundred miles of Berlin.

In the meantime, the German high command began a massive transfer of troops and armor from West to East. But fuel was precious, and the railroads and autobahn were racked and ruined from Allied bombing. Desperate, Hitler countered in both the East and the West with his Volkssturm, or Home Guard, made up of youths and old men.

Although most of the 740th tankers led the good life for the next couple of weeks, the downtime for C Company was unexpectedly brief. With hardly any time to lick their wounds, C Company's First Platoon was split off and attached to the 82nd's 517th Parachute Infantry Regiment on January 12. They moved out quickly for Stavelot, and rolled to the attack the very next morning.

The Second and Third Platoons were totally uprooted and temporarily attached to the 424th Infantry Regiment of the badly battered 106th Infantry Division, which was holding between Trois-Ponts and Stavelot. They went into division reserve temporarily, where occasional mortar and artillery fire did little more than keep them edgy and on their toes.

Meanwhile, on January 16, patrols from the U.S. First and Third Armies linked up in Houffalize, just twenty miles to the south, cutting off the leading edge of the German penetration through the Ardennes. It was the beginning of the end of the "Battle of the Bulge," and a precursor of the end of the war. General Eisenhower pulled the U.S. First Army, including the 740th Tank Battalion, out of Montgomery's 21st Army Group and placed it back under Bradley's 12th Army Group command.

Hitler, who had been directing the Ardennes offensive from his headquarters in Rastenburg, arrived that same day in Berlin, never to leave his bunker again. His health deteriorated rapidly, probably from the unhealthy conditions in which he lived—mostly underground, and from the attentions of an apparently incompetent doctor. Although, some historians believe he suffered from the aftereffects of the bomb explosion in the assassination attempt, which very nearly took his life. For whatever reason, he considered his generals useless, even traitorous, and became more and more difficult for his minions to deal with.[26]

The shuffling of C Company's three tank platoons continued during the next several days, in and out of attack and defensive positions in the area. First Platoon tanks remained in support of the 82nd's 517th infantry, blasting out some die-hard German snipers in Henumont, supporting the attacks on Coulee and Logbierne, and setting up defenses in the vicinity of Petit-Thier. The Second Platoon led the Second Battalion of the 106th's 424th infantry in the capture of Ennal. The Third

Platoon advanced to Wanne with the 424th's Third Battalion. They were all within a high-flung cannon shot of one another.

The company was detached from the 106th's 424th Infantry on January 19, and moved to Farm Bronromme, south of Winamplanche. The First Platoon rejoined the outfit in sections during the next two days, and the company was finally reunited.

30. Photo credit: Franklin D. Roosevelt Presidential Library and Museum

An overturned German tank lies in a shallow stream alongside a rebuilt bridge in war-ravaged Houffalize, Belgium.

The only real casualty in all of this activity was the First Platoon's Sergeant Jefferson L. Miller, who was caught out of his tank on the 20th, and wounded when artillery shrapnel came slashing in unexpectedly. Earlier, Sergeant (later Staff Sergeant) Willie F. Morris' tank nudged over into a bomb crater, stripped the big gun gears, and had to be evacuated.

While C Company was banging about in the snow, A, B, and D Service Companies busied themselves with maintenance—cleaning guns, patching up engines and tracks, and whitewashing their vehicles for camouflage in the snow-covered terrain.

Adequate cold-weather clothing just wasn't available. Much of what the tankers wore was either unserviceable or the worse for wear by this time, and there was a definite shortage of combat suits. The tankers were miserably cold. Arctic clothing from the U.S. was apparently coming into the European Theater but had not been allocated directly to separate tank battalions, nor through the units to which they had been attached.[27]

Staff Sergeant and C Company Supply Sergeant, Burtis M. Tyler said, "We never got the new shoe pac boots with the moccasin style rubber bottoms for our guys. All we had were the old combat service boots—composition soles and two-buckle leather cuffs added to the tops. And we were desperate for socks. I remember getting in two hundred pairs of socks and had no idea how to distribute them fairly. Finally, at a lull in the fighting, I just put out the word and gave one pair each to the first two hundred men who showed up."[28]

31. Photo Credit: Wikimedia Commons/U.S. Army

The bitter cold, the lack of warm winter clothing, and the hilly, heavily wooded terrain over which the battle of the Ardennes was fought, was tough on the tankers, but the infantrymen, God bless 'em, had it worst of all . . . in so many ways.

Chapter 16

FDR's Inauguration, 1945
The Drive to the West Wall

January 20, Washington D.C. An inch of snow had fallen on the nation's capital overnight and became sleet by morning. A cold winter day. Not as cold as it was in the Ardennes. But cold.

It was early, and the White House was already buzzing with activity. The President had to be ready. It was Inauguration Day.

Arthur Prettyman, Franklin Roosevelt's trusted black valet, lifted the President's frail body from his bed and deposited him gently into the bathtub, then helped him wash and shave. Later, Prettyman and Roosevelt's son, Colonel James Roosevelt, helped him dress. It was painfully apparent to those close to him that the President was gradually failing.[1]

Church services were held in the Rose Room, with two hundred fifty of the "official family" in attendance. The hymns included "Oh, God, Our Help in Ages Past," and one prayer was even included for the enemy.

It was time. The President was lifted into his wheelchair and moved to the south portico, where the Supreme Court justices, cabinet members, and presidential advisors with their families waited. A crowd of thousands awaited his arrival, including fifty wounded service men in wheelchairs, looking up from the south lawn.

At exactly noon, as the law set forth, Franklin D. Roosevelt's fourth-term inauguration as President of the United States began. FDR came out on his son's arm, moving slowly and painfully to his seat as quickly as his cruel iron braces would allow. The Marine Band trumpeted "Hail to the Chief" as he waved to the crowd, shivering in the thirty-three degree temperature. The Episcopal Bishop of Washington gave the invocation. Vice President Henry A. Wallace stood and held the Bible for the man who would take his place, as Harry S. Truman, Senator from Missouri, took the oath of office.

The President clasp his hands around his son's neck, and with the help of a Secret Service man, pulled himself clumsily to his feet. Just one arduous step and he was able to grasp the lectern. Holding the Roosevelts' family Bible, Chief Justice Harlan Fiske Stone delivered the oath of office, ending with FDR's "So help me

God" in a firm, clear voice. With that, he began his thirteenth year as President of the United States.

His inaugural speech was brief—only 573 words. He noted that God had blessed our country in so many ways, and that it was "His purpose that we shall not fail." Then he spoke primarily of peace. A durable and lasting peace.[2]

Back inside the White House, Roosevelt collapsed in his wheelchair. Additional Secret Service agents were assigned to Vice President Harry Truman shortly thereafter, and sworn to secrecy, on the assumption that the worst could happen at any time.[3]

That same day, Russian tanks entered Germany proper for the first time—no more than one hundred miles from Berlin. The exodus began. With their often meager possessions, thousands upon thousands of Germans clogged the roads westward to escape the Russian retribution.

On January 22, *Time Magazine* reported heavy casualties coming out of the German thrust through the Ardennes. "The Allies claimed some 50,000 Germans dead or wounded, 40,000 taken prisoner. Last week, Secretary [of War Henry L.] Stimson gave a preliminary count of 40,000 American casualties, including 18,000 missing, but this obviously did not include all the categories of losses."[4]

With the snow at least three feet deep back in the Ardennes, the 740th tankers were using bulldozers to clear the roads between companies in an effort to get back and forth. It was a blessed respite—a hot shower, clean clothes, and they were away from the miserable conditions and ceaseless anxiety at the front.

By this time, they had grown to admire the troopers of the 82nd Airborne, and managed time for some coordinated tank-infantry training. In turn, the 82nd sent movies and orchestras to play for the tankers. "The kind deeds bestowed on us and their open praise of our fighting ability made us feel that we both belonged to the same school," Lt. Col. Rubel said.[5]

Rubel learned on January 24 that the next action was scheduled for January 28, and that the job of the 740th would be to "move to a line extending from Malmedy south to St. Vith, drive to the northeast, pierce the *Siegfried Line,* and hold the position until relieved—

"The First Infantry Division was to attack abreast of us on the northern flank. Patrols of the 32nd Cavalry Reconnaissance Squadron were to operate on the south flank—terrain over which we were to attack almost completely devoid of roads . . . country rough and hilly and covered with an almost unbroken forest, through which an occasional fire lane had been cut."[6]

The 740th was attached to the 325th Glider Infantry on January 25, except for C Company, sent to the 504th Parachute Infantry, and the Assault Gun Platoon, sent to the 319th Glider Field Artillery Battalion.

At dusk the next day, the battalion rolled out of Winamplanche. It was near midnight when the tankers closed in bivouac at Recht, Belgium. The weather grew fiercer during the night, and the tankers had to fight deep snow drifts heaped up by the hard-driven wind.

Because of the snow, the tank retrievers saw plenty of action in Recht, and not without some elements of heart-throbbing terror. A German fighter plane roared overhead and strafed the area as a retriever crew was pulling a tank out. Most of the crew scrambled to safety in the retriever, but Private First Class Lloyd C. Rule dived under the tank into three feet of snow, and narrowly missed tumbling over the precipice into a fifty-foot well. He remembered that as the "hottest snow" it had been his misfortune to encounter.[7]

On January 27, the usual shuffle of the 740th before the battle began. A Company was sent to the Third Battalion of the 325th in regimental reserve, then later shifted to the 508th Parachute Infantry. B Company's tank platoons were split among the 325th's various battalions and moved into the Medell area, and the Third Platoon encountered two anti-tank guns en route. Fortunately, the infantry reacted smartly and took out both big guns before they could do any damage, and there was no serious resistance during the advance.

Meanwhile, C Company's three tank platoons were separated and moved into position with three different battalions of the 504th. D Company wound up with the 505th at Myerode.

In the early morning darkness, the 82nd Airborne moved through the shadows of the 7th Armored Division, and attacked with the 325th Glider Infantry on the left (to the north), and the 504th Parachute Infantry on the right (to the south). The 505th and the 508th were in reserve.

The bitter weather was about as close to unbearable as it could get. The snow, waist deep. Enemy strong points, dug in and waiting. The way ahead was freezing, mind-numbing, and racked with the unknown. As the cold seeped up through the steel floor of the tanks, the tankers' feet numbed, and their bodies shivered and shook, at times uncontrollably.

On foot, the 82nd troopers simply could not negotiate the snow. The tank commanders encouraged as many as possible to climb up on the back of their tanks and ride until trouble hit, then be prepared to leap for cover. Still, most of the infantry had to follow along in the wake of the tanks.

Lt. Col. Rubel said, "In this attack a tank was a strange looking object. [In addition to the] ten to twenty men riding on top —[the tanks were] usually towing a trailer loaded down with rations, machine guns, tripods, and the usual miscellany of gear that a combat soldier takes along with him. [Also] the tankers had placed sandbags on the front slope plate of the tank, the sides, and sometimes around the turrets for protection against *Panzerfausts*.

"The [usual] load on the back of tank [also included] a liberated heating stove, two or three joints of stove pipe, frying pans, [big multi-purpose] black pots used for converting snow into drinking water, washing clothes, cooking food, and pouring gasoline—[and] extra boxes of .30- and .50-caliber ammunition."[8]

Add to this conglomeration at least five multi-blanketed bedrolls and a liberated radio or two, and the camouflage was complete. Rubel facetiously noted that from a distance, no German lookout could possibly identify such an outrageous looking vehicle as a tank coming at him.

Small arms and machine gun fire crackled from hot spots along the way, but resistance was generally light as C Company's Third Platoon tanks moved to the attack on the morning of January 28. In support of the Third Battalion of the 504th, the tankers were about two miles northeast of St. Vith, north of Wallerode, rumbling in an easterly direction. In the vicinity of Herresbach, word came back that the Germans were counterattacking. First Lieutenant Powers moved the platoon to the head of the infantry column, loaded the 504th troopers aboard his tanks, and roared down the road to meet the Germans head-on. On contact, the tanks and troopers opened up with everything they had, and absolutely routed the surprised enemy column in just a few minutes' time.

When his tanks ran out of ammunition, Powers dismounted and directed the action under heavy enemy fire. Later reloaded, he led his tanks in repulsing another counterattack, knocking out a German tank in the process. In all, several hundred enemy soldiers were killed or captured, without suffering a single American casualty.[9]

The next day, D Company's First and Second Platoons advanced northeast from Meyerode in support of the Second Battalion of the 505th Parachute Infantry. Resistance was light, and the scattered small arms fire was easily taken out as they rolled onto their objective: the high ground north of Holzheim.

The attacks were relatively smooth that day for B Company's Second and Third Platoons. Although their tanks attracted both small arms and artillery fire, the Second Platoon moved successfully to the high ground east of Wereth, along with the Third Battalion of the 325th Glider Infantry. Against minimal opposition, the Third Platoon rolled into the little town of Valender with the 325th's First Battalion.

C Company had a relatively quiet day until well into the night. The Second Platoon ran into a couple of machine gun nests, which they managed to subdue, but then a tank rolled over a land mine as it lumbered through Herresbach with the 504th's Third Battalion. No one was hurt in the explosion, so the advance continued until Second Lieutenant John E. Callaway's tank slid into an artillery shell crater and was upended. Calloway had to be evacuated, and Staff Sergeant Homer B. Tompkins took command of the platoon.

With a determined infantry at their side, the platoon went on through the night to secure their objective, the high ground southeast of Herresbach. Still supporting the 325th Glider Infantry on January 30, B Company tanks attacked from Holzheim toward the town of Lanzerath. They advanced steadily without serious resistance, rumbling over several machine gun nests and taking a number of prisoners. Their columns slowed long enough to shoot up two German tanks and a number of enemy vehicles and anti-tank gun emplacements.

The same day, C Company tanks rolled out with the 504th Parachute Infantry, its three platoons split among three infantry battalions. Medendorf was quickly overrun. Staff Sergeant (later Second Lieutenant) William H. Nemnich's section of the First Platoon moved with a company of infantry into the town of Eimerscheid, destroying two horse-drawn artillery pieces along the way. A third gun escaped his fire.

Third Platoon tankers thought they were getting a break as they moved with infantry into the town of Holzheim, against nothing more than small arms fire. However, when they pushed through to Chateau Igelmonderhof at the top of a hill, they ran headlong into a hornets' nest. As the lead infantry broke out of the woods across open ground, the attack was unexpectedly bushwhacked by powerful, flat-projectory weapons' fire—anti-tank guns!

32. Photo credit: Chris Clarke/U.S. Army. Image and description courtesy of the Harry S. Truman Presidential Museum and Library.

Tanks of the 740th Tank Battalion and G Company of the 504th Parachute Infantry, 82nd Airborne Division, push on through the snow towards Herresbach, Belgium, during the Battle of the Bulge.

The tanks spread out, and First Lieutenant Powers, the platoon leader, and Staff Sergeant Loopey led the charge up the hill, blasting away with everything they had. The attack was bold and devastating. Loopey's tank set two trucks, filled with Germans, afire with star shells. When the tanks reached the Chateau, the bow gunners jumped from their front right hatches with tommy guns spitting fire, and rounded up the Germans who were left alive. When the infantry arrived to take over, the prisoner count varied from one hundred, all the way up to two hundred.

D Company assembled at the railroad underpass southeast of Honsfeld, Belgium, and attacked in the middle of the night with the 505th Parachute Infantry's Second Battalion. First Lieutenant (later Captain) Raymond E. Smith's First Platoon led the attack eastward, with a hodgepodge of tanks cobbled together for the mission. Smith had only one of his M5 light tanks left, but managed to commandeer a couple of M4 Sherman mediums from B Company. Two M8 self-propelled howitzers filled out the platoon. The M8s were variants of M5 tanks with open tops and stubby 75 mm pack howitzers, normally used as close support vehicles, and not for direct fire.

33. Photo credit: Wikimedia Commons/U.S. Army History Images

Troops of Headquarters Company, 3rd Battalion, 504th Parachute Infantry Regiment, 82nd Airborne Division advance in a snowstorm behind a tank of the 740th Tank Battalion, in an attack on Herresbach, Belgium.

With 82nd troopers on the backs of the tanks, and the heavier Shermans leading the way, the column encountered little resistance until they neared the German border — they even took out a couple of enemy anti-tank guns. Their good fortune changed, however, just northeast of Losheimergraben, when the infantry commander in charge unwittingly ordered one of the M8s up front — ostensibly to "speed up" the attack. The tankers were stunned. The M8 just wasn't fitted to spearhead such an attack.

The night was bitterly cold. The way ahead slippery, with deep snow on the road. And Private First Class Clarence R. Horn was the gunner in that tank. He said they had just been "tagging along," when ordered up front. And it wasn't too hard to imagine what was ahead.

Their big gun was mounted on a light tank chassis and designed for high angle firing at low velocity – no contest against another tank or an anti-tank gun. They were not equipped for direct fire, and there were no machine guns.

With nothing to shoot but that big assault gun, Horn figured he was expected to "shoot from the hip." It was a recipe for disaster.

As daylight neared, the column ran head-on into an established roadblock, and enemy flares quickly lit the sky overhead. "They started shooting at us from all sides with every kind of weapon the Jerries had," Horn said. "My tank was hit on the sprocket with [Panzerfaust], which knocked the track off."

Out of action, they were sitting ducks. The crew scrambled out. Horn felt for his own limbs to make sure he was still alive, and then he scratched out a hole in the snow with his bare hands.

Sergeant Clayton D. Curtis, who commanded the only M5 left in the company, started around the knocked-out assault gun tank to assume the lead. He was head and shoulders out of the turret hatch. Still knee-deep in the snow, Horn watched helplessly in horror as yet another *Panzerfaust* exploded directly into Curtis, killing him instantly.[10]

Corporal Glenn H. Lewis, Curtis' gunner, was wounded in the melee, but kept on firing his gun until the tank was hit a second time and set afire. Waiting until the last moment to leave the tank, he crawled back to the aid station with enemy flares still lighting the landscape, and was evacuated. "After I made it through that, I figured I could make it through the war," Lewis said.[11]

And, he did make it.

Although the bitter fighting chewed up most of the day and night, D Company finally secured the battalion objective, a line running southeast of Losheimer Graben to a point just east of Lanzerath. Eventually, it became impossible for the tanks to maneuver in such deep snow, and they had to withdraw. By ramming the snow banks with their tanks, then backing up and ramming them again to break through, they finally pulled up into a defensive position on the high ground southwest of Neuhof.

It was the morning of January 31. The rains came, and the temperature rose several degrees. Three feet of morning snow sloughed into knee-deep slush as the ground thawed. The tanks quickly became road-bound again. Not that there were any roads nearby. The deep-stick mud, and the massive bomb craters that abounded throughout the forest, literally stacked up the 33-ton American tanks. At one point, an entire five-tank platoon of the behemoths sank into the slush and mud craters, until only the turrets were above ground. Some tanks just had to be left where they were, their cannons nose down in a crater, and their vulnerable backsides up in the air. Or worse, completely upended, tracks still circling slowly in the freezing sleet and rain.

Company A's platoons were split among battalions of the 82nd Airborne's 508th and 505th Parachute Infantry Regiments, in both attack and defensive positions. The First Platoon moved out at 3:00 a.m. toward Holzheim in a special mission to hook up with the 508th's Second Battalion and shut down a German counterattack of tanks and a couple hundred infantry. Artillery fire broke up the attack before the tanks could be utilized. The tanks then moved southeast of Losheimer Graben to organize a defense of the area with the Third Battalion of the 508th.

The Second Platoon was in regimental reserve. The Third Platoon moved to support the First Battalion of the 505th Parachute Infantry in an attack just northwest of Losheimer Graben. The attack sputtered, however, and the tanks were confined to the area under artillery and mortar fire.

The maintenance and repair people provided herculean service throughout the miserable winter, but it was particularly noticeable in these tense times. Technical Sergeant Paul W. Lipp, acting as maintenance officer of A Company, dodged a lot of artillery and small arms fire in the forward zones. He not only helped repair disabled tanks under enemy fire in the worst weather, but he never failed to keep his company's tanks supplied with ammunition, fuel, and rations.

Private First Class Walter T. Garrett, and Technician Fifth Grade James A. Duncan of Service Company, also engaged in similar action without regard for their own personal safety.

The Assault Gun Platoon fired well over five hundred rounds during this four-day period. It was credited with breaking up an enemy counterattack that included both infantry and tanks in the Lanzerath area.

At month's end, Lt. Col. Rubel knew that the officers and men of the 740th had driven themselves to the point of complete exhaustion. And the *Siegfried Line* lay dead ahead.

Area map studies of the defense of the dreaded West Wall showed Rubel the closest, and probably best spot to smash through and into enemy country —a gate midway between Udenbreth and Neuhof, Germany.

With the thaw setting in, Rubel knew the 740th would not be able to spread out in line formation and attack with all its firepower on a wide front. If the battalion was to breach the *Siegfried* here, it meant that the tanks would have to stay to the road, and rumble forward in column to attack. It also meant that losses would be heavy.

The Battle of the Ardennes began on December 16, 1944, and on January 28, 1945, SHAEF declared the battle to be officially ended. In just over six weeks, the allies had blunted the powerful German blitzkrieg and driven the Nazis back to the original lines of the attack. Unknown to the 740th tankers, the "Battle of the Bulge" became a campaign, and they were entitled to a Bronze Battle Star to be worn on their European Theater ribbons.

The tankers, well, they just gritted their teeth and prepared themselves, each in his own heart, and in his own way, to go into the breach once again. The famed Siegfried Line and all of Germany was dead ahead. The fanatical enemy now fighting for the fatherland — their backs to the wall.

By this time, the 740th had built a long list of credits. The statistical after action report for January 1945 lists ten enemy tanks destroyed, twenty-eight anti-tank guns, sixteen half-tracks, a host of machine gun nests, mortars, assorted cargo and supply trucks, and other German vehicles, including a Flak Wagon and horse-drawn wagons loaded with American bazookas. In addition, a proud number of tankers had received awards and citations for individual actions that were above and beyond the call of duty.

On the other side of the ledger: The battalion had lost nine M4 tanks with 75 mm guns, five M4 tanks with 76 mm guns, and one M5A1 tank with a 37 mm gun. Ten of the tanks were lost to anti-tank fire and three to anti-tank mines — two turned over, one was in a bomb crater, and the other slipped off the road.

More importantly, one officer and six enlisted men had been killed. Three officers and twenty-five enlisted men were wounded, or otherwise out of action.

The largest and most vicious battle for the Western Front was finally over. Hitler's last gamble had failed. Estimates of enemy casualties vary, but the figure remains between 80,000 and 120,000 of the half million German soldiers involved.

The pitched battle was a daunting lesson for the Allies as well. The surprise breakthrough had its successes, including setting back the final Allied offensive by six weeks. And, of the 850,000 Americans who eventually took part in the battle, nearly 81,000 were casualties. In his book, *Citizen Soldiers,* military historian Steven Ambrose notes that January 1945 was the costliest month of the northwest Europe campaign for the U.S. Army, with a total of 10,276 Americans killed in action, 47,493 wounded in action, and 23,218 missing.[12] Other similar estimates include some 15,000 captured. Of the 55,000 British soldiers participating, some 200 were killed and 1,200 were otherwise casualties.[13]

Each side lost approximately eight hundred tanks, and the Germans had one thousand planes destroyed. The big difference was that the Americans quickly replaced their equipment while the Germans had no way of doing so.[14]

It is not generally understood that it was General Courtney Hodges' U.S. First Army in the north that withstood—then turned back—the major German thrust through the Ardennes.

Still, it was the colorful, but enigmatic General George Patton who garnered most of the publicity back home. Much of the history of the Battle of the Bulge has been written about Patton's U.S. Third Army's spectacular turnaround and hard-fought battle from the south northward, to relieve the beleaguered 101st Airborne in Bastogne.

Hitler's great gamble in the Ardennes offensive was to split and rout the western Allies en route to the capture of Brussels and Antwerp. It was not until after this grandiose scheme had been thwarted in the north, that Hitler turned his panzer armies south to attack Bastogne in force, hoping to hold there. Until Patton broke through from the south to relieve them the day after Christmas, the 101st Airborne, surrounded and cut off ten days earlier, made a magnificent stand in Bastogne against vastly superior forces.

Chapter 17

Cracking the Siegfried Line
A Glimpse of the Yalta Conference

February 1945. Still with Gen. Hodges' U.S. First Army, and attached to the 82nd Airborne Division, the 740th tankers were attacking day and night. They had penetrated the extensive outer defenses of the *Siegfried Line* at Neuhof and Udenbreth, Germany.

Lt. Col. Rubel reported that "Weather and gunfire had taken a heavy toll on both men and machines. Many tanks had been hit and burned. Many more had dropped out due to mechanical failure, while others were stuck in the mud. Casualties ran high on the human side of the ledger in direct proportion to the vehicular losses. Frozen feet, or 'trench foot' as the medics called it, accounted for two thirds of the casualties. Regiments were about the size of a battalion. Tank companies, instead of having the seventeen tanks authorized for each company, at this time had about seven left in running condition."[1]

The tankers got precious little rest. One regiment of the 82nd would attack through another, picking up the 740th tanks as they continued the advance. Those days, a tanker pretty well had to get his tank shot out from under him to get any sleep at all.

The battalion was scattered among the various regiments of the 82nd in the areas of Wereth, Losheimer Graben, Honsfeld, and Hasenvenn that first day in February. The tankers had been on the wrong end of heavy artillery fire all day and night, and as a result, seldom strayed from their tanks. Artillery is especially vicious in heavily wooded areas. A lot of casualties, particularly troopers caught out in the open, resulted from tree bursts. The hell unleashed when an artillery shell exploded in the top of a huge tree was absolutely mesmerizing. The ground trembled, the tree flamed across its breadth, then fired its branches like jagged shrapnel out from its cracked and blackened trunk. Bad, mean stuff.

D Company's tanks were split up and chewed up. Three of its regular light tanks and two assault gun tanks, were still hung up in the clammy mud and slush of a creek bed after days of an impossible struggle to drive them out or pull them free. The company's other assault gun tanks had been farmed out to the battalion's other tank companies to haul supplies through the snow.

This left only the First Platoon still in action. Attached to the Second Battalion of the 505th Parachute Infantry, the platoon advanced during the day all the way to the German border, just southwest of Neuhof. The vicious looking dragon teeth of the famed *Siegfried Line* staggered in double rows no more than twelve hundred yards away.

At midnight, the 740th, except for D Company, was ordered into action with the 82nd Airborne's 325th Glider Infantry. After fighting steadily for the past five days in the fiercest weather and combat conditions, the tankers were about to be thrown into the breach again. Jump off time in just four hours. Objective: Neuhof!

Reconnaissance reports showed this section to be one of the most heavily defended along the entire *Siegfried Line*. Staggered rows of "dragon's teeth," with heavily fortified pillboxes, were scattered all about in the slopes and crevices of the surrounding hills—organized crossfire with big guns, many of which were zeroed in on the single road that passed through the line.

It was cold and pitch black at 4:00 a.m. on February 2 as the B Company tankers moved to the attack with the 325th's First Battalion. Small arms and mortar fire grew in intensity as the tanks rumbled forward, and the infantry began to stagger and fall in the snow. Suddenly, a self-propelled rocket burst into First Lieutenant Arthur P. Hartle's tank, creating havoc.

The enemy opened up with anti-tank guns. Sergeant Charles E. Boler's tank was immediately hit by anti-tank fire and burst into flames. Casualties were staggering. Lt. Hartle was the only person out of the two tanks not evacuated; and although he was slightly wounded, he took command of another of his platoon's tanks, and went on that day to destroy two Mark IVs and an armored half-track.

First Lieutenant Raymond E. Davies moved up his Second Platoon, destroyed a Mark V Panther tank that afternoon, and the two platoons managed to blast their way through a number of pillboxes zeroed in on the battle area.

Company A rolled in then with two of its three platoons attacking with the 325th's Third Battalion of infantry. These tanks came under heavy fire, and First Lieutenant Allen C. Christie's tank took a round from an anti-tank gun, and burned. Fortunately, the crew came out safely.

The advance had been effectively stopped, and the fighting was fierce. After getting off three or four rounds at the AT gun position causing all this trouble, Sergeant J. L. Montgomery's own gun jammed, and he had to withdraw. He called Sergeant Charles B. Harrell to alert him to enemy gun positions but was unable to raise his tank on the radio. Montgomery dismounted his tank, and in a heavy barrage of mortar and artillery fire, led Harrell's tank into position to take out the target.

Incredibly, Montgomery was struck and killed by incoming shrapnel.[2] Compounding the tragedy, Harrell's tank was then hit and burned by that same

German gun. Harrell was slightly injured, but the rest of his crew escaped without injury.

Corporal Maurice E. Logan, Montgomery's driver, described the series of events as one of his darkest hours. When his tank commander was killed, Logan immediately backed his tank behind an old house for cover. But the Germans had them spotted and really opened up—throwing everything they had, concentrating on their position. And with Sgt. Harrell's tank burning in front of them, and Lt. Christie's tank burning behind them, he said it was pure hell.[3]

The Third Platoon was quickly pulled back to regroup, being reinforced by crews from the Second Platoon. As events proceeded, Staff Sergeant Hall's hand was crushed in the recoil of one of the 75 mm cannons, and he had to be evacuated.

Because of the fanatical German resistance at Neuhof, the tanks of both A and B Companies had to be committed to reach the objective.

Late that morning, C Company tanks picked up the attack with the 325th's Third Battalion of Glider Infantry, rolling north from Neuhof towards Udenbreth. The Third Platoon was in the lead with the First Platoon as backup. The Second Platoon followed in reserve.

"The attack on the *Siegfried Line* at Udenbreth will live in the minds of the men who fought the battle. Men of the 82nd Airborne Division say it was their toughest battle. It certainly was our roughest show. We had been fighting for five days and nights when we went in," said Lt. Col. Rubel.[4]

Technician Fourth Grade Mike O. Smith (later to become First Sergeant) remembers the time all too well. The company was continually short of men in key positions on the line and regularly robbed Peter to pay Paul. As a company mechanic, Smith was well back of the front lines and about to sack out for the night when they came for him.

He was needed at the front, the messenger said, and he was to report immediately to Sergeant J.D. Keen. Well, he knew Keen as a tank commander, of course, he had worked with him, and he liked his attitude. Keen always said that his wasn't "foxhole religion," but that he never let the day go by without thanking God for His grace in making the day. And Smith was somewhat comforted to know that Keen's tank was named *Grace Sufficient.* He had, in fact, been involved in the naming of the tank.

A number of tank commanders and crews painted names on the sides of their tanks: *Hellzapopp'n, Comin' Berlin, Zig-Zag, Sno-Tex, Ranger, Lil Abner, Love Sick,* and others, perhaps, just as well left unnamed.

Keen, a favorite among the tankers, and eventually a fifty-year minister of the gospel, named his first two tanks *Dorothy I* and *Dorothy II,* after his devoted wife who waited all those years for him back home. After losing both of those tanks to enemy fire, he had considered changing the name of his third tank to *Self Sufficient.*

However, Smith said, at the time, nobody there knew how to spell "sufficient." It just so happened that Smith carried in his shirt pocket a little pocket bible, to which he referred for the correct spelling. It had to be there. Smith thumbed through the pages, and suddenly, there it was for all to see. "My grace is sufficient for thee." Second Corinthians 12:9. That was it, of course. They all agreed: *Grace Sufficient.* "And you know," Keen used to grin and say, "It really was."

When they came for him that particular night, Mike Smith didn't have to be a brain surgeon to understand that he was headed for a drastic change of responsibilities up front, in the middle of the night, with the bullets flying and all. He dutifully reported up front as ordered, albeit with considerable trepidation— well founded, as it turned out. For that's when he learned he was going to be Keen's tank driver on the next mission—*an attack on the Siegfried Line was to begin in the next few minutes!*

Now it also happened that in crossing the *Siegfried Line, Grace Sufficient* fell into a tank trap and was disabled. Keen, Smith, and company, greatly discouraged, had to give up on that tank and abandon her. Next morning, however, in one of those baffling enigmas of war, *Grace* appeared in front of their bivouac, all perky and ready to go. Once again, they were on their way with their namesake, with which they would finish the war, and without a scratch. Although, they never did find out how she got there.[5]

"We spearheaded the cracking of the *Siegfried Line,*" said Technician Fourth Grade W.A. Nipper. "We hit the [*Siegfried*] in line formation up to the dragon's teeth, and then moved into a column to cut through the line to take the town of Udenbreth."[6]

C Company's lead tanks roared into the town with guns blazing some thirty minutes or so before the infantry arrived, and proceeded to shoot up everything that moved against them, or even looked like it might move against them. Staff Sergeant Loopey's tank destroyed three Mark IVs and an anti-tank gun in less than an hour. This tactic—blast everything in sight—worked well until about noon, when suddenly, First Lieutenant Powers' tank was clobbered with a high-velocity 88mm round, and Powers' gunner, Corporal Jack D. Ashby, was killed. Powers was wounded in the skirmish, and Loopey took command of the platoon.

Corporal Ashby's unfortunate death was uniquely tragic. Just days before, he had been cited for gallantry in action when he dismounted his stymied tank in the face of intense ground fire and personally shot up a large number of the attackers. Then, with other members of his crew, went on to capture some two hundred of the enemy.[7]

As the battle continued, Sergeant Thomas P. Reiley's tank took eight hits from anti-tank fire, blowing Reiley clear out of the tank, killing a crewman, and seriously wounding others.

"We had just gotten stopped when—*Wham! Wham!*—all hell broke loose. Our tank and Sergeant Reiley's tank were knocked out," said Staff Sergeant James E. Lewis. "I tried to get out of the tank but couldn't—the 75 mm [barrel] was over my hatch. The rest of the crew dismounted, and then I got out of the bow [gunner's] hatch and took cover behind a building—constant artillery fire—wondering if we were cut off from the rest of the company, for we had no communication with them. Two of my closest friends lost their lives."[8]

34. Drawing courtesy of John Smith, son of Mike O. Smith

With two of the platoon's five tanks knocked out and burning, the remaining tanks hastily took cover behind a small building left standing. Technician Fourth Grade Samuel A. Crandel, the tank commander, and his crew, nosed their tank out just enough to draw fire, enabling his fellow tanks to spot and zero in on the AT guns which were giving them such a fit. Later, they managed to destroy a concealed enemy tank with the same trick.

Seven tankers were cited for heroic conduct in this action. With two of five tanks knocked out by enemy armor and anti-tank guns, the remaining three tanks took cover as best they could and fought back. In one instance, Private First Class James K. Windham stayed with his tank as it was used as a decoy to draw enemy fire, and as a result, the enemy guns were eventually located and taken out."[9]

Three German counterattacks came hard at them during the day; they threw everything they had at the Americans. Supported by tanks and self-propelled guns, the fanatic Nazis rushed forward shouting *"Heil Hitler!"* at the top of their lungs. In turn, each attack was driven back. And it didn't stop there. Three more attacks exploded on them that night. These were also beaten back, with heavy losses in both men and equipment on both sides.

"One company of the 325th counted a total of one officer and seven men that night," Lt. Col. Rubel said. "At sundown that night, seven of our tanks were still blazing furiously, adding columns of smoke to that of the enemy vehicles still on fire.

"Several hundred bodies remained where they had fallen. Many of the wounded, too weak to crawl, froze to death before aid could reach them that night. To add to this picture, several houses in each town were on fire. Thirty-two enemy pillboxes had been blasted to pieces during the shooting," he said, "and large chunks of concrete also littered the area."[10]

Rubel went on to say that "Surviving paratroopers, who had jumped in Africa, Italy, Normandy, and Holland, said this was the roughest fight they had ever witnessed."[11]

The enemy continued to lambaste both towns with mortars, artillery, and direct fire, ensuring a fitful night for the Americans, and disrupting their resupply operation.

Even in the heat of battle, funny things happen. Near sundown, a young German lieutenant unwittingly led a column of twenty enemy soldiers and a horse-drawn gun up the road to Neuhof, and proceeded to set up his own defenses, smack dab into the midst of a well-camouflaged 740th roadblock. The four American tanks, along with a scatter of 82nd paratroopers, simply held fast at the ready while the enemy made all the necessary preparations and did their thing. Just as the Jerries got their big gun all set up and were getting ready to lock and load, the 82nd infantry captain eased out from behind a tree, pistol drawn, and announced to the astounded German officer that he was now a prisoner. The rest of the Americans moved out from under cover and relieved the Germans of their weapons.

Still, it wasn't over. Having entered Germany at yet another juncture, Second Lieutenant Burlin V. Wilson and his crew were slowly leading a column of tanks around 3:00 a.m., when their guns suddenly quit working. This was not an uncommon occurrence in the heat of battle, but it did tend to cause a brief flurry of panic and a certain tightening in the chest.

Wilson pulled his tank over to the side of the road so his second tank could take the lead, just before a German self-propelled gun rolled into view up ahead. The crews of both tanks began to sweat. The Germans were no more than thirty yards away before the new lead tank could clear enough road to open up. They got the enemy gun in the nick of time, but moments later, a German Panzerfaust exploded into the last tank in the column, and set it on fire.

Making a bad situation even worse, Wilson got a call from the infantry that an enemy tank was clanking forward no more than seventy-five yards farther on up the road. The tankers went into a mad scramble to get their guns working again.

With the tank burning in the darkness behind him, the lieutenant figured they were sitting ducks. "Luck was with me," he said later. His guns clicked in, and he let loose with several "guess" shots from his cannon, even before the enemy tank hove into view, knocking the confounded German out before he ever knew what hit him.[12]

Thinking they had done their due for the day, Technician Fourth Grade Orbie J. Floyd and his crew spread out their bedrolls in what was left of an old house they had liberated in town, hoping for a brief respite, even a couple hours sleep. No doubt they were preparing to say their prayers for the infantry, giving thanks that those guys were out there, had secured the area, and posted guards nearby. The tankers loved those guys. And the infantrymen continually showed their appreciation to the tankers, not the least of which was bringing them fresh eggs. It just so happened that this time, the infantry outposts were no more than one hundred yards from the enemy. Not good.

Suddenly, an infantryman burst in on them screaming, "The Jerries are on our necks!"

The Germans were, in fact, on them, and had captured the outpost guards and infiltrated the barn attached to the very house the tankers were in.

Clutching their pants, their paraphernalia, and guns, the tankers poured out of the house and scrambled into their tanks, taking several prisoners on the way. It was hard to tell who was more frightened.

The first tank to get fired up and going, and to pull out onto the road, was smacked dead-on by a Panzerfaust.

Floyd's tank was next in line. Somehow, they managed to get off enough kill shots to take out the Panzerfaust guy, just before their guns jammed and quit firing. Still, it didn't turn out to be anywhere near as bad as it could have been. The next tank pulled up past them — its machine guns flashing, and spitting death in the dark, and led the way out.[13]

Earlier that day, on the island of Malta (at the time, a British Crown Colony off the southern tip of Sicily in the Mediterranean Sea), Winston Churchill, in a blue uniform with brass buttons, broke into a huge smile and waved his cap from the deck of *H.M.S. Orion* when he saw the American President. His great Navy cape flowing about him, Roosevelt was seated on the open bridge of the American cruiser *U.S.S. Quincy* as it eased carefully through the submarine nets and steamed slowly past into Valletta harbor. Bone tired and exhausted from the long trip aboard ship, the President summoned that famous smile of his and waved back.[14]

It was beautiful, sunny day, and a "splendid scene," Churchill was later to relate. "With the escort of Spitfires overhead, the salutes, and the bands of the ships' companies in the harbour playing *The Star-Spangled Banner*."[15]

Malta was a stopover for the two Western leaders who were en route to a

February 4 through 11 meeting of the "Big Three." Joseph Stalin was at the seaport of Yalta on Russia's Crimean coast, in what was destined to become their most important, and ultimately controversial, meeting. The transition from planning for war, to planning for peace, would determine post-war relations for many years to come.

It was said that Hitler often scoffed at these high-level meetings when they came to his attention, contending that the more the Allied leaders met, the more they would disagree.

As a matter of fact, the British and Americans were bitterly divided over the American plan for final victory in the west. The Combined Chiefs of Staff had been haggling for three days in preparation for their report to Churchill and FDR.

General Eisenhower believed that one final, aggressive campaign on a broad front would deal a "death blow" to Hitler's Germany. His plan was to destroy the enemy west of the Rhine, then, with some seventy-five reinforced divisions, cross the last natural barrier to the German heartland in two major assaults: the heaviest assault to the north by the 21st Army Group, under Field Marshal Montgomery, and a secondary attack to the south by the 12th Army Group, under Lt. Gen. Bradley.

The British opposed the plan, arguing for one major assault to the north, with Montgomery as overall Ground Commander-in-Chief, effectively kicking Ike "upstairs." The implication was that there were "national considerations" in the American plan.

Neither Eisenhower nor Montgomery was present at the Malta meeting. Ike was represented by his Chief of Staff, Lt. Gen. Walter Bedell Smith. However, General Marshall had met secretly with Ike in Marseilles, just prior to the Malta meeting, and came away fully convinced that the broad front initiative would win the war. He stood tough and firm, therefore, on the American plan. And that was that.

Knowing that Montgomery was behind much of the criticism of Ike and American strategic planning, Marshall went on to recount how troubling it was to the Americans that Churchill and the British chiefs continued to pressure Ike to place Montgomery in control of the ground war.

America's top soldier stood solidly behind Ike all the way, and it finally became crystal clear to the British that there would be no ground commander appointed as long as George Marshall was the American Chief of Staff and Eisenhower was Commander of SHAEF.

The Yalta Conference, February 4 – 11, 1945. *While Roosevelt and Churchill were striving to come to terms in Malta, Generalissimo Stalin and his entourage were steaming by train to Yalta, some nine hundred miles south of Moscow. All three of the Allied leaders* *were in their sixties, and each most certainly had different aspirations for what was to come.*

The American president, born in 1882, had just celebrated his 63rd birthday, but was quite ill and further weakened by the long sea voyage. It would be FDR's last such meeting.

His primary goals were relatively simple and clear-cut: to finalize the division of a defeated Germany; to settle problems with the Soviets in the formation of the United Nations; and to get Stalin signed on to help in the war with Japan. Anything else would be icing on the cake as far as FDR was concerned. And he fully expected to give, as well as get.

Six years the President's senior, the British Prime Minister was the oldest of the three. He was deeply concerned about bringing the war to a quick conclusion, and the settlement of German affairs. However, he was perhaps more anxious about the political issues regarding France's role and British influence in the post-war balance of power. Only after these matters had been agreed to by the great powers, would the United Nations come into play, as far as he was concerned. And Churchill felt quite strongly that he and the President were clearly not on the same page with respect to Russian occupied territory.

The wily old 65-year-old Soviet dictator knew exactly what he wanted, and ultimately got: massive reparations from Germany and loans from the United States for economic reconstruction. He would agree to intervene in the war with Japan by invading Manchuria sometime after the Germans surrendered — in return for the territories lost in the Far East after the Russo-Japanese war of 1904–1905. Finally, he would insist that "friendly" governments be established in all of the East European countries between Russia and Germany.

While Roosevelt, Churchill, and even Stalin talked of "democracy and free elections" in the liberated countries, the Soviet dictator gambled steadfastly that the U.S. and Britain would never interfere in the Russian zone of Eastern Europe, once it was established.[16]

And so, when the three great Allied leaders gathered at Yalta on February 4 through 11, the eventual agreements hammered out included: (1) the unconditional surrender of a defeated Germany, with the zones of occupation to include France; (2) the road to the United Nations paved and cemented; (3) the fate of the liberated countries of Europe determined; (4) the land and power that Stalin demanded in the Far East given. Controversial, even secret, decisions that would profoundly affect the participants and the world for years to come.

Still, anything else might have "fractured the Grand Alliance before Germany and Japan could be defeated. And with a war yet to win —"[17]

While the Big Three were settling the fate of the world in Yalta, American and British air forces continued the unrelenting saturation bombing of German cities. In Berlin, fires smoldered throughout the bombed-out ruins of the city. Food and fuel were scarce. Refugees by the thousands lived helter-skelter as best they could. To the east, the Russian hoard was at the Oder River, less than fifty miles away.

The noose was tightening.

Nearly one thousand American B-29 Superfortresses slammed the capital city with high explosives and incendiary bombs on February 3, in one of the toughest tests of the German will to date. "Deserters and foreign slave workers were beginning to appear, scavenging and terrorizing in the streets."[18]

35. U.S. Army Signal Corps photo from the files of the California Connection

British Prime Minister Winston Churchill, U.S. President Franklin Roosevelt, and Soviet Leader Joseph Stalin at the historic Yalta Conference, February 1945. Note the President's haggard appearance.

But the war was far from over. The tankers had been fighting in death's grip night and day for a week, when word came down that they would be relieved by the 99th Infantry Division and the 750th Tank Battalion on February 4. No more than eighteen tanks were operational in the entire battalion, and both gunfire and the weather had taken their toll on the crews.

Lt. Col. Rubel noted that the battalion had drawn on Service and Headquarters Companies for men to fill out tank crews. "Several radio operators, some of the cooks, and the Intelligence Sergeant of Headquarters Company were in the line at that very time in tanks. We were practically fought out," he said.[19]

And relief did come, although it wasn't until February 5. Elements of the 750th Tank Battalion began to filter into 740th positions that morning, and it took most of the day, and on into the night. The Third Platoon of B Company had to wait for dark to maneuver around the enemy anti-tank guns zeroed in on their breakout route. It was February 6 before the battalion was finally able to regroup in Hebronval, Belgium. Sleep, blessed sleep. First, their tanks had to be serviced, of course, before they could hit the sack. And some new (well, serviceable) tanks, and some replacements, were coming in.

It was to be a short reprieve. "Just before midnight of the sixth a breathless messenger dashed in. He stated that he was from Division Headquarters and had an urgent message for me," said Lt. Col. Rubel.

The 740th had been transferred to the First Army's VII Corps and attached to the Eighth Infantry Division, and was to *move immediately and secretly* to the vicinity of Gressenich, Germany, just east of Aachen. "Grab your hats, Tankers, here we go again," Lt. Col. Rubel told the company commanders.

Any markings that could reveal the identity of the battalion were to be painted or covered over. *Rigid secrecy* was stressed among the men. The name of the battalion was sacrosanct from that moment on, and not to be revealed to anyone. There was that feeling again, emanating from the pit of the stomach. *What the hell is going on here?*

Lt. Col. Rubel protested. The 740th needed time—time for rest, time to get caught up and reorganized, and time to secure the necessary replacement vehicles lost in the last weeks of fierce combat. He was told to move on out: the battalion could do all these things when it arrived at the designated assembly area—if there were time.

Major Graddy H. Floyd gathered up the forward Command Section and rolled out for Gressenich the very next morning, February 7, while Lt. Col. Rubel made a dash to the 82nd Airborne Headquarters in Stavelot to bid his *adieu* to Gen. Gavin. Rubel was high on the 82nd, and believed them to be the "best fighting organization in any man's army."[20]

He was somewhat taken aback when the general handed him a letter, already prepared, which he was about to pass on to the message center. The 740th Commander's face must certainly have taken on a look of fierce pride as he read:

HEADQUARTERS 82ND AIRBORNE DIVISION [21]
Office of the Division Commander

APO 469, in the Field,
7 February 1945

SUBJECT: Letter of Appreciation.
TO: Commanding Officer, 740th Tank Battalion.

I would like to express to you my appreciation for the splendid performance
of your battalion during its period of attachment to this Division. During that
time the Division, with your able assistance, has participated in the attack to
pinch off the ARDENNES salient, destroying the 62nd Volks Grenadier Division.
Following that, it has advanced into Germany to the east, penetrating the
SIEGFRIED Line and seizing the key defenses at UDENBRETH. These
accomplishments were only possible with the courageous and zealous assistance
of the personnel of your battalion. Their esprit and elan have been the subject
much favorable comment by all members of the Division. It has been a pleasure
and a privilege to have had you serve with us and I sincerely hope that the
fortunes of war will bring us together once again. I am proud to have served
with such fine soldiers.

/s/ *James M. Gavin*
JAMES M. GAVIN
Major General, U.S. Army, Commanding

36. Copy of original letter from the author's collection.

Chapter 18

Veritable and Grenade

As scheduled, the 740th rolled into its newly assigned area late in the afternoon on February 8. Headquarters, Service, and D Companies billeted in Kornelimünster, just south of Aachen. A, B, and C Companies bivouacked in the vicinity of Schlich, a little village about a mile west of Duren, in a forest said to be strewn with mines.

The entire area in the environs of Duren was devastated. It seemed that just about every building, every square foot of ground, and even the surrounding fields had been bombed or chewed up by artillery and mortar fire. Dead and bloated livestock littered the landscape, apparently killed in their tracks. Cows and horses were still hitched to their plows and wagons. The stench was almost unbearable.

Schlich, where the battalion command section set up along with a divisional artillery battery, had been abandoned. However, it was still within range of enemy fire. And battalion vehicles were axle-deep in mud from the overflow of a drainage ditch onto the main road. Basements and ground floors of many of the buildings that were still standing were filled with slush and water. The February thaw had begun. But it was still brutally cold.

The tankers would now have to fight the mud, slush, and miserable rain, as well as the enemy. They continually scraped and shoveled the angry mud from their tank tracks. The slime crept up over the tops of their boots, onto their pants, and down into their socks. Diarrhea was rampant among the troops, along with the attendant abdominal cramps, and all too often, fever. On the move, it was not unusual to see a tanker's cold, bare bottom hanging over the back end of a slow-moving tank that was sometimes under fire.

In general, the 740th had most of the supplies they needed except for overshoes and socks. Their biggest worry was trench foot. But nothing like the doughboys––forever out there in the midst of the most miserable conditions. Those poor guys were really hurting.

The tankers desperately needed time for rest and tank maintenance, and it was obvious that they were not going to get much of a respite with random mortar fire raining down on their heads. So Rubel appealed to Division to be allowed to relocate, at least out of mortar and artillery range, while they waited for the attack to begin. After all, he'd been promised time to rest and retrofit. Rubel said that Division, however, was "entirely unmoved" by his arguments, "and [they] stated that if I expected to do [all] that —I should have done it before coming up here."[1]

B Company was ordered to the nearby town of Gey on February 9. Like Schlich, Gey also stood on top of a hill. When the tanks moved in, the Germans quickly laid out a blanket of artillery fire, and several infantrymen were killed.

The 740th's Staff Sergeant Ivy L. Kelley and his food service crew found the going rough as well. "My kitchen was set up in an old roofless farmhouse in Gey, within artillery range of the Germans," he recounted. That afternoon, the " —.88s started coming in, and shrapnel peppered the ground all around us. Each round hit a little closer to our kitchen." It wasn't long, he said, before his staff began to grab up the 10-gallon pots for helmets and dive into the muddy water under the kitchen table. Kelly said when he finally got his wits about him, he found himself wedged between the wall of the house and an old iron bake oven. That was one he'll never forget.[2]

A warning came down to the battalion that same day that the 8th Infantry, Major General William G. Weaver, commanding, would attack across the Roer River in the mask of darkness at 0510 hours the very next morning, February 10.

In addition to the 8th Infantry, the VII Corps at this time included the 104th Infantry and the 3rd Armored Divisions, along with the 4th Cavalry Group, and was commanded by Major General J. Lawton "Lightning Joe" Collins. The job: seize crossings over the Roer River at Duren and protect the right flank of the XIX Corps, which was scheduled to cross the Roer about five miles northwest, in the Jülich area.

The plan was for the 8th Infantry, with the 740th tanks attached, to cross the river and seize the south half of Duren and the town of Stockheim, a mile to the south. The 104th Infantry Division was to attack left of the 8th and capture the north half of Duren. Having established this bridgehead, the two infantry divisions would allow the 3rd Armored Division to roll through and make a drive for Cologne.

Two battalions of infantry were to cross the Roer in assault boats and ferries under cover of darkness, and drive at least one thousand yards into Duren. As soon as a bridgehead had been secured, the engineers would begin to construct foot soldier bridges, infantry support vehicle bridges, and finally, treadway bridges strong enough to support the 740th's 35-ton Sherman tanks.

It was a tense and exacting time. The tankers and infantrymen were briefed on the order of events which were to take place. The engineers hauled in their heavy equipment throughout the night, stacking it up and down the river. Some five hundred assault boats came first, closest to the river. They would be used in the first wave. Farther back were all the elaborate construction materials. And behind all this turmoil, infantry practiced for the assault —picking up the boats, carrying them to the water's edge, then jumping in, shoving off, grabbing oars, and rowing like all get out.

And wouldn't you know: torrential rains flashed up and down the Roer Valley that next morning. The river rose an inch an hour. Air reconnaissance showed the entire dam system full and overflowing the spillways. The melted snow from the surrounding hills began its rush downhill to the river.

Worse, the Germans still had control of the series of dams which regulated the flow of water of the Roer River and its tributaries. The enemy could, at will, open the flood gates and wash out any temporary bridges downstream. This would flood the surrounding fields, making troop movement almost impossible, and isolating any Allied troops making it across the river. When the order came down at midnight that the attack would be postponed for twenty-four hours, Lt. Col. Rubel and his tankers were hardly surprised.[3]

On February 11, B Company's Third Platoon was stunned when it was ordered up to the river at Lendersdorf. Best they could figure was they had been invited over to share in the misery of the formidable mortar fire that the Third Battalion of the 28th Infantry Regiment was receiving.

The 740th's Corporal Ray F. Newman remembered Lendersdorf quite well. He guessed he'd been spotted one afternoon because mortar fire exploded all up and down the road when he was taking chow up to the tankers. As he zigzagged his peep into town, a round dropped nearby and spun crazily under his vehicle. He sat frozen in time, his whole life flashing before his eyes, until he finally realized the round was a dud.[4]

Meanwhile, engineers of the First Army's V Corps made a heroic grab for the huge Schwammenauel Dam. When withering rifle fire drove them from the spillway, they slid down the two-hundred foot face of the dam, overcame the startled German machine gunners, and entered an exit at the bottom. Although the Americans expected the massive dam to blow at any moment, they found no booby traps nor prepared explosives. Instead, the Germans had cleverly damaged the power room machinery and blown the discharge valves the night before. This, along with similar action at the Urft Dam, produced a steady flow of water throughout the Roer River Valley and stopped the American advance in place.[5]

The plan was for Montgomery's "Veritable" and "Grenade" offensives to destroy the Nazis west of the Rhine in the northern sector, thus paving the way for the main thrust into the heart of Germany. This was to take place in three stages, according to Gen. Bradley. The first stage was the seizure of the dams. The second stage, to begin on February 8, was Operation Veritable, a massive assault of some 400,000 British and Canadian troops attacking southeast from Nijmegen. And the third stage was Operation Grenade, to begin

February 10, with Lt. Gen. Simpson's U.S. Ninth Army of about 300,000 troops, attacking to the northeast from the vicinity of Jülich, in a giant pincer movement. "Lightning Joe" Collins' VII Corps of some 100,000 men, including the 8th Infantry to which the 740th Tank Battalion was attached, was to jump off with the U.S. Ninth Army and cover their right flank.[6]

It was a fitting plan. The problem was that the dams were spewing water down the valley, and the situation worsened daily. The river was no more than one hundred yards wide where the 740th was slated to cross, but the rush of water swelled and picked up speed by the hour.

The massive buildup of soldiers, vehicles, and supplies for the Allies new offensive mounted, and Operation Veritable moved forward to its inevitable climax. The British and Canadian Armies of Montgomery's 21st Army Group jumped off with an enormous roar in the cold and rain of February 8—the creeping fire of fourteen hundred big guns pounded German positions, announcing the coming. It was an awesome set-piece engagement, literally exploding out of the woods at Nijmegen.

But German resistance was fierce, and the rain cutting. Enemy reinforcements poured in. Every foot of soggy ground had to be desperately won. As the tanks and armored personnel carriers began to bog down in the mud and mine fields cross-country, the troops slogged doggedly forward on their own. But progress was painful and slow, and when the main supply route eventually stalled bumper to bumper, the attack gradually ground to a halt.

Just to the south, the U.S. Ninth Army's planned pincer, Operation Grenade, scheduled to launch on February 10, was completely stymied by the flood waters. The powerful "big right hook" organized to link up with the First Canadian Army, simply could not get out of the mud and across the rushing river to support the "Veritable" assault.

On the Ninth Army's right, the First Army's VII Corps, which included the 8th Infantry Division, along with the 740th Tank Battalion, was helplessly on hold as well. Sitting ducks from the shelling across the river.

Word came down that "Grenade" was postponed. Indefinitely.

On learning that the Americans were completely stalled, Field Marshal von Runstedt, Hitler's titular Commander in the West, began to move troops to the north to counter the massive British and Canadian attack. Interestingly enough, even as the German field commanders were reading von Runstedt's Enigma signal that ordered troops northward, American and British leaders were carefully evaluating the same top-secret message.[7]

Aside from the atomic bomb, the best kept secret of the war was that the British had broken the code for the German radio traffic, and had brought the Americans in on it shortly after Pearl Harbor.

Hitler believed he had the most secure system ever developed, based on an electrically operated cypher machine known as Enigma, a big portable typewriter-looking thing packed in a wooden box. Theoretically, messages could be decoded only by someone equipped with another Enigma machine, and there were millions of possible settings.

The British, however, had secured a copy of the Enigma machine from the Poles, and developed a harbinger of the computer to "read" these messages. The translated messages became known by the code name ULTRA. The secret work was done at Bletchley Park, a secluded enclave in England, and only a handful of key people knew about it. Only in the Ardennes offensive was German secrecy so tight that the Allied command failed to grasp the warning signals in time.

The 740th still needed reinforcements and repair. Forty-five replacement tankers came in to the rear CP on February 11, and they got in some target practice and training outside Kornelimunster. But generally, for the tankers, life on the Roer was cold and miserable. Regular "incoming mail" (artillery and mortar fire) from across the river, made any kind of rest or tank repair all but impossible. Practically any movement, loud noise, or bright light would bring down the wrath of enemy guns. And there was always "outgoing." Lt. Col. Rubel tried again to get part of the battalion moved back in order to get *some* work done while the tankers waited, but to no avail. All he got was the now familiar, "Should of done all that before you got here."

Tanks, riflemen, artillery, engineers, fighting vehicles, and hardware of every imaginable military persuasion were stashed throughout the woods, in or behind every available ditch, house, barn, building, or underpass. Movement of any kind always had to be quick and silent, and in the dark of night—if the matter could possibly wait. It was eerie in the morning fog. And ghostlike at night.[8] When the jolting crack of a rifle or the menacing burst from a machine gun splintered the silence, the freezing cold was temporarily suspended—but not the shivers.

The infantry, all up and down the bank of the river, took the brunt of it, as usual. Boat patrols probed the far bank of the frigid river every night for minefields, gun emplacements, or to try to capture prisoners. All too often, the rubber boats capsized, or the gutsy guys in them got shot up or captured, and never came back.

Infantrymen on the line crawled cautiously from foxhole to tree to outpost, at times almost to the water's edge—there to remain motionless for hours until frozen stiff, and then relieved. Any fleeting shadow or flash of light, especially match light, drew rifle or machine gun fire. Wet. Cold. Scared. "You know, those German boys—just across the river—they've gotta be just as cold and scared as we are."

Some would say that it really began on February 3, when nearly one thousand American B-17 Flying Fortresses pounded what was left of Berlin into near devastation. That brought the scavengers—especially the foreign slave workers and the deserters — out into the streets, terrorizing the already desperate and totally unnerved populace that remained in the capital city.

But while the 740th was shivering in and around their tanks at the flooded Roer, the saturation bombing of German cities by the Allies between February 13 and 16 was by any count, the most awesome of the war.

Virtually every city in Germany had been hard hit by this time. But the most disastrous and controversial raid of the war was the one that destroyed Dresden on February 13 and 14. Nearly 1,200 British RAF and U.S. Eighth Air Force bombers roared over the old German city of the arts in wave after wave, dropping thousands of incendiary and high-explosive bombs. The resulting firestorm created "hurricane-like winds and temperatures up to 1,000 degrees Fahrenheit or higher."[9]

Not a block of buildings in the inner city remained unscathed. The killing fires raged for days through the narrow streets and could be seen for two hundred miles, according to the historian Stephen Ambrose. The Germans announced the death toll at 135,000, but Ambrose puts the figure at 35,000, noting that "no one knows for certain, as Dresden had many refugees in the city."[10]

Saturation bombing had been an accepted method of retaliation ever since the terrible Nazi destruction of London and across England. Now, however, since there was little in Dresden of military or industrial concern, and the terrible destruction was out there for all the world to see, neither Britain nor America were quite so sure any more.

Still, this was war. For survival. And, although the political uproar never really subsided, the mass bombings continued until the last big American raid on Berlin nearly two months later, when it was determined that such action was no longer necessary to win the war.

Marching orders for which the 740th had been waiting finally came down on a rainy Friday, February 16. Word was that it was "Go!" for February 23 and that "The attack will be launched come hell or high water!"[11]

Lt. Col. Rubel figured the word "launched" was used deliberately, since it certainly appeared as if the exercise were likely to "be more of a naval operation than a land attack, for there had been no letup in the rains."[12]

But the tankers knew what was coming and moved quietly off for a private moment by themselves, or gathered in small groups and talked in hushed tones with their buddies. Stomachs tightened a bit now that the time had actually come.

German air activity began to pick up considerably over the area, and the Americans would often see groups of four or more enemy planes at a time. However, the Allies were generally in control of the sky and daylight raids were rare, no more than an occasional Luftwaffe pilot screaming past. This allowed the artillery observation planes to fly a number of the 740th platoon leaders and sergeants across the heavily fortified eastern bank, and even over the city of Duren for familiarization purposes.

Out of the blue, the tankers spotted one of Hitler's revolutionary Messerschmitt 262 jet-propelled fighter-bombers on February 20, obviously on a reconnaissance mission, since it did not choose to slow and fight. It simply ran away from the Thunderbolts and Mustangs that rose to challenge it, no matter the angle the attacking propeller-driven fighters put on it.

As the jet flyby became a regular occurrence, it became quite frustrating to watch them roam the skies at will, the American planes playing catch-up in their wake. And ack-ack huffing and puffing explosions of black and white still farther back. It became so frustrating that when one of the new jets hove into sight, as if on cue, all the tankers in the area opened up with everything they had: .50 calibers, carbines, Tommy guns, and even pistols. When the fireworks started, it was a sight to see. Of course, nobody ever hit anything. Although, they all felt better when it was done. "We probably inadvertently shot at more Thunderbolts than we did Jerry jet jobs," Lt. Col. Rubel said.[13] Not to mention the fact that a number of tankers were wounded by the falling flak.

The new German Messerschmitt 262 jets not only frustrated the ground troops, but were somewhat unnerving as well. Those damnable planes could literally strike from out of the blue. Bolting through the sky, they could suddenly idle their engines, dive silently, and bomb and strafe unsuspecting Allied troops. Although they could outrun and outmaneuver anything the Allies had, they were not invincible. Just days later, Battery C of the 557th Antiaircraft Artillery Battalion somehow found the range and snagged a couple of the ME-262s as they swooped in to bomb Roer River bridges. Cheers went up as the second jet exploded in a fiery ball in a near vertical climb after losing his bombs.[14]

The rumor mill, of course, ground on. Were there still more of Hitler's "secret weapons" out there, yet to be unleashed, which could change the fate of the war?

Two light tank platoons from D Company were shifted to the division's "Task Force Crawford" in mid-February, and moved to the village of Scherpenseel on February 22. Their special mission was to assist in the protection of the south flank of the division after the river crossing the next day.

The Germans knew it was coming, of course. By now, there was not much effort at concealment back of the front lines. On every passable road, thousands of trucks packed dangerously high with ammunition, bridging materials, steel girders, pontoons, assault boats, and rafts, and supplies were slowly converging on their allocated target areas. The Third Armored Division filled every nook and cranny of a host of little towns in the area, making no effort to hide. Newly painted staff cars with ranking officers with neckties on and chin straps buckled, shuttled back and forth through the area, "inspecting" this or that, and checking how the "battle" was going.

During the afternoon of February 22, American artillery began to lay out interdiction fire on all the roads across the river, then area fire on known enemy concentrations. After dark, the huge assault force edged closer to final staging areas. The night was wet and bitterly cold, and the moon too bright for what had to be done. Infantrymen slowly made their way through the muddy, knee-deep slush, up to the hidden assault boats on the banks of the river. No sleep for anyone. Just shake, shiver, and pray.

At 2:45 on the morning of February 23, the twenty-five-mile Roer River line erupted—literally burst into flames. By all accounts, it was one of the fiercest bombardments over such a wide area in the entire war. Two thousand artillery pieces in the Ninth Army laid out some forty-six thousand tons of ammunition: 240 mm cannons to 40 mm anti-aircraft guns; rockets and mortars; direct fire from tanks; and machine guns and rifles. Even pistols were fired across that river: " — every weapon the Americans had [was] hurled against the enemy [in] a forty-five minute deluge of bullets and high explosives designed to stun, kill, or drive him [the German] from his position."[15]

C Company tanks fired three concentrations: five hundred rounds on Merzenich, three hundred rounds on Binsfeld, and two hundred rounds on Rommelsheim. The 740th Assault Gun Platoon fired thirteen missions (1,002 rounds) on Duren, and A Company fired direct fire missions into Duren to support the 13th Infantry crossing of the river. Positions were along the west bank of the river at Rolsdorf.[16]

Across the river in Duren was utter devastation. Buildings shattered or crumbled. Broad fields in and around the city churned and belched fire and smoke. It was like Hades at first glimpse.

When the barrage lifted, the infantry began their assault. After such a terrible pounding, the Germans were surely dazed, devastated, or dead in their tracks. Still, the GIs moved cautiously through the darkness and smoke to the river to launch the assault. Shock and dismay raced through the ranks as they found themselves facing heavy enemy fire. From then on, almost everything went wrong.

Although temporarily driven back into shelters and basements in the city by the initial barrage, most of the Germans seemed to have survived and were now back at their gun emplacements. Assault boats were riddled by enemy fire as quickly as they were launched. Power boats fared little better. Too many wouldn't start in the damp, murky weather. And it seemed that as if by some miracle, a boat made it through the gunfire to midstream, it would more than likely be upended by the raging currents. This was disastrous, since the orders were for the boats to come back for more troops after each crossing.

Those waiting their turn from the bank could hear the wounded screaming as they were swept downstream in the darkness. All through the night, one after another, an increasing number of the assault teams made it across, and wild firefights ensued. Those gutsy doughboys slowly but surely cleared the far shore, and the bridgehead was established.

Meanwhile, the engineers of VII Corps worked feverishly against time, the weather, and enemy fire to lay out their bridges. Low-level machine gun fire chopped away at them, but when one man dropped, another took his place. That was bad enough, but when the pre-registered mortar and artillery fire started coming in right on target, even in the darkness, whole sections of bridges and workers were blown away almost as quickly as they had been maneuvered into position.

Although the infantry gradually expanded its foothold on the far side of the river, the tanks did not make it across until the next day, when a prefabricated Bailey bridge of lattice steel was finally laid out across the ruins of the main highway bridge into the city.

The engineers of VII Corps took 154 casualties, eight killed, and one missing, in constructing this, and eight other bridges for the 8th and 104th Divisions.[17]

Company A tanks moved into prepared positions along the west bank of the Roer and opened up on targets called in by the infantry, as well as targets of opportunity. Fires flamed up in barracks and a factory area, and at least one self-propelled gun was spotted and knocked out. The A Company tanks rolled across the Bailey bridge the morning of the 24th and supported the 13th Regiment as it fought its way through Duren. There was not a lot of firing as the infantry preceded the tanks on this occasion. The only casualties were to Sgt. Nello Fasoli's crew, which was scrambled by mortar fire while they were temporarily out of their tank. The company set up defenses for the night on the eastern edge of the city.

B Company's Third Platoon was ordered to move immediately from Duren to Niederau as quickly as they crossed the river, then on toward Stockheim to breakthrough to the 28th Regiment's Third Battalion, which was surrounded in a heavily wooded area and running low on ammunition, food, and water. Also, there were the wounded.

The platoon made it to Niederau without a fight, but the road from there to Stockheim was known to be mined. When assured by regimental command that the road had been cleared, the tanks moved out. By mid-afternoon, however, three of the Shermans had been ravaged by mines, and the platoon was both stunned and stymied. Later, they learned that the mine sweeping detail sent out to clear the road had been driven back by small arms fire before being able to complete the sweep. Sadly, this information slipped through the cracks and never made it up the chain of command.

Meanwhile, the tanks of B Company's First and Second Platoons crossed the river at Rolsdorf, but were unable to make contact with infantry because both the roads and the surrounding fields were mined. They wound up at Niederau for the night.

C Company was attached to the 121st Infantry Regiment late that afternoon and moved their tanks into Duren under cover of darkness. As they should have guessed, the First Platoon was attached to the Third Battalion of infantry, the Second Platoon to the First Battalion, and the Third Platoon to the First Battalion. "This to confuse the enemy no doubt," Lt. Col. Rubel later reflected. "It certainly confused me."[18]

At one point, a group of infantrymen ran headlong into a nest of enemy anti-tank guns and found themselves pinned down on the wrong end of a bad situation. The German gun crews were having a great time of it until Staff Sergeant Joseph "Buck" Southers and Corporal (later TEC 4) Morris E. Copeland's tanks pulled up in the middle of the fight, completely exposed, and laid high-explosive shells right on top of their lead gun. After that shocker, the sight of that Sherman tank turret traversing rapidly in their direction must have completely unnerved the three other AT crews, for they suddenly decided to take the rest of the day off, scrambling out and away from their gun emplacements with a fever born of necessity.[19]

D Company, still with Task Force Crawford, had crossed the bridge late that morning, and its tanks were attached to different platoons of the 8th Reconnaissance Troop in Niederau. And there they stayed the night, completely cut off by mine fields.

Most of the 8th Infantry Division's combat units made it across the river February 24, eventually overwhelming the east bank defenses. The battered city of Duren was pretty well cleared by nightfall.

Still, it was by no means over for everyone. "I hope never to spend another night like [that] one," said Corporal Donald F. Beebe. "It was a cold, rainy night, dark as pitch."

Beebe ended up driving his liaison peep through that bomb-ravaged city all through the night. Always looking over his shoulder. Never knowing what kind of surprise was around the next corner. Trying to find his way around the deep bomb craters and mangled piles of debris. Without letup. "Every time I returned to the CP, there was another errand to run. Daybreak couldn't come soon enough for me," he said.[20]

High command, clear up to the corps commander, was getting impatient, according to Lt. Col. Rubel. The 104th Division, on the left, was already across and ready to roll. However, the 8th Division's entire right flank was wide open, and a battalion of the 28th Regiment was being gradually cut to pieces at Stockheim.

The 740th's B Company moved out toward Stockheim in the early morning darkness, but was of little immediate help because the road was heavily mined. Both tanks and infantry came under heavy fire during the morning. Around noon, however, the Third Platoon moved to the attack with infantry, overran an anti-tank gun, and rounded up forty-eight prisoners near the town. Things looked somewhat brighter.

As the Second Platoon moved to help capture the town, First Lieutenant Raymond E. Davies' tank was blown by mines. Fortunately, no casualties, but the minefield effectively stopped the platoon in its tracks. As a result, the tanks were reassigned to the Third Battalion of infantry with a new objective: a pre-dark attack to clear the nearby towns of Binsfelder Burg, Rommelsheim, and Burgbernheim, all standing in the way of the advance.

The First Platoon, working with a company of the First Battalion from the 28th Infantry, was successful in its attack on the little town of Stepperath. "Successful," that is, until disaster struck. It was growing dark before they were in control of the town. Even then, First Lieutenant Arthur P. Hartle, the platoon leader, felt comfortably secure as he dropped down from his tank and walked over to check with one of the infantry captains. Without warning, a German mortar whistled in and exploded in their midst. Hartle was mortally wounded; he died instantly. An incredible coincidence, tankers said. Staff Sergeant Mack J. Fleenor took command of the platoon.

Private First Class John A. Amann, Lt. Hartle's loader, said when the sudden death of Hartle began to sink in, "We were devastated, in a state of shock. How terrible it was to lose such a good man. What insanity. And it just goes on and on."[21]

Still with the 121st, C Company attacked the towns of Binsfeld and Girbelsrath. With the Third Platoon held in temporary regimental reserve, the Second Platoon was split in two sections, each supporting a different company of infantry. It was touch and go from the start, but the First Platoon was the first to hit the buzz saw.

By early afternoon, the First Platoon was nearing Girbelsrath and came to an open field, some three thousand yards across. The field was flat, except for some suspicious looking haystacks on a slight mound near the center of the field—an obvious spot for anti-tank gun emplacements, especially if they were zeroed in. Clearly concerned that his tanks and the infantry involved were under the gun, the platoon leader, First Lieutenant David Oglensky, called for smoke and artillery fire before advancing. His request was refused, and he was given a direct order to move out.[22]

With the hackles rising on the back of his neck, he ordered his tiny task force forward—some twenty-five infantrymen advancing uneasily abreast of the five tanks. They were no more than five hundred yards out when the trap was sprung. The haystacks exploded! And a battery of 88mm AT guns opened up from the front and the right flank. In just thirty seconds, three of the tanks were burning and destroyed. Oglensky was dead. Sergeant Ira M. Case was dead. TEC 4 Herbert Howell was dead. TEC 5 Grady Morris, Jr. was dead. And eight other tankers were wounded.

A vicious firefight erupted. Small arms fire swept the area from dug in enemy riflemen and well-camouflaged machine gun positions all about the field. The ambush was complete.

Private First Class Paul L. Gittings, bow gunner in Case's tank when it was hit, said that the German shell slammed into the tank directly behind his seat. The terrifying smell of gasoline and black gunpowder filled the air, and the tank exploded. All he could see was flames. But miracles do happen of course, as every soldier knows, and he and TEC 4 Arlie A. Wells, the driver, somehow made it up and out, and crawled to the safety of a ditch. The rest of his crew —Case, the tank commander; Howell, the gunner; and Morris, the loader —were all dead.[23] There was no immediate count of infantry lost in the battle that followed, as the desperate little task force was driven back.

Staff Sergeant (later Second Lieutenant) William H. Nemnich took charge of what was left of the tank platoon, and ultimately pulled back to Duren under cover of darkness.

The Third Platoon's First Lieutenant Charles B. Powers was struck by mortar fire and evacuated that same day, and Staff Sergeant Charlie W. Loopey took command of that platoon.

Leaving most of D Company in Niederau, the Third Platoon, now under the command of First Lieutenant Lloyd P. Mick, rolled out for Stockheim with the 28th Infantry. En route, Mick's tank hit a mine and burned. Since there were no severe casualties, Mick led the balance of his platoon into town to help relieve the battered infantry forces still fighting there.

By the time D Company's commander, Captain Raymond R. Smith, arrived on the scene, German armor had entered the town from the south, wreaking havoc; the badly outgunned infantry was preparing to withdraw. Smith's arrival encouraged the infantry to hang tough with his tanks, and together they eventually cleared the town. However, another tank was lost in the process, knocked out by an SP gun.

With so many tanks lost, Lt. Col. Rubel struggled to combine elements of the various companies in order to meet all the assignments of the battalion. Lack of ammunition completely stalled the Assault Gun Platoon. Still, on February 25, the regimental commander was determined to make a "Combat Command" out of the available tanks and infantry, and use it as a "small force of opportunity" to make a breakthrough when a weak spot in the line developed. The very next day, however, the division commander released the tank platoons from the various infantry battalions, and ordered them scattered among the nearby towns of Frauwüllesheim, Binsfeld, and Binsfelder Burg. Then, with the day not yet done, the bulk of the tank battalion was ordered to the vicinity of Girbelsrath, to become part of Task Force Greer—a mobile reserve force being organized to repel counterattacks from the division's south flank.

"From this point to Cologne, our entire action was a nightmarish routine of attachment and detachment from one Regiment to another," said Lt. Col. Rubel. "On a good many occasions, before one order could be complied with, it would be rescinded and another attachment would be made, so that platoons crisscrossed each other, and having moved all night or all day would be back with the same outfit a few hours later."[24]

Complicating the situation, German artillery kept nerves raw and on edge, whether the tankers were at a dead stop, scattered in camouflage positions, or rumbling down the road in column. Such action made the delivery of gas and ammunition extremely dangerous, of course, and the situation was unusually tenuous that particular day.

While on a routine delivery, Technician Fifth Grade James H. Thomas was caught in an especially withering barrage. Bouncing along, his truck rocked like a bucking bronco as incoming shells whacked first, one side of the road, and then the other. Being a rather bright fellow for his young age, it didn't take long for him to determine that there simply had to be a better plan—him sitting right on top of that gas and ammo and all.

Jamming his truck under cover at the side of the road, he infiltrated the lines on foot, through enemy fire, up to where the tanks were, so they'd know help was on the way. Then, as the shelling eased off, he maneuvered his way back and brought his explosive cargo on up to his guys—carefully weaving his way through the huge black potholes in the road.[25]

Meanwhile, in a parallel advance to the north, the Third Armored Division, with the 13th Infantry Regiment attached, abruptly swung south just before reaching the Erft Canal and overwhelmed the town of Blatzheim. This eased the pressure on the 8th Infantry and the 740th, and the attack up and down the line began to move more smoothly.

On February 27, with both A and B Companies now in mobile reserve with Task Force Greer at Girbelsrath, C Company collected two of A Company's platoons and moved into Blatzheim, after its capture by the Third Armored

Division. Service Company and the Battalion Maintenance Platoon also moved into the town and immediately set up shop.

The battalion was always short of tanks, and since replacements were frozen by the First Army, Service Company scavenged parts and pieces where they could. As a rule, they could find what they needed only on one of the battalion's own knocked-out tanks back down the road—and all too often, while they were under enemy fire.

It was close to midnight on February 27 when Lt. Col. Rubel received notice that the division's mission was to seize crossings over the Erft Canal in the vicinity of Mödrath. It seemed that the 28th Infantry Regiment, with which the 740th had been fighting all this time, was being passed through by the 121st Infantry, and the 740th tanks (with the exception of B and D Companies, which still had fighting jobs where they were) would be continuing the attack with the 121st! No rest for the weary.

A mammoth new German artillery piece, mounted on a King Tiger tank chassis, heightened the tension that night. The huge gun had a range of 7,000 to 15,000 yards, and fired shells weighing 700 pounds and measuring 380 mm in diameter.

These thunderbolts suddenly began blistering the area every few minutes, continuing all night. And that mammoth gun was still lobbing shells into the area, off and on all the next day. Lt. Col. Rubel, in his book *Daredevil Tankers,* tells of an entire regimental staff of the 104th Infantry being killed when one of these monster rounds crashed through the roof of a four-story building, drilled down floor after floor, and exploded twenty feet below the basement, leveling the building. [26]

With American air superiority clearly dominating in the daytime, enemy airplanes generally stuck close to their bases. Nighttime, however, was a different matter. The German airplanes buzzed into and out of the front lines at all hours, bombing and shooting up anything that moved, especially road traffic and big gun positions. There was little sleep for the tankers.

Elements of D Company, working with an infantry recon outfit as flank guard to the main attack, pulled up to an old stone farmhouse just recently vacated by the Germans in the outskirts of Blatzheim. They made themselves at home, figuring this was as good a place as any to regroup and grab a bite to eat, according to Technician Fifth Grade Guy D. Knight. They set up a flank guard, as was their mission, and then settled in opening tins of 10-in-1 and K Rations for a big breakfast. They even tidied up the place after the departed enemy marauders.

Knight goes on to tell what happened then. He says that although the area was shelled intermittently, the tankers felt pretty secure in the big stone house, while keeping a sharp eye out with their field glasses. When someone figured out that much of the fire seemed to be coming from a fairly large settlement of farm houses and barns a couple of thousand yards to the southeast, a volunteer infantry patrol went out on foot to check it out.

The patrol quickly ran into trouble, and three tanks, commanded by Sergeants Clarence C. Wolverton, Tadeus R. Gawrych, and Royce A. Samples, roared off to help.

Knight and his crew, with Staff Sergeant Jimmie L. Wise as tank commander, pulled their light tank out of camouflage and onto the road to lay down covering fire.

As a fierce firefight developed in the village, Wise and his crew, out on the open road, began to realize their tank was under the gun as well. When their 37 mm shells failed to penetrate a suspicious looking haystack and started ricocheting off even after direct hits, they figured they were in for it. Then came the artillery and mortar fire and shrapnel zizzing about — striking the tank and clanging away. A high-explosive shell suddenly exploded on his gun shield, and it was all over. Wise was killed, and the rest of the crew was badly shaken. Knight went on to maneuver the tank into a defiladed position so the crew could evacuate to safety.

Within minutes, the three tanks returned from the village carrying infantry casualties, and the beleaguered group called for help as the Germans continued to pound the area. Apparently, their own artillery had changed locations since they were unable to make contact.

Private First Class Cox took off to get the tank destroyers on the radio and managed to get through to them, but was wounded by shrapnel on the way back, Knight said. Relief finally came from the TDs and their own artillery.

Sergeant Clarence C. Wolverton assumed command of the platoon until his own tank was knocked out, and he was wounded.

Citations and awards fell on D Company following this action, and Corporal Knight's and Sergeant Wolverton's were just two of them.[27]

At yet another area from which D Company was receiving fire, First Lieutenant (later Captain) Raymond R. Smith spotted a couple of haystacks that appeared strangely positioned, out-of-whack somehow. Since German haystacks were always suspect, he had two of his medium tanks ease into position to lay down direct fire. The Shermans leveled their big guns on the haystacks, only to see their tracers ricochet toward the heavens. The 75s must have made their point with the Germans who were inside those haystacks. As one of the stacks caught fire, the other haystack quickly drove away. It was like a Keystone Cops episode, and although really more scary than funny, it sure relieved the tension, and the tankers broke out laughing.

C Company's First and Second Platoons, along with A Company's Second Platoon, moved from Blatzheim to Kerpen with the Third Battalion of the 121st

Infantry Regiment, on the night of February 27. And, as they should have expected, they were reassigned on arrival—to the 121st's First Battalion.

Combined elements of C and A Companies moved to the attack the next morning, February 28, with infantry riding the backs of their tanks. In their sights: the heavily defended town of Mödrath.

A blown bridge over the Erft Canal brought the tanks to an abrupt halt at least a thousand yards short of their target. Unfortunately, it turned out to be a real hot spot.

Dismounting, the infantry waded through the shallows of the canal to the relative safety of a high railroad embankment, and prepared to move on the town. While the tanks covered their advance with a blanket of machine gun and cannon fire, they attacked.

German small arms fire crackled, then a deluge of mortar and artillery shells blew in—the explosions gouged ugly black holes in the earth. Infantrymen staggered and fell. Sergeant Hubert J. Bast's tank rocked with anti-tank fire and was knocked out.

The tanks were elevated and road-bound, as in a carnival shooting gallery, with two feet of water clogging the fields on both sides of the road. Large trees loomed on either side, providing fodder for enemy tree bursts. Division engineers' attempts to bring up bridge-carrying trucks were driven back with still more devastating fire. Casualties ran high, and it was clear the tanks were not going to cross at this point of the canal.

The 104th Infantry Division had gotten across the day before to the north, and it seemed imminently sensible to Lt. Col. Rubel to send a 740th tank company up into their sector to cross. The tankers could then flank back on Mödrath, and once the town was in friendly hands, the engineers could then build their bridge in a semblance of safety. "My suggestion that we use the 104th Division's bridge was not favorably looked upon," Rubel noted later. "There seemed to be an attitude of 'build your own bridge or bust.'"[28]

That same afternoon, just twenty-five miles or so to the northwest, a high-ranking soldier in trim battle dress was visiting army commanders in Monchengladbach, heading for a quick tour of the Erft River battle scene. The balding, 54-year-old chain-smoker stared in fascination as one of those incredible German ME-262 jet fighters blazed high through the blue and white sky above his jeep. It was the first jet he had ever seen. And when the anti-aircraft guns opened up in series, and jagged steel fragments from the exploding shells began thwacking at the ground around him, Ike Eisenhower, the Supreme Commander of the Allied Expeditionary Force, was seen scrambling for his steel helmet, just like all the GIs around him. It was one of the few times during the war he ever had one on.[29]

Not a man to be stymied for long, Lt. Col. Rubel did his own reconnaissance to the north, and found that tanks could cross through the 104th Division zone without that much of a problem—in spite of what he'd been told. And, as the standoff at the Erft eased, he alerted B Company to be prepared to move.

Before daylight on March 2, the 740th was rolling again. B Company crossed the canal in support of the infantry attack to the north on Mödrath. The town was still a hotbed of activity and turned out to be the toughest nut to crack along the canal. Even as the tanks moved in, they took direct fire from three enemy 75 mm self-propelled guns at a range of no more than fifty yards. Although the tankers got two of the devilish guns, the third knocked out two tanks—Lieutenant Raymond E. Davies' 76 mm gun tank, and Sergeant George M. Reeves' 75 mm gun tank—before the infantry was finally able to close in and neutralize it.

Just minutes later, an 88mm anti-tank gun on the eastern edge of the town hit and destroyed Private First Class James N. Wilson's tank. Wilson, the tank commander, and Private Joseph P. Riden, the gunner, were seriously wounded. Private Carrol E. Harkey, the driver, and Private Lawrence W. Gerardo, the bow gunner, were killed. Miraculously, the loader escaped injury.[30] But, in the bloodbath that followed, this same 88mm gun killed and wounded a number of the accompanying infantrymen before the 740th Assault Gun Platoon was called in to pound this deadly nemesis into oblivion.

Working in coordination with battalion headquarters, the Assault Gun Platoon was busy all afternoon—firing some one hundred twenty rounds of high-explosive shells and ten rounds of smoke. Tank platoon leaders called in coordinates on the radio, and then made adjustments as necessary to get the fire in support of specific operations.

In a frontal assault on the town, the Second Platoon of A Company moved against fierce resistance as well. Blazing away with everything they had, First Lieutenant Thomas T. Munford's tankers quickly took out the first line of entrenched machine gun nests and mobile Panzerfaust teams. But strategically placed strong points slowed both tanks and infantry to a dangerously vulnerable pace.

On the edge of town, Lt. Munford's tank was hit by a self-propelled gun and burned. The gunner, Corporal Raymond E. Johnson, was killed. Munford was severely wounded in the leg and arm, and Corporal Elbert G. Wilcox, the loader, was wounded on his face and eye. Private First Class Boyd L. Graves, the driver, and Technician Fifth Grade Carl A. Shores, Sr., the bow gunner, escaped injury, and managed to evacuate the wounded and administer first aid, exposing themselves to heavy enemy fire in the process.[31] Staff Sergeant Jessie M. Hendrix took temporary command of the platoon.

C Company also took it on the chin, greeted with intense artillery fire when they rolled into town late afternoon. However, no tanks were lost. D Company, dealing with maintenance most of the day in Blatzheim, did not arrive until after dark. The First Squad of the Mortar Platoon from Headquarters Company rolled in with D Company, along with the company tankdozer. Before darkness fell, the Germans had been pretty well routed, some two hundred prisoners captured by the tanks and infantry, and most of the 740th tankers settled into reasonably secure defensive positions for the night.

Lt. Col. Rubel planned to move the Battalion Command Post from Blatzheim to Mödrath the next day, March 3, but the town was so shot up that there were hardly any habitable buildings. And the few that were at all usable were already crammed with his exhausted tankers and a completely frazzled bunch of infantry who needed a respite in the worst way. So Ruble set up shop in Kerpen and called in his company commanders to finalize plans for the next attack, just hours away. The assignment: Frechen. The last German stronghold before Cologne on the Rhine River.

With the 104th Infantry on the northern flank, and the Third Armored rumbling through town after town still farther north yet, the 8th Infantry Division was finally ready to move on Frechen. Little reconnaissance was available, however, from the south. The tankers could see fires burning in the nearby towns of Turnich and Balkhausen, but battalion headquarters could only guess as to how much of the battlefront was in friendly hands.

Frechen was going to be tough. The Germans had been placer mining for coal in the region, and excavation had left huge, circular holes in the ground, up to one thousand yards across and three hundred feet deep. The sides were straight down, and small lakes filled the holes—some as much as fifty feet deep. Roadways leading to the town were no more than narrow defiles, perfect traps for tanks in a column.

The tankers knew how the Germans played this game. With their anti-tank guns zeroed in on all the passable spots, they would whack the lead tank, then the last tank, and then have a field day duck shooting at all those immobilized in between. Not a fun game to play.

Such an assault in the daytime was out of the question, so the infantry division commander ordered the attack for that night, with the infantry leading. The day was spent registering division artillery on known German gun emplacements, to pave the way once the assault got under way.

The division was on the move. Coming up on Frechen in dawn's early light of March 4, the tankers could see the twin towers of the famous Cologne Cathedral, which stood over five hundred feet high. It had been touch and go all the way across the Cologne Plain, and they were looking forward to a well-deserved respite once they closed on the Rhine River. Wishful thinking?

In support of the 28th Infantry Regiment, B Company was the first to maneuver through the defiles and debris of the coal mines. The three tank platoons had to line up and roll through in order. Lt. Col. Rubel noted that " —passing through the maze of coal mines was almost the same as a river crossing and priority had to be set up on the use of the road."[32]

The First Platoon of tanks was assigned to the First Battalion of infantry, the Second Platoon of tanks to the Second Battalion of infantry, and the Third Platoon to the Third Battalion of infantry. The tankers got a kick out of that, considering the way the 740th was usually scattered. Still, they didn't have much time to concern themselves with the coincidence.

The First Platoon immediately encountered enemy tanks on the western edge of Frechen, but drove them back into town with a withering cordon of fire, where they ran headlong into the Second Platoon's blazing guns coming in from the southwest. The Third Platoon joined the slugging match later that morning.

With those dauntless infantrymen routing snipers and Panzerfaust teams on the flanks, the tankers advanced, spraying the streets with machine gun fire and blasting away at the buildings with cannon shots. Against this classic coordinated effort, the enemy tanks and the self-propelled anti-tank guns that were still alive began to pull back toward the east and the Rhine River. When the artillery was called in, the Germans decided that was enough and fled.

Lt. Col. Rubel, anxious to get into Frechen and establish a forward Command Post, sent First Sergeant Charles W. Edwards and Technician Fifth Grade L.C. Dunn into town to beat the infantry commanders to the best available location. As Dunn told the story, they knew the town was still "hot" when they began to see dead German soldiers scattered about in the streets. As they turned their peep down a side street in search of a still habitable house or building, what was left of the civilian population filled the windows, waving white "flags," white shirts, bedsheets, or anything white they could get their hands on, calling out *"Kamerad, Kamerad."* Not knowing exactly what they meant by that, Dunn said, "I had my doubts as to whether or not they were our comrades, and letting the doubt get the better of us, we turned the peep around and immediately headed for the American side of town."[33]

En route, they ran into an infantry officer who told Sergeant Edwards that he thought they were a bit early, since he personally was well forward of the troops and looking for an Observation Post,[34] no doubt to help bring his people up. This bit of new information hardly added to the CP hunters' sense of well-being at the time.

It all worked out well for the tankers, and the colonel was well pleased. The battalion CP ended up in a Nazi Party town hall " —courtesy of the local Nazi Bigwigs who had moved out at our request," Rubel said. "It proved to be quite a place—replete with a bar at which beer could still be drawn. An immense warehouse adjoining—the building [which] held a large store of food —including several tons of a very excellent marmalade. Also a considerable quantity of flour, lard, butter, and several barrels of sauerkraut." Much had been made of the near starvation of the German working class, Rubel noted, but the Nazi Party members in Frechen were sure not suffering a food shortage at this time.[35]

Fighting their way through the coal mining district had been ugly. Not only was the terrain fraught with difficulty, but the weather was miserable—cold, damp, drizzling—bringing on the cold sweats, and filthy underwear sticking to dirty clothes. To make things worse, the division was up against the north flank of the LVIII Panzer Corps. With Frechen virtually in the bag, however, the 8th Infantry was now finally ready to strike at Cologne.

That morning, the 740th received a message from the new commanding general of the 8th Infantry, Brig. Gen. Bryant E. Moor,[36] ordering unit commanders to "instruct all members of your command not to fire [on] or otherwise damage the Cologne Cathedral."[37] The magnificent old cathedral was a landmark of the famous "Cathedral City," the fourth largest city in Germany, a Rhine River port, and a major cultural, industrial, and trade center. The medieval cathedral, some six hundred years in the making, had already sustained damage from Allied bombing but was still standing majestically over the ruined city, seemingly indestructible. Some called it divine intervention.

The Third Armored Division rolled into Cologne on March 5, the 104th Infantry later that same day. But the 740th Tank Battalion, still supporting the 8th Infantry, would not make it to the Rhine until they battled their way through a slew of small towns.

It took all day into dark for the First Platoon of A Company to clear Gleuel and its suburb, Neu Zieskenen, then roll on through Burbach and into Alstadten. The tanks knocked out a number of sniper and machine gun nests as they went, but had to call in the Assault Gun Platoon when two German tanks blocked their way briefly outside Burbach. One of the enemy tanks was completely destroyed by the artillery barrage, and the other chose common sense over valor, and backed out towards the Rhine.

B Company ran into small arms fire as the tankers moved to the edge of Frechen for maintenance, but had little trouble clearing the area before settling down for business.

Earlier that morning, C Company moved out with the First Battalion of the 8th's 121st Infantry Regiment. En route to Frechen, the tanks hit a minefield and had to hold while the engineers cleared the road. The two companies of infantry were ordered to move on without the tanks. Though the Germans had already begun to filter back in, the companies succeeded in seizing the small towns of Horbell, Sielsdorf, and Burbach.

As the German strength began to build in the area, the infantry in Horbell came under a heavy counterattack and the direct fire of a number of self-propelled cannons. An entire company of infantry was nearly decimated. However, the tanks were on the way.

C Company's Second Lieutenant Homer B. Tompkins organized a rescue party from his Second Platoon of tanks, a platoon of tank destroyers, and a chemical mortar platoon, and rushed up to engage the Germans and eventually routed them in some fierce back and forth fighting. The mortar platoon laid down a spectacular wall of smoke to screen the last stage of the attack as the tanks roared into Burbach at high speed.[38]

Still with the 121st Infantry, C Company tanks moved on the next day to attack through Hermulheim, Kendernich, and Fischenich, setting up roadblocks along the way to cut off possible enemy breakouts from Cologne to the west.

37. Photo credit: National Archives (111-SC-206174)

Bombing and shelling of Cologne was so intense as to leave the great Rhineland city in shambles. Both air and ground forces had orders not to fire on the magnificent Cologne Cathedral, and it remained virtually unscathed.

The stricken city was in ruins, gutted and blackened after years of allied bombing, its existing population living "like moles amid the rubble." Despair and disease were epidemic, and those civilians who remained numbered hardly a tenth of the peacetime population of more than three quarters of a million. And now, even as the Americans were moving in, refugees by the thousands were fleeing the city west, toward the American lines, clogging the roads.[39]

The 740th was just south of Cologne on March 7, within sight of the Rhine River, literally catching hell from three sides. The river angled crookedly through the southern edge of the city forming a huge bend or "pocket" several miles deep and across into which what was left of the enemy forces had retreated. And the deeper the tankers blasted their way through the small towns in the area the greater the concentration of fire that was drawn down upon their heads. Enemy guns from the east punished them from across the river on two sides of the river bend, and they were getting flanking fire from guns to the south as well.

The First Platoon of A Company had moved quickly through the little towns of Altsadten and Hermulheim during the night, and ultimately shot their way into Rondorf just after daylight. There they took a lot of incoming, but no tanks were hit. Then, when the Germans drove a battalion of infantry out of Immendorf to the south, the platoon was ordered to retake the town.

Immendorf was in open terrain where mine fields were known to exist, along with a number of anti-tank gun positions, including the dreaded dual purpose 88mm tank killers. In addition, a number of enemy tanks and SP guns had apparently been driven up into the area.

Although the plan called for the attack to be supported by smoke and artillery fire, it never developed. So Second Lieutenant Ledbetter loaded five infantrymen on the backs of each of his four tanks and roared out in sort of a "blunt arrowhead" arrangement with all guns blazing. Ledbetter was supposed to hold up outside of town and let the infantry guys off to sweep up behind him, then blast his way on in. However, luck was with them: the tanks missed the mines, and the AT guns missed the tanks. In fact, things were going so well, he never even slowed down, and as the infantry guys began to yell "Hey! When do we get off?" he kept hollering back, "Not yet!"

The tanks were still blasting away with everything they had as they rolled into and on through town with the courageous doughs on their backs, routing the Germans that were left, and setting any number of buildings on fire.

It's not known for certain that the Supreme Commander kept tabs on the tankers of the 740th everywhere it fought, but that same day, a beaming Eisenhower showed up just west of Cologne to give the tankers' corps commander, Major General Joe Collins, a big pat on the back for seizing the fourth largest city in Germany only twelve days after jumping the Roer. Ike liked "Lightning Joe" and told him that if another field army was created, he would command it. Collins, the youngest corps commander in the American army in the ETO at forty-eight, was grateful for the confidence Ike had in him, but told the Supreme Commander he'd rather lead VII Corps on into Berlin.[40]

Berlin? When the tankers heard that word, they hung their heads and sighed, figuring they'd just be spread out among the ill-fated chosen, and expected to lead the charge. That is, if they made it alive out of this damned pocket along the Rhine.

B Company was spread among the First and Second Battalions of the 28th Infantry in their attacks, and pushed through heavy artillery fire most of the day. Meschenich was captured. Second Lieutenant Mark J. Cohen was injured in a peep accident and evacuated, and Staff Sergeant (later 2nd Lt.) Glen D. George took command of the First Platoon. Staff Sergeant Mack J. Fleenor had been slightly wounded in the shoulder by shell fragments, but was not evacuated.

C Company's three platoons were scattered in Hermulheim, Kendenich, and Feschenich. D Company moved to Meschenich, relieving an infantry battalion.

Jump off time was 5:00 a.m. on March 8. Company A's First Platoon, with K Company of the 28th, moved on Rodenkirchen, a southern suburb of Cologne along the Rhine. The town was cleared by the infantry before the tanks even moved in. The infantry then rode the backs of the tanks from there on the attack on Weiss, just at the edge of the Rhine, deep in the "pocket."

Having joined the attack on Weiss, the Second Platoon spotted a large barge escaping across the river with two enemy tanks and a personnel carrier aboard, and cut loose with such a barrage of fire that they soon had the thing burning fiercely.

B Company attacked in support of infantry to capture Surth and Gondorf to the south and southeast, and overwhelmed the towns rather quickly, although a lot of shooting took place. They spotted three enemy tanks hot-tailing it to the east, and it was later thought that these were some of the vehicles A Company caught retreating by barge across the river.

All elements of the 740th reverted to battalion control on the night of March 8 through 9, and by nightfall of March 9 had assembled in Knapsack, just outside Cologne. Knapsack had an enormous power generator, which had apparently supplied Cologne and the valley round about it with electric power; at least it must have done so before the Allied bombers had come to play havoc with it. Electricity or not, each tank crew was looking for a warm, dry place to sack out, perhaps even real beds in real houses if they were to be found in the town. They were, to the man, exhausted, desperately needing a good night's sleep, and hopefully, time to rest and refit.

Lt. Col. Rubel sent for the burgermeister on arrival, and informed him that all weapons had to be surrendered, and that any shooting on the part of Germans would bring swift reprisal. "The first night some shooting did develop whereupon we burned one of their houses down. After that we had no trouble," the colonel said.[41]

Twenty some miles to the south, the Americans were streaming across the Ludendorff Bridge at Remagen, in the face of withering fire. They had surprisingly come up on the last intact bridge across the Rhine, with enemy soldiers still retreating across it. Even as the German engineers struggled frantically to blow the bridge, some gallant guys from a task force of the 9th Armored Division, zigzagged, crouched, and ran in a mad dash to get across the huge railroad bridge alive, before it blew. The Germans rushed up massive reinforcements, and resistance toughened all up and down the Rhine. The next few days were hectic at Remagen, and the Luftwaffe and heavy artillery finally took the bridge down. By then, however, the Americans had three pontoon and treadway bridges across. The First U.S. Army had a bridgehead over Rhine, the final natural barrier into the heart of Germany.

This didn't sit well at all with Hitler. In the days that followed, his minions set about court-martialing those officers who had "allowed" this travesty to happen. The bridge's security guard leader, a Captain Willi Bratge, was sentenced to death (in absentia, since he was by that time interned in an American prison camp). Other such "cowards and betrayers" were found guilty of high treason and dragged outside and shot. The trials were well publicized, and the message went forth to all German units on the Western Front that this would be the fate of all such traitors.[42]

In the course of the eleven-month campaign for northwest Europe, Hitler executed some fifty thousand for desertion or cowardice. Interestingly enough, in the U.S. Army, "One deserter only went through the process from confession, to court-martial, to sentence, to execution by firing squad, to death."[43]

Back in Knapsack, the men of the 740th breathed a huge sigh of relief when the 8th Infantry Division was informed that they would have a least a week's rest––maybe two. Elements of the 104th Division were said to be moving up to relieve them.

The tankers had been up to their rear ends in alligators day and night since the day they jumped off from Duren. They were dog tired and dirty and looking for a place to sleep. They began to pull their tanks up beside the best available houses (facing out, of course, for a quick getaway) and commandeered whatever living areas remained. Any family members still around just doubled up or moved out to their barns, or down in their basements.

When Lt. Col. Rubel moseyed on over to Division Headquarters at Frechen the next morning, March 10, to see what was going on, he found the top brass in a genial mood. Gen. Moore said a plane was leaving for London on March 12 and asked him if he'd like to take a week's leave. As might be imagined, the colonel broke out in a big smile and accepted with sincere appreciation.

Relaxing for the first time in a long while, he stayed on at division headquarters for lunch. About 2:00 p.m., his orders for London were handed to him. *Praise the Lord. It was really going to happen. Blessed R&R. He'd have to work on leaves for some of the men. And quickly.*

However, it was not to be. Just minutes later, the general's chief of staff called him in and handed him another order. He was terribly sorry, but there'd been a change in plans. This new order informed the colonel that the 740th Tank Battalion was temporarily attached to the Seventh U.S. Army, and was to report immediately to the XXI Corps in Lieutenant General Jacob M. Devers' 6th Army Group.

The order went on to say that the 740th Tank Battalion must arrive in the vicinity of Morhange, France, no later than March 15. They were being called on to crack the *Siegfried Line* again.[44]

There went London for the colonel. And there went blessed R&R for his beleaguered battalion. Only last night, the young tankers had at long last lain their worn bodies down to rest, placing their scattered nerves on hold. No tension nor fear, only dreams of home and visions of soft and loving girls in la-la land dancing in their heads. Oh well, there was a war to be won.

The Seventh U.S. Army, on Lt. Gen. George Patton's right (south) flank, was commanded by Lieutenant General Alexander M. Patch, who also had operational command of the First French Army. His Seventh Army and Patton's Third Army were engaged in a fierce struggle to clear the Saar-Palatinate in order to establish bridgeheads over the Rhine between Mainz and Mannheim. It was expected to be a long and bitter battle.

The Saar-Palatinate area was of great strategic importance to the German war machine, second only to the Ruhr as an industrial stronghold. South of the Moselle River, it included not only the heavily industrialized Saar and the old Bavarian Palatinate, but also sections of the Rhineland and Hessen provinces, as well as a stretch of French territory along the Franco-German border in the northeastern corner of Alsace. And, menacingly, along the southern edge of the area, stood the strongest segment of the entire Siegfried Line, by all accounts more heavily fortified and defended than anywhere else.[45]

The "vicinity" of Morhange was back across the French border, way south, around Patton's Third U.S. Army, down past and west of Trier and Saarbrucken. Lt. Col. Rubel would have to consider a roundabout route for the 740th in order to avoid battle and supply lines. It could easily be a 350-mile trip. He needed help with his plan, and there wasn't much time.

Early the next morning, Rubel took off for First U.S. Army Headquarters, now moved up to Duren, to get a quick grip on things, taking his top staff and company commanders with him. It was March 11. There he coordinated with the people who could get things done. In the emergency, railway transportation would be made available immediately, and the tanks would go by rail. After backtracking to Aachen, the tanks would be loaded onto flatcars. The tankers would accompany their tanks. Each company commander would be in charge of his section of the train, and he and the tank crews would ride in a boxcar attached in front of the flatcars carrying his company's tanks. The wheeled vehicles and half-tracks would march overland and meet them in Morhange, where further orders would await. Once again, the 740th was heading into the breach.

No use griping, boys, just get packing. Happened every time they were about to get a break.

38. Author's collection

The highways were too slow, so whenever someone called for help, the 740th loaded on railway flatcars and raced from one hot spot to another. Crews rode on the backs of their tanks. This is a Second Platoon C Company tank crew: Al Balentine, driver; Rex Taylor, gunner; the author, Paul Pearson, tank commander; Joe Gutawski, bow gunner; Jack Earhart, loader.

Back in Cologne, a flight of Thunderbolts screamed low over representatives from all of Lightning Joe Collins' VII Corps, gathered in parade formation for the victory celebration over the capture of the old Cathedral City. Men who wore the golden arrow shoulder patches of the 8th Infantry Division were there—guys with whom the 740th had been joined at the hip these last weeks—all scrubbed up and clean for the occasion, saluting as the band struck up "The Star Spangled Banner." And the Stars and Stripes was raised over the city. It must have been a proud moment for them all.[46] Too bad the 740th tankers had to miss the big celebration.

With a workable plan in place and scrambling to meet the March 15 deadline, Lt. Col. Rubel took off with the advance party on March 12 and pulled into Morhange the next afternoon. The 740th was immediately attached to the 70th Infantry Division in the Seventh U.S. Army's XXI Corps.

Major Richard G. Otto, on special assignment to the battalion, led out with the wheeled column of the 740th at daybreak March 13, with final orders to march overland back west to Aachen, all the way south and west to Verdun, France, then back southeast to Morhange. The tanks followed the tail of the wheeled column to Aachen, loaded up on the flatcars, and rolled out south almost immediately, on a wild train ride the tankers would not soon forget.

Having learned that the 70th Infantry Command Post was located at Merlebach, France, a town about five miles west of Saarbrucken, Lt. Col. Rubel had Maj. Otto and the wheeled column meet en route and divert to Merlebach.

They pulled in dog tired and dirty mid-afternoon on March 14. The train arrived in Morhange the next day, and the tankers unloaded their tanks from the flatcars and pushed their lumbering giants as hard as they could go to Merlebach, arriving just before midnight on the 15th, the deadline. They made it by thirty minutes.

All the arrangements had been made for the 740th tankers to support the 70th Infantry Division in the proposed attack through the Siegfried Line, within the next forty-eight hours, to capture Saarbruken. While the tankers struggled to collect their scattered nerves and get their act together in the few hours they had before the forthcoming jump off—cleaning their guns, maintaining and arming their tanks, getting something to eat and trying to settle down in preparation for another big battle—Lt. Col. Rubel got new orders.

The 740th was detached from the 70th Infantry and reassigned to the 63rd Infantry Division. That division CP was in Auersmacher, Germany, a good twenty miles south of where they were as the crow flies—but at least forty miles by road. "Here we go again, boys!" Rubel said.

It was another mad scramble, but they did it by noon, March 17. They were there to relieve the 70th Tank Battalion, which had been sent up just two days before to support the 63rd Infantry. The 63rd's chief of staff told Rubel "that the weight of this proposed attack had been shifted from Saarbruken to Ensheim, and instead of the 70th Division making the main effort, it now fell to the 63rd Division and the 740th tankers to make a breakthrough."[47]

The plan was for the division to breach the *Siegfried Line* north of Ensheim, then push on to occupy the high ground about a mile north. Tanks with infantry support would go on to capture St. Ingbert. The job of the 740th was to blast its way through the *Siegfried* defenses and then allow the 6th Armored Division to roll through and exploit the breakthrough.

Chapter 19

Operation Undertone

Undertone was a 6th Army Group plan to destroy German Army Group G in the Saar-Palatinate, as soon as the 12th and 21st Army Groups arrived at the Rhine River.[1]

Lt. Gen. Devers' 6th U.S. Army Group, which included operational control of the First French Army, was assembled and ready to attack through the West Wall defenses between Saarbrucken and Haguenau, and then advance through the Palatinate highlands. The plan was to converge with a surprise attack by Patton's Third U.S. Army east from Trier, then southeast across the Moselle toward Mainz behind German Army Group G, trapping the Germans between them.

Undertone could thus take out a significant German force, and put both Dever's 6th Army Group and Patton's Third U.S. Army in good positions for crossing the Rhine River.

Within the 6th Army Group was Lt. Gen. Patch's U.S. Seventh Army, now reorganized, fourteen divisions strong, and including Maj. Gen. Louis E Hibbs' 63rd Infantry Division and the 740th Tank Battalion.

Deep anti-tank ditches had been dug across and in front of the vicious looking dragons' teeth of the *Siegfried Line* in the area. The few narrow roads which had provided passage through the line had been heavily blasted, leaving huge craters in their wake. Massive concrete bunkers were strategically placed in pairs, guarding even these passageways—bunkers with walls up to six feet thick and often outfitted with 75 mm high velocity anti-tank guns. Behind all this, yet another line of seemingly impregnable pillboxes made up a secondary line of defense.

According to Gen. Bradley, "The Germans were dug in deep [here] at the *Siegfried Line* with insane orders from Hitler not to yield a foot."[2]

The four tank companies of the 740th moved out in four different directions from Merlebach, in the early morning of March 18, in support of the 63rd Infantry Division. Company A to Eschringen with the 253rd Infantry Regiment. B Company to Ensheim with the 254th Infantry Regiment. C Company to Ommersheim with the 255th Infantry Regiment. And D Company to a point a couple of miles east of Eschringen, in reserve for the 253rd.

Relieving a company of the 70th Tank Battalion, the 740th's B Company moved into the line near Ensheim that afternoon, and all three platoons spread out and opened up with all they had—an earth-shattering barrage of direct fire. In an all-out effort to soften up the German defenses before going in, the tankers pounded *Siegfried Line* pillboxes and other enemy installations with some fifteen hundred rounds of high explosives and armor-piercing shells. Although German artillery and mortar fire was heavy throughout the area, the tanks were able to move about and advance under the protective cover of a smoke screen laid down by chemical mortars from division.

Private First Class John Amann said that they were close enough to the German pillboxes to fire directly into their gunports while the infantry moved into position. "When [the infantrymen] were ready, we'd momentarily stop firing. Then they would throw [a Bangalore torpedo or satchel charge] through the gunport of the bunker, and it would totally destroy [those inside]. No one could survive that kind of blast," Amann said. Yet, "[our] infantry was paying a terrible price, because of the cross firing German machine guns." The tankers kept their own machine guns hot "to give these poor souls as much cover as we could."[3]

Then things must have gone really crazy. Suddenly, an artillery or an anti-tank shell exploded right at the top of his tank, directly above him, and a piece of shrapnel penetrated the turret and slashed into the top of his forehead. All Amann remembered was waking up in a room full of German soldiers. He had a huge turban on his head and a terrible headache.

When a guy in an American uniform came in, Amann asked if he was a prisoner. "Son," the doctor said, "you're in the 93rd Evacuation Hospital in Sarreburg, France. American, I assure you, I was your surgeon last night. You have a bad concussion and a groove in your skull bone from the shrapnel, which by a hair would have exposed your brain. You were lucky.

"You're supposed to be in a different room. This one is for German prisoners only. I was looking for you in another room and wondered where you disappeared to," the doctor said. "Tomorrow we're sending you to the 36th General Hospital in Dijon, France, where they'll continue treatment."

Amann began to feel better right away. "I wasn't dead," he said. "I wasn't blind or crippled or maimed. My head? We'll see."

A strong and virile man, John Amann made a remarkable recovery, was given a Purple Heart Medal, wished good luck, and got a salute from an officer.[4] After a circuitous and adventuresome journey, he was back at the 740th with his old tank crew, Baker 1-1, somewhere around the first week of April—the best he could remember.

Welcome home.

Meanwhile, the day on into night that Amann was hit and evacuated wasn't by any means over for his tank and crew. Not by a long shot. After dropping back to care for Amann when he was wounded, Sergeant (later Second Lieutenant) Glenn D. George, tank commander and Platoon Leader, pulled right back up into action, with that nasty little hole still in the top of the turret, and continued to pound pillboxes on the *Siegfried*. George's bow gunner, Private First Class William D. Hamilton, had taken over Amann's position as loader.

Later, as George moved his tank toward a hole in the dragon's teeth that looked as if it could be breached, he was stopped dead in his tracks by a large crater blown in the road. By the time a tankdozer could be brought up from another division, the incoming mail was getting choppy and mean again. And when it turned out that the dozer crew wasn't too excited about working in that kind of hostile environment, Lt. Col. Rubel took them in charge.

Then George, Hamilton (who had replaced Amann as loader), and other crew members dismounted, crawled up into the tankdozer under a hail of murderous fire, and filled in the crater themselves. George then led two tanks and a tank destroyer, along with some infantrymen, through the gap, breaking into the Germans' secondary defenses.[5]

"Chemical mortars, attached to the Division, did a fine job maintaining smoke screens for the tanks to work under," Lt. Col. Rubel recalled. "Their fire was extremely accurate, and when a small gap began to appear in the screen, they dropped a round just where it would do the most good. This smoke screen was built up in about fifteen minutes and was maintained for over four hours. It was over four thousand yards long, and a pretty sight."[6]

As darkness moved in, the First and Second Platoons withdrew to Ensheim, while the Third Platoon held its position in order to repel any counterattack that mounted over overnight.

Enemy aircraft activity was picking up considerably, and a number of dogfights developed over the area by the time the 740th's C Company moved into the line that afternoon, relieving another company of the 70th Tank Battalion. Corporal Ernest H. Swanson was a replacement bow gunner in the Second Platoon when his tank moved up to engage the enemy at the *Siegfried*. "We took up a column formation and prepared for the first attack. Doughboys were moving up to positions for the fight. Up in front of us, an airplane burst into flames and fell to the ground. We moved up over the hill at full speed, squared off, and started firing at pillboxes. Our tank had only thrown a few rounds when a round hung and we had to pull back. The Jerries were throwing in artillery for all they were worth. Shells were landing on nearly every foot of ground. I was new to this business and scared as hell."[7]

It was give and take at the *Siegfried Line* near Ommersheim until daylight faded. C Company then pulled back into fairly secure locations to wait while the

19th Engineers, under cover of darkness, worked furiously to blast out enough dragons' teeth for the tanks to make a run for it.

Sitting bundled up and exhausted in their tanks that night, struggling to keep warm, and catching only snatches of sleep, the tankers waited for the call. They didn't have long to wait before the word came down. Jump off was set for 4:00 a.m. Then, no sleep at all.

C Company's three tank platoons were spread out among different battalions of the 255th Infantry Regiment. And as the tanks began to rumble forward through the *Siegfried Line* in the face of artillery and small arms fire, it was stop and go. The tankdozer had to be called up again to drag and fill a crater here, and struggle with a dragon's tooth there, so the tanks could maneuver through. Then the chemical mortars started lobbing in protective smoke again, coming to the rescue. Until, finally, the tanks were able to move again. But the going was tough, and every stop was especially dangerous. Incoming fire was frustrating throughout the night and into the next day, although not that effective after the smoke descended throughout the area.

As the attack moved forward the next day, one section of the Second Platoon, along with some TD's, moved up to take the lead when one of the tanks broke through a makeshift bridge the engineers had thrown across an anti-tank ditch. The tank thudded heavily down into the ditch, still right-side-up but at a half-cocked angle, halting the advance. The crew was still able to traverse the turret and fire their guns, however, and hung in there with both .30 caliber machine guns chattering, and their 75 mm cannon booming as the Germans counterattacked.

With enemy artillery literally plastering the area, the other tanks and TD's had to pull back temporarily, but Second Platoon tanks came roaring back in time to repulse the counterattack and hold the position until their downed tank could be extricated.

As the 740th continued to pound pillboxes up and down the *Siegfried*, the battalion's ammunition supply dump had moved up as close to Ensheim as possible, and the day became a real shoot-out for B Company. Each of the three platoons in turn would fire a load of ammo, then shuttle back to the supply dump for more, keeping up an almost continuous fire on the line. Together, they shot up over twenty-five hundred rounds. When two massive enemy bunkers still held tough, Lt. Col. Rubel ordered up the Assault Gun Platoon with their six big assault guns, and they finally put the quietus on those seemingly intrepid pillboxes, with more than two hundred rounds of high explosive/anti-tank direct fire.

Things get rather dark when tragedy strikes. First Lieutenant Bill Shaw moved a section of his First Platoon tanks up to within one hundred yards of the dragons' teeth, then climbed down and walked over to talk with the infantry company commander. "He [the infantry commander] was in a shell hole about twenty yards to the right front of my tank," Shaw said. "I had no more than got in the shell hole with him, when the Jerries started throwing 170s at the tanks. The damn things were falling around us like rain. One of the shells made a direct hit on the top of my tank turret, exploding inside, and killing two men and wounding the other two. Things can be rather dark for a tanker sometimes—especially if he is in a front line foxhole with the doughboys and his tank is burning only a few feet away."[8]

39. Author's collection

Corporal Ernest Swanson, left, TEC 4 Al Balentine, center, and Corporal Jack Earhart, right, prepare to mount up and move out in an all-out attack on the *Siegfried Line* near Ommersheim, Germany.

Corporal Clarence W. Munger, the gunner, and Private Carl A. Schroeder, the loader, were killed. Both the driver, Technician Fourth Grade Jack H. Gammons, and the bow gunner were wounded and evacuated.

Almost all of the platoons were pretty well decimated by this time. Second Lieutenant Tompkins had only two of his five tanks left when his Second Platoon was called on to support an infantry attack into a heavily forested area, just west of Ober-Wurzbach. It was beginning to grow dark, and Tompkins and his people were uneasy moving into the woods. This was just no place to make a fight.

Sergeant Rex Taylor, who was the gunner in the second tank at the time, remembered the action very well. "I can recall several bad situations I have been in, but I believe the worst was when we were on the 7th Army front. We had cracked the *Siegfried Line* and had taken up a position. Just at dark, the infantry got an order to attack, so we had to go along as support.

"They moved into a patch of woods to the front of us and called for us. When we reached them, they had started back out as the Krauts were infiltrating their lines. However, we went on with the attack and fell into a tank trap," Taylor said.[9]

As the tanks moved into the attack, it was pretty clear that the infantry had decided that that particular patch of woods was no place to make a stand, and was beginning to pull back. Tompkins and his tankers grabbed up a handful of them as they filtered by, and coaxed and cajoled them into hanging tough with the tanks, which by that time were pretty well hedged in and always vulnerable without infantry.

To make matters worse, when the tanks tried to ease into a better defensive position, the second tank, which Taylor was in, slid helter-skelter into an anti-tank ditch, coming to a jarring halt at an odd angle. The disabled tank could still traverse manually and fire its guns, however, and Tompkins maneuvered his tank so as to cover their blind side, just before the Germans came at them again. "We had to stay there the rest of the night, sitting, [and firing] at a forty-five-degree angle. Having to traverse manually isn't any easy job. But we did it," Taylor said.

The two tanks and that gallant little band of infantrymen who stayed to help, managed somehow to beat off that counterattack; the tanks raking the woods time and time again, with blistering barrages of machine gun fire, using the cannon where they could.

Interestingly, two infantrymen hauled a captured German prisoner up to the tank in the ditch, said they couldn't handle him, and asked the tankers to keep him—in the tank. Now an occupied Sherman tank makes a very poor stockade of any kind, since there is hardly a square foot of extra space in any direction. So the tankers could not have taken in the prisoner even if they had wanted to, which they did not. The infantry guys, angered at the rebuff, and stuck with their prisoner, mouthed some obscenities, which amounted to something quite different from "Thanks a lot!" and filtered away through the shadows, obviously deciding that this particular spot was no place to die. There were no shots fired right away, so the tankers figured the two doughboys just let the German go.

Enemy artillery was vicious all the next day, and the tankers were on the receiving end of just about every big gun in the German arsenal, from 210 mm on down. Fire was especially heavy in Ensheim, Omnersheim, Eschringen, and Ormesheim, with three to four thousand rounds pounding Ensheim alone. Casualties ran high, to tankers and infantrymen alike. And the shelling was not limited just to the advancing troops and tanks.

The First and Second Platoons of D Company commanded the light tanks of the battalion, and were newly located dead in the center of Ensheim, catching some of the heat. The Third Platoon, mounted in the larger Sherman tanks, was temporarily attached to A Company, also in town for the day. Both companies were in reserve and looking forward to a hot dinner. It was just not meant to be.

Fortunately for the tankers, the main body of Germans had no idea the tanks were almost out of ammunition and in such a desperate situation, and made no further attacks.

As D Company's Staff Sergeant Alfred A. Giangregorio and his staff were preparing a special meal for his guys, enemy mortar fire started coming in. The first round splattered about fifty feet from his kitchen truck, and he and the crew hit the ground. When the second round exploded the truck, and set it and the food trailer on fire, the kitchen crew jumped and ran for the nearest cover.

"We took cover in the cellar of a house, but soon had to leave it because mortar fire was knocking [the house] down on top of us," Giangregorio said. "The truck burned all that evening and until the next morning. There I was, with no kitchen and no food for my men. It was rough, but we got by with what we could get from the other Companies in the Battalion."[10]

A G-3 Report that day noted that 70th Infantry Division on the left, and the 45th Infantry Division on the right, were also probing the Siegfried Line and making "substantial gains against determined enemy resistance."

Other reports indicated that elements of Lt. Gen. Patton's Third Army had made a breakthrough near the Rhine and was no more than thirty miles to the northeast, pushing south. The Third Army was trying to cut off any escape route the Germans might have from the St. Ingbert/Saarbrucken area, where the 740th was on the prowl.

When the firing suddenly died down about midnight, Lt. Col. Rubel became convinced that the Germans were unloading their ammo and pulling out, afraid of being encircled. He headed for the Regimental Command Post and recommended that patrols be sent out to determine the facts.

"Jerry had a trick of firing his maximum rate of fire for two purposes," Rubel reasoned. "The first: when he would relieve and replace troops in the line, he would step up his artillery and automatic weapons fire considerably while one unit replaced another. The second: he would fire everything he had before a general retreat, with the exception of small arms. He usually saved this. On this night there was practically no small arms fire, so I suspected that instead of a relief of positions by other units, he was withdrawing. His idea was to get across the Rhine before General Patton could cut him off."[11]

Although no patrols were sent out, the First Platoon of A Company moved out in the middle of the night toward St. Ingbert, in support of the First Battalion of the 253 Infantry. It was March 20. Their objective was the high ground just south of Sengscheid, from which they could attack the pillboxes just east of there the next morning. Not a shot was fired. The eerie silence pervading the area was almost unnerving.

40. Photo credit: 2nd Lt. Jacob Harris, U.S. Army Signal Corps, March 20, 1945
From the files of Harry Miller.
**Medium tanks of the 740th Tank Battalion move through the Dragon's Teeth of the
Siegfried Line in the Wurzbach area of Germany.**

Captain Cecil A. Wright, Jr., the A Company commander, collected Second
Lieutenant Ledbetter and moved cautiously on foot into St. Ingbert. Nothing. Not
a sound. They edged even more carefully toward the center of town. It was a
moonlight night. Tense. Figuring things could begin to pop at any moment. But
the town was deserted. The two officers began to breathe again and went back to
report to the infantry commander. Later, the infantry filtered quietly but swiftly
across the low ground, all the way to the pillboxes, finding them deserted as well.

At mid-morning, the First Platoon of B Company, with infantry, rolled over
eight pillboxes near Heckendalheim without firing a shot. The entire area deserted.
By noon, the infantry with C Company had taken all of the objectives in their area
without incident, and the tanks had returned to Ommersheim to await further
assignment. Elements of D Company moved down the valley and into the village
of Reichenbrunn, to find that village deserted. *The Germans had withdrawn from the
Siegfried Line during the night.*

Enemy resistance had collapsed, and a division task force was quickly
organized to exploit the breakthrough and move on to Homburg. Tanks from the
First Platoon of A Company loaded infantry from the Third Battalion of the 253
Infantry Regiment on their backs, and highballed it through Kirkel, Alstadt, and
into Homburg, only to find that a Third Army group was already there.

Elements of the Sixth Armored Division passed through the holes the 740th had hammered in the *Siegfried,* and the job became one of collecting prisoners and destroying enemy weapons.

Maj. Gen. Hibbs, commanding the 63rd Infantry Division, came before the 740th tankers on March 24 to commend the battalion for its breakthrough of the *Siegfried Line.* He went on to say that he had requested permission for the 740th to be permanently attached to the 63rd. Lt. Col. Rubel expressed his appreciation, but noted that the battalion was on loan from the First U.S. Army, and that he felt certain the 740th would be ordered to return. Gen. Hibbs then presented awards to several members of the 740th, including an Oak Leaf Cluster of the Bronze Star to Lt. Col. Rubel.

Having been the first to cross the Rhine River, on March 7 at Remagen, Gen. Hodges' First Army continued to enlarge the bridgehead and was poised, ready to breakout. Next across, on the night of March 22 to 23, elements of Patton's Third Army slipped quietly across at Oppenheim, to the south without fanfare, in rafts and assault boats, and with very few casualties.

The irrepressible Patton called Gen. Bradley that evening and shouted into the phone, "Brad, for God's sake, tell the world we're across [the Rhine]. I want the world to know the Third Army made it before Monty starts across." [12]

It remained for Field Marshal Montgomery to unleash his massive set-piece crossing to the north, code-named Operation Plunder.

Meanwhile, at Station X in Bletchley Park near London, Ultra was awash in intercepted signals from the enemy's super-secret Enigma encoding machines. It seemed the German commanders in the area between Duisburg and the crucial road/rail hub of Wesel, were in a panic, sensing the huge Allied buildup, and expecting an airborne assault at any time.

Following an immense and lengthy buildup, Field Marshal Montgomery, forever given to jingo, finally said, "Over the Rhine, then, let us go." It was the night of March 23 to 24, and "Operation Plunder" attacked along a seventy-five-mile line of smoke. More than one million men, an earth-shattering three-hour artillery barrage, a monumental airborne assault, and a mass parachute drop and glider landing behind the lines. It was the virtual equivalent of the D-Day assault on Normandy and included British, Canadian, and American combat divisions.

As the shadows lengthened that evening, the 740th tankers' old fighting friends from the "Old Hickory" 30th Infantry Division were moving up for their turn to cross the river. Tense, wrapped in their own thoughts, no one paid much attention to the solitary figure that suddenly appeared out of the shadows and moved silently into their ranks. He was just another soldier as far as they were concerned, although obviously an officer of some kind, with a necktie yet. Rear area personnel, they assumed, up to see the war.

The officer fell in step and moved right along, until he caught up with one young soldier who was walking along with his head down, obviously deep in his own thoughts about the forthcoming battle.

"How are you feeling, son?" the Supreme Commander asked.

Startled, the young man took in that familiar grin of the old soldier by his side, blinked a couple of times and shook his head. He seemed to straighten up as he replied, "General, I'm awfully nervous. I was wounded two months ago and just got back from the hospital yesterday. I don't feel so good."

As shells crashed along the far bank of the Rhine up ahead, Ike said to him, "Well, you and I are a good pair then, because I'm nervous too. But we've planned this attack for a long time and we've got all the planes, the guns, and airborne troops we can use to smash the Germans. Maybe if we just walk along together to the river we'll be good for each other."

"Oh," the soldier said, "I meant I was nervous. I'm not anymore. I guess it's not so bad around here."

And Ike said, "I knew what he meant."[13]

The tankers moved to Potzbach on the 25th, anticipating a Rhine crossing with the 63rd Infantry, and then roaring off in pursuit of the fast retreating Germans. But it was not to be.

On the morning of March 28, General Bradley's 12th Army Group ordered the 740th Tank Battalion to "return at once to the First U.S. Army and the 8th Infantry Division." The 8th Infantry was knee-deep in the battle with the remnants of three German armies in the "Ruhr Pocket." The Ruhr Valley was a heavily industrialized area north and east from Cologne. Caught in the trap were German survivors from the Pas de Calais, the Battle of the Bulge, old men of the *Wehrmacht,* and even teenage recruits from the *Hitler Jugend.*

Having suffered heavy losses in their initial attack on Siegen, a town on the southern edge of the pocket, the 8th Infantry was calling repeatedly for the 740th to "come on back" before going in alone again. "Here we go again, boys!" Lt. Col. Rubel thundered.

The tankers rolled out of Potzbach on March 30 and closed on Sarrebourg, France, that night. There they learned that the tanks would be moved by rail and the other vehicles by motor convoy. The next morning, Lt. Col. Rubel and his advance party loaded in their peeps and headed back up north for First Army Headquarters, which they understood was in now Duren, Germany, a city with which they were quite familiar. However, Duren was deserted upon their arrival, and they had to chase army headquarters first to Bad Godesberg, and finally to Marburg, where it was now in the process of settling in.

41. Photo credit: A/P Images

His soldiers took heart from Ike, who was at his best with the troops as they went into battle.

The 740th's commander knew that his men urgently needed rest before being committed to battle again. He knew also that the tanks desperately needed maintenance and rehabilitation. Then he learned that the infantry had gotten time off while the 740th had been busy breaching the *Siegfried Line* down south. He appealed for, and got a three-day rehabilitation period for men and machines, and managed somehow to make arrangements with an ordnance battalion in Bonn to work on the tanks.

April 1 was Easter Sunday in 1945, and three long trains chugged out of Reding, France, a suburb of Sarrebourg, that beautiful Easter Sunday morning, carrying all the tanks and crews of the 740th Tank Battalion, headed north to Aachen, Germany. Best guess was the tankers were heading into a fistful of trouble with their good friends of 8th Infantry again. Seemed like they'd been there, done that.

Lt. Col. Rubel managed to get the tanks routed on through Aachen to Odendorf, just a few miles from Bonn, where the convoy of wheeled and half-track vehicles was already in place. The battalion was reunited on April 4.

The rear echelon ordnance guys had not worked directly with real fighting tankers before, and both sides came to know and appreciate the jobs each of them had, at the front and at the rear. For three days and nights, these soldiers worked their hearts out, making engines hum again, welding steel and racks, changing tracks, testing sights and gun tubes, fixing this and restoring that, and gradually becoming valued friends of both tankers and their tanks.

Lt. Col. Rubel, suffering from a killer back pain since the first of the year when a stray round exploded nearby, finally found time to seek relief at the hospital in Aachen, and Major Floyd, battalion exec, assumed command of the battalion during his absence.

Chapter 20

Into the Ruhr Pocket

While the 740th tankers were riding the rails northward to reunite with the 8th Infantry Division to go in and help clear the Ruhr Pocket, the First and Ninth U.S. Armies linked up at Lippstadt and Paderborn, locking the pocket up tight.

The ring around Field Marshal Walther von Model and what remained of his German Army Group B was complete. An estimated 400,000 enemy troops were caught in the vast Ruhr industrial district trap, and Nazi Germany had lost its industrial heartland and greatest source of weaponry. With leaflets and radio messages to the Germans, General Eisenhower called on the enemy soldiers to surrender and the people themselves to begin planting crops.[1]

Thousands did in fact throw off their uniforms and join the civilian population, never to utter the word Nazi again. Still, a hard core of fighting men continued to do battle—Waffen SS, Hitler Youth, officer candidates, fanatics, and ordinary soldiers who were just unable to betray the Fatherland, or were more afraid of the Gestapo and the firing squad than the Americans.[2]

So the fight was still on in the Ruhr Pocket. German Field Marshal Model knew he wasn't going to surrender and figured the best place to break out was to the south. And the 740th Tank Battalion was rushing headlong into the midst of it.

The tankers pulled out of Bonn on the morning of April 8, and crossed the Rhine River on a massive pontoon bridge the size of a two-lane highway. American ingenuity. Seven hours later, a motorcycle escort of military police met the dusty column of tanks just outside of Siegen, about eighty miles east of Bonn, and led the battalion to a bivouac area just south of there in the vicinity of Niederdielfen.

Major Floyd, still in command of the battalion, was hardly out of the saddle when he was smacked with orders for the attack toward Olpe. The tank companies were quickly parceled out to various infantry outfits throughout the 8th Division—A Company and the First Platoon of D Company to the 13th Infantry, B Company and the Second Platoon of D Company to the 28th Infantry, and C Company and the Third Platoon of D Company to the 121st Infantry.

Floyd couldn't help but think *Here we go again!* when yet another reshuffle began no more than an hour later. B Company was detached from the 8th

Division's 28th Infantry, attached to the 86th Infantry Division's 342nd Regiment, and ordered to move out immediately to the 86th Infantry Division area at Feudingen, about thirty-five miles east of where they were presently hunkering down. The tankers sighed, *It figures.*

That night, A Company moved with their infantry into Siegen, and C Company split up, moving northeast with their infantry over to Deuz, Netphen, and up to Lutzel.

The plan was for the 740th tanks to spearhead the attack of the 8th Infantry Division and blast their way on the run right up through the center of the Ruhr Pocket. The 86th Infantry Division on the right and the 78th Infantry Division on the left would protect the flanks and keep the supply lines open. Into the breach, again.

The attack jumped off shortly after midnight on April 8, the tankers moving at high speed, packing as many of the infantry as possible on the backs of their tanks. When resistance reared its ugly head, the infantry jumped off, spread out, and helped overcome the problem. Then they'd mount up on the tanks again and fast forward into whatever was next.

Where possible, the columns of tanks kept off the main highways. German roadblocks were treacherous. A barricade of trees and logs usually meant *Panzerfaust* teams, dug in machine gun nests, and anti-tank guns. Sometimes the dreaded 88s.

Still, the rumble of approaching armor, and ultimately the sight of the column of oncoming tanks, had a tendency to unnerve a lot of enemy infantrymen, regardless of Hitler's orders to "fight to the death." Many times, they just gave up, came out with their hands up, and were marched to the rear. When they chose to fight, they more often than not knocked out the lead tank, and a brief skirmish would ensue until the tanks' overwhelming power shattered the defenses and overran the position.

There were times when the tankers found that the Germans would not fire unless fired upon. The tanks would just charge the barricade, bulling right on through. It was a heart-thumping procedure, because the lead tank crew knew they'd had it if the Germans decided to fight at the last minute.

The First and Third Platoons of A Company, with the First Battalion of the 13th Infantry riding their tanks, took Staatsforst Siegen without opposition, then moved on through Kreuztal and Stendenbach. Some AT guns opened up on them as they left Stendenbach, but the tanks managed to overwhelm them with superior firepower and without damage to themselves, and move on to Krombach. Almost out of ammunition and low on fuel, the company held there until supplies could be trucked up.

By early afternoon, they were rolling on Altenkleusheim and caught heavy fire before finally capturing the town. No losses yet. But there was real trouble ahead.

They took the village of Rhonard on the run by midafternoon and headed for Olpe, moving into the town as darkness began to close in. Sergeant (later First Sergeant) Carlton D. Dyball and his crew were leading the column when they rounded a curve in the road and ran headlong into a German Mark IV.

Corporal Douglas F. Greenwalt, the gunner, said they were on the outskirts of the town when they spotted a convoy of German vehicles beginning to retreat. "We fired a few rounds to disrupt them, and then started around a curve to take the town. At that moment, we were hit by a Panther tank. Goen and I jumped off together and ran side by side towards a barn.

"They fired another round of HE [high explosives] and the shrapnel killed [Private Stanford N.] Goen. I made a beeline for the barn with my Tommy gun, and ran smack into a squad of Jerries who had probably had the same idea I had. I ducked behind some boxes expecting to be fired at, but to my surprise they didn't fire. I started to check my gun to get it ready to fire in case they started anything and found that there wasn't a damn round in the magazine. To this day, I don't know why they didn't fire, but I guess my days weren't up yet."[3]

After Dyball's tank was hit, Sergeant (later Staff Sergeant) Frank M. Quick dismounted, went up on a hill with infantry, and spotted the big German tank that had done all the damage. He ran back down to his tank and had his driver, Technician Fifth Grade Clarence O. "Chigger" Webster, move around Dyball's disabled tank.

Retreating back around a wide curve in the road, the German tank stopped momentarily, fired, and killed a number of infantrymen who had gathered around Quick's tank. With the ground around them littered with dead GIs, it was a sobering experience for the tankers. That German S.O.B. was going to be waiting now around the curve.

An infantry lieutenant wanted Quick to go after them. Quick's reply was, "Are you crazy?" or words to that effect.

Captain Bill Wright, Quick's company commander, rolled up about that time and quickly agreed that the idea was indeed crazy. The infantry officer walked off mouthing his dissatisfaction, but outranked.

In short order, he was back, apologizing to the tankers. "Tell you what. We'll slip through the woods and see what's around the curve," he said. "You guys ease on up to the curve and back us up if we run into trouble."

Quick knew that big tank was around the curve, just waiting for them. It looked like a suicide mission to him.

However, he talked it over with his crew. After a big discussion, Private First Class George "Kingfish" Courtney, the bow gunner, finally said, "Hell, let's all have a drink—and go get 'em." With that, he produced a bottle of rye whiskey, took a big slug, and passed it around.

Quick said the decision was made right then and there. And swears to this day that he didn't know that bottle of whiskey was in the tank.[4]

He told Webster to "Back her up, so we can get a head start. I want to hit that curve wide open."

It wasn't like the crew took a vote or anything, but they were all agreed and figured that that ugly German tank was going to be at 11 o'clock just around the corner, so they would go in firing.

Webster backed her up, slapped her in gear, and took off around that curve like a scolded dog. And there was that big German—precisely at 11 o'clock.

Corporal M.W. Chism, the gunner, immediately let loose with his 76 mm and narrowly missed to the right. The German was too big and thick to be any more than jolted anyway, unless they'd got in a lucky shot. He had an 88mm and fired back at the same time.

"The round hit us almost center front, about four inches to the right of my head," Webster said. "Came busting through and ricocheted up into the gun shield. "We were shocked and helpless, but our engine was still running. So I pulled the tank hard left, cut between two trees stripping the bark off them, and rammed into a nearby building so the crew could get out."

Webster wound up with shrapnel wounds and broken ribs. No one else was hurt. "I guess the Old Man from Above was keeping me around for something. It could have been a lot worse," he said. "You know, I still have the piece of metal that shell knocked out of our tank."[5]

The Second Platoons of both A and D Companies, attached to the 13th Infantry's Second Battalion, jumped off in the wee hours after midnight on April 8. Night attacks were becoming more frequent, as it was learned that they seemed to be less costly in casualties than dawn attacks.

Sergeants (later Staff Sergeants) Herman R. Beard and Jesse M. Hendrix's tanks destroyed an even dozen active 88mm dual-purpose guns in and around Oberhus, and Beard's tank knocked out a Mark IV Panther tank at Kreuztal. Incredibly, Beard and his crew took out nine of the big guns at Oberhus. "I consider myself very lucky," Beard said. "I suddenly discovered that I was in a nest of 88 AT guns, and a large artillery gun was pointing directly at me. I really thought my time had come, because I had already spearheaded seventeen miles and my ammunition was about gone. However, I had enough to do the job. My bow gunner kept the crews of the Jerry guns pinned down while my gunner knocked them out."[6]

The attack ended at Drolshagen, the final objective for the day.

Each of B Company's three tank platoons moved out separately from

Feudingen on April 8 and 9 with a different battalion of the 342nd Infantry Regiment in the 86th Division's zone. For the most part, resistance was light — small arms and automatic weapon fire, with an occasional SP gun sighted on the run. Rumbling slowly in a northwesterly direction, they worked their way through Erndtebruck on the Eder River, Vormwald, Hilchenbach, Kohlhagen, Womelsdorf, and Wurdinghausen. They rolled into some of the villages without a shot being fired. Three tanks were lost along the way, however, due to mechanical trouble. There had been little time for maintenance since the tankers had left Bonn.

Still with the 121st Infantry, C Company moved on through Hilchenbach, Hillnhutter, Dahlbruch, and Musen, catching only sporadic light resistance most of the way. The fighting picked up as First and Second Platoon tanks attacked Littfeld, where German infantry and a number of anti-tank guns decided to make a show of force at the entrance to the village. A brief firefight ensued, but the tanks routed the stubborn enemy patch with a fierce display of firepower.

C Company's Third Platoon picked up the fight at Littfeld, and pushed on through Rahrbach toward Welschen-Ennest. As two massive 70-ton Jagdtiger self-propelled 128 mm guns raced away from the attacking tanks, Lt. Loopey's tank pumped high-explosive rounds through their rear escape hatches, which were unexplainably open, and destroyed both vehicles. They were obviously on the run, but catching them going away was a pure piece of luck. Their frontal armor was a full nine inches thick, and side armor was three to four inches thick. Loopey said the guns looked like railway artillery they were so huge.[7]

Second Lieutenant Jeremiah C. Ingersoll, D Company's First Platoon leader, was hit that afternoon. Corporal Earnest Abney was Ingersoll's gunner. "Eight tanks jumped off at twelve o'clock and had taken five villages by daybreak," Abney said. "We stayed at the last village until three o'clock in the afternoon when we jumped off again. We had gone about a mile when we ran into some action.

"The lead tank was knocked out by a *Panzerfaust*, but the rest of us kept going—my tank commander [Ingersoll] was shot by a sniper and fell to the floor of the tank—I had to keep firing. We finally took cover behind a house. TEC 5 Lawrence Jacobson and I got Lt. Ingersoll out of the tank under fire and took him into the house—then got the medics who treated him. We were pinned down by enemy fire—and couldn't get back to the tank for quite a while. When the fire slowed—we got back into our tank and again went into action."[8]

Staff Sergeant Roy Parks assumed command of the platoon.

While the 740th roared fast-forward eighteen miles the first day of the attack, it was much tougher going for the 78th Infantry Division on their left flank, between them and the Rhine River. The 78th was encountering armor in ever-growing proportions, with King Tigers reported rearing their ugly heads in the area. It was touch and go for the Seventh Armored Division, as well on the eastern edge of the pocket, slugging it out with heavy German armor.

Although the 740th's Sherman tanks were faster and more maneuverable than the German tanks, it was never an even match. A German Tiger could knock out a Sherman at up to four thousand yards, while the Shermans had to close to within three hundred yards to even have a chance with a Tiger—then it takes a lucky shot. "A Sherman tank attempting to fight a King Tiger has about the same chance as a trawler has of sinking a battleship," Lt. Col. Rubel said.[9]

With the 740th spearheading, the 8th Infantry Division was advancing so fast that the orders always seemed to be Go! Load up the doughboys and race forward. Surprise the sons of bitches! Bust in on 'em. Give 'em hell.

It was like a deadly game of leapfrog. Infantry from one regiment would load up on the backs of the tanks and go for broke until they gave out, then another regiment would pass through, and new infantry would climb up on the tanks to keep the attack going. The problem was that the tankers never stopped, except to reload with fuel, ammo, and a fresh bunch of doughboys.

The tankers were constantly on edge. Drivers were continually hard at work, responding to commands in a very physical way, with foot, and left and right hand control levers. Gunners were always tense; searching for targets through their telescopic sights, gripping the machine gun trigger on the power turret traverse handle, foot hovering over the cannon's firing solenoid on the turret floor. Loaders were forever straining to see through their periscopes, always at-the-ready to grab up the next shell on command and thrust it into the cannon's breach. Bow gunners watched anxiously through their periscopes, fingers on the triggers of their .30 caliber machine guns, ready to take out a target or rake either side of the road.

Tank commanders, most often in a half-crouch, helmeted heads stuck out of their turret hatches, directed the movement and fire of their tanks over the headsets connected to the radio intercom, always searching the front, sides, and rear for signs of trouble, or targets to react against. It was tense, exhausting, and often frightening work for every member of the crew.

Noticing his tank commander's knees trembling in the middle of a firefight on a moonlit night, a gunner teased, "How come you're shaking so hard, Sarge?" He got a curt reply. "Listen, meathead, you'd shake too if you could see what I see out here!"

The First and Third Platoons of A Company rolled forward with the First Battalion of the 13th Infantry Regiment in the early morning hours of April 10. As they attacked northwest toward Meinerzhagen and Kierspe, they caught only scattered small arms and automatic weapons fire.

Suddenly, two lengthy German truck convoys crossed their path, making a run for it—practically bumper to bumper. The tankers unloaded on the convoys, and the tracers from their machine guns set fire to one, then another, until the whole roadway appeared to be in flames. Some two hundred enemy trucks were destroyed in the conflagration. Still more escaping trucks were razed as the tanks moved on farther up the road.

B Company moved slowly through Oberveischede, Kirchveischede, and Kirchhundem with the 342nd Infantry, advancing eventually to Konzell, against sporadic small arms and light artillery fire. C Company continued the attack to the northwest. The First and Second Platoons, with the First Battalion of the 121st Infantry, captured Rahrbach before dawn on the 10th, and then rolled through the little villages of Rehringhausen, Stachelau, Lutringhausen, Hohl, and Stade, en route to Valbert, and destroyed a number of enemy artillery pieces and trucks along the way. At Valbert, they joined forces with their Third Platoon.

The Third Platoon had taken the towns of Mittl Negger, Listernohl, Hunswinkel, Hosinghausen, and Valbert, and with the Second Battalion of the 121st Infantry, captured some two thousand prisoners and destroyed well over one hundred fifty enemy vehicles, both motor and horse-drawn.

"The attack was going at steeplechase speed," said Lt. Col. Rubel, when the battalion closed at Olpe in the early afternoon on April 11. "The roads were literally clogged [going northward] with every type of vehicle imaginable— howitzers, ammo and gas, medical, reserve components, engineer trucks loaded with pontoons and bridging equipment, and replacement tanks trying to get to the front.

"Traffic going south [to the rear]—every kind of vehicle loaded to the overflowing with prisoners—[and] thousands [of prisoners] marching along by themselves, not particularly happy."[10]

Jumping off from Meinerzhagen on the morning of April 11, A Company faced a concentration of anti-tank guns all day. The mood of the tankers was high. Sergeant Beard continued his onslaught on the big guns in the area, and knocked out three of them just minutes after moving out. His luck ran out an hour later when his tank was knocked out by yet another AT gun. Although immobile and shaken, Beard and his crew hung fast and laid down a blistering blanket of fire that destroyed the crew of the enemy gun that got them. The platoon went on to reach its objective, the village of Halver, late that afternoon, but most of the company remained under the gun all day.

A firefight erupted when Sergeant (later 2nd Lt.) Leadbetter ran headlong into a cluster of big guns. He and his crew came out unscathed in that one, but an 88mm AT gun knocked his tank out of action just a few hours later. Tragically, Private Grover Plaunt was killed, and the crew was badly shaken up. Sergeant (later Staff Sergeant) Milburn A. Francis took command of the platoon and reorganized it for the fight ahead.

B Company's First Platoon attacked northwest out of Oberveischede toward Attendorn, catching only light artillery and 20 mm flak fire. The Second Platoon ran into a hornets' nest in their attack on Neiderhelden. Fortunately, there were no casualties, but both 1st Lt. Chauncey C. Lester's and Sergeant Gerald L. Wood's tanks took direct hits from an 88mm dual-purpose gun just as they entered the town. Lt. Lester took over one of the other tanks and continued the attack on into Attendorn.

C Company was split up as usual. Just after midnight on the night of April 10, the First and Second Platoons were switched from the First to the Third Battalion of the 121st Infantry Regiment. They jumped off from Blomberg before daylight. Against only scattered, light resistance, they took the towns of Lengelscheid, Werkhausen, Fernhagen, and Bechinghausen. Several hundred prisoners were collected, and a multitude of enemy vehicles were destroyed.

The Third Platoons of both C and D Companies combined to seize the towns of Reblin, Stottmert, Kalme, and Stillering. They, too, captured hundreds of prisoners and shot up dozens of vehicles. They held in Homert that night.

"Attachments and detachments from one outfit to another were so rapid that throughout most of the day [April 12] it was impossible to tell what battalion the tanks were attached to," said Lt. Col. Rubel.[11] All the shuffling about didn't mean the going was easy, however. During the day, the Second Platoons of A and D Companies ran into heated anti-tank fire en route to Wellringrade. A Company's First and Third Platoons hit trouble at Radevormwald when AT gunfire ricocheted off the bow gunner's hatch on Sergeant Clarence W. Davis' tank, injuring the bow gunner, and taking the tank out of action.

While reconnoitering a bypass for the infantry, First Lieutenant George W. Merritt's tank platoon came under heavy fire from the high ground. Merritt dismounted his tank in the midst of the fracas, located the guns dealing them such misery, and then led two tanks on a frontal assault across open terrain to overrun the enemy position. Three anti-tank guns and two flak wagons were destroyed in the process.[12]

B Company, now attached to the 86th Infantry Division's 343rd Regiment, moved rapidly against Kuckelheim, Holtzhausen, and Plettenberg, against light resistance.

C Company, still with the 8th Division's 121st Infantry, attacked with its First and Second Platoons from Bollwerk through Berken, Kierspe, Wegenhof, and Halver. Resistance was scattered all the way to Kierspe, where anti-tank and flak fire began to dog them. As artillery and mortar fire started coming in, the infantry scrambled down off the tanks, and they were all pinned in place for a time. They went on to destroy several big guns and wheeled vehicles, and captured about one hundred prisoners during the day.

When the tank that Corporal Oren W. Blakely was driving was hit by a bazooka, he came out of his tank with a mad-on and succeeded in capturing five of the enemy soldiers. After marching them to the rear, he returned to the front lines, recovered the tank from the Germans, and set about rounding up and bringing in almost fifty-five more enemy soldiers.[13]

The Third Platoons of both C and D Companies roared out of Homert early on the 12th and pushed through Reininghausen, Oberbrugge, Ehringhausen, Dahlhausen, Berge, Heesfeld, and Ockinghausen. They not only overcame the bazooka men on the two roadblocks, but they also destroyed a number of enemy vehicles and rounded up about four hundred prisoners by nightfall.

Lt. Loopey was wounded in the face and neck by shell fragments at Oberbrugge, and was evacuated. Staff Sergeant Fleming commanded C Company's Third Platoon in Loopey's absence.

Chapter 21

The President is Dead

The train ride down to the "Little White House" in Warm Springs, Georgia, just before Easter, left President Roosevelt spent and exhausted. He had to be carried into the cottage and into bed.

The place always tended to work miracles for him. There, he felt protected from the onslaught of day to day in the capital city —away from the scheming, and the travails of world leadership, and the terrible war that was killing the cream of America's youth.

He brightened considerably as the days passed. Of course, there was the daily pouch from Washington to be worked through, but there was time to doze and read and engage in small talk while mixing cocktails for a few old friends.

There was no real escape, however. The holocaust deep in Germany was becoming well-documented—photos and eyewitness stories regarding the mass murders, the ovens, and the gas chambers. People were starving in the liberated areas of Europe. And the English people had to be fed.

There was the problem with Stalin, who seemed determined to undermine the hard-won decisions hammered out at Yalta. And Winston—forever pressing, differing from the President in thought and style.

Of course, he was still involved. Early on, he sent a top-secret message to the implacable Stalin, but it is not clear that he dictated it personally. More and more, he left such details to key aides: his personal Chief of Staff Admiral William D. Leahy, or the trusted Army Chief of Staff General George C. Marshall, and even Secretary of State Ed Stettinius.

His hand often trembled so badly he could hardly fit a Camel into his cigarette holder. There were times he ignored urgent papers and just worked on his stamp collection.

He kept in touch with Mrs. Roosevelt at Hyde Park by phone. His old friend, Henry Morgenthau, secretary of the treasury, called and came by for soup and waffles one night, pushing his favorite subject —making Germany an agricultural society by breaking the country into small, pastoral states. But all the President wanted to talk about was old times and the people they knew who were now gone. He contacted Lucy Mercer Rutherfurd and arranged for her to visit.

When he was up to it, he worked on the plans and organization of the first meeting of the United Nations, upcoming in San Francisco on April 25.

April 12, 1945: The President slept late, and he woke with a headache and some stiffness in his neck. Around noon, he sat in a big leather chair in the living room, in his dark Navy cloak, with a rolled scroll in his right hand, trying to hold his chin up for a formal portrait. He enjoyed chatting with the women and making small talk. Polly Delano and Margaret "Daisy" Suckley were cousins, and favorites of his, and had come down with him on the train. Lucy Rutherfurd was there watching him quietly, smiling when he looked up at her.

When the Washington pouch came, he had a small desk placed in front of him and read and signed state papers for a bit, his cigarette holder at a jaunty angle.

Suddenly, a throbbing in his head caused him to put down his cigarette and raise his hand to press against his temple. He clutched his forehead. "I have a terrific headache," he said. His eyes almost closed, and he slumped to his left. It was 1:15 Central War Time.

"Franklin, are you all right?"

There was no response. The President seemed to be asleep.

Someone screamed.

Aides rushed in and lifted him ever so gently into his bedroom. His doctor was at his side in minutes, and other specialists were called. But, it was all too late.

Franklin D. Roosevelt, age sixty-three, the 32nd President of the United States, died at 3:35 p.m. that afternoon, just eighty-three days after being elected for the fourth time. A massive cerebral hemorrhage.[1]

"Harry, the President is dead," said Eleanor Roosevelt. Stunned, the dapper little man in glasses and a bow tie struggled to absorb what the First Lady was saying to him.

Pulling himself together, Vice President Harry Truman asked, "Is there anything I can do for you?"

Quietly, Mrs. Roosevelt replied, "Is there anything we can do for you? For you are the one in trouble now."[2]

As the news spread around the world, the chief of German propaganda, Joseph Goebbels, exulted, "My Führer, I congratulate you. Roosevelt is dead. It is written in the stars that the second half of April will be the turning point for us. This is almost Friday, April thirteenth. It is the turning point!" Vindication undoubtedly sprang into Hitler's heart.

Eisenhower, Bradley, and Patton, sat and talked until 2:00 a.m., reminiscing about personal experiences with Roosevelt, and calculating what kind of man America now had in Harry Truman.

At FDR's home in Hyde Park, St. James Episcopal Church's bell began a somber toll. A senior warden had just died.

In addition to their bold headlines, some newspaper editors inserted a notice in the list of local soldiers and sailors killed or missing in action:

"ROOSEVELT, Franklin D. Commander in Chief U.S. Armed Forces, at Warm Springs, Georgia."[3]

Chapter 22

Friday the Thirteenth

"Friday the 13th was a 'black cat' day for the 740th Tank Battalion," Lt. Col. Rubel said. Call it superstition if you like, he went on to say, but ". . . the fact remains that the enemy did considerable damage to this Battalion on this day.

"The logical answer, however, was that the enemy was being compressed into a smaller area by our relentless drive. He would fire and fall back. Then, too, although the Division doughboys had been leapfrogging one Battalion through another, the 740th Tank Battalion had had no such luck.

"By this time a tanker's eyes looked like burned holes in a blanket. Our mobile hospital was carrying quite a number of men who were utterly and completely worn out," said Lt. Col. Rubel.[1]

Going all-out to destroy or capture all enemy forces in its zone, the 8th Infantry Division rattled its sabers and slashed forward in its attack. The 740th was scattered, as usual.

With elements of the 28th Infantry Regiment, the Second Platoon of A Company and the First Platoon of D Company roared out of Wellringrade before daybreak. The problems began at Huhlschen, where D Company's Staff Sergeant Roy Parks' tank was bushwhacked by a Mark VI. Then, when 1st Lt. Merritt maneuvered his tank around the spearhead tank and assumed the lead, his tank took the brunt of head-on enemy fire just short of Schwelm. The tank was literally shot to pieces; at least seven rounds pierced the front and went right on through, scrapping the engine in the rear. Technician 4th Grade John R. Mercer was killed. Lt. Merritt and two other members of the crew were severely wounded.

Staff Sergeant Hendrix took command of the Second Platoon, and went on to continue with the attack for three days and nights without rest, eventually getting wounded himself.[2]

In the meantime, A Company's First and Third Platoons moved up into position to provide more firepower, and they all pulled back into defensive positions at Schwelm for the night.

To the east, B Company's First Platoon attacked from Kuckelheim with the 343rd Infantry Regiment, toward the village of Herscheid. Staff Sergeant George, who was commanding the platoon at this time, was seriously injured, and evacuated when his tank tumbled over into a drainage ditch as they neared their objective. Fortunately, Corporal Henry Anderson, the gunner, was only slightly injured, and the rest of the crew was unhurt. Sergeant Russell L. Lucas took command of the platoon, continuing the attack until finally reaching Brugge.

B Company's Second and Third Platoons, with the infantry riding the backs of their tanks, attacked northwest through Plettenberg, and Werdohl, to Brugge, with artillery and flak threatening off and on all the day long, and received only random small arms fire.

The tankers of C Company's Second Platoon got their first look at a German labor camp as they moved into the tiny hamlet of Halver. As the gates were broken down, the tattered and enfeebled Polish/Russian prisoners still able to do so, poured out of their ramshackle quarters, cheering the Americans on. The prisoners immediately surrounded the German guards who remained, and beat them to the ground as best they could in their pitifully weakened condition.

As things settled down, the meat market across the dusty street was broken into, and the prisoners turned loose to grab and gobble up the raw meat. It was a heart-wrenching scene.

The day before, General Eisenhower got his first look at a foreign slave labor camp in the village of Ohrdruf in the Third Army sector, after inspecting a major find of Nazi loot in nearby Gotha. "I have never felt able to describe my emotional reactions when I first came face to face with indisputable evidence of Nazi brutality and ruthless disregard of every shred of decency," Eisenhower said. The Supreme Commander called on Washington and London to send in editors and national legislators to make certain the unfolding Nazi atrocities were placed before the American and British publics.[3]

The smell of death at the Ohrdruf-Nord "work camp" was overpowering. It contained facilities for torturing inmates and for executing those too weak to work. A barracks area and "hospital" housed still-living inmates lying shoulder-to-shoulder, awaiting death. The corpses of people who were shot in the head were stacked in a pile, awaiting burial in a nearby pit. In surrounding fields, more than three thousand rotting bodies lay about in piles near railway ties, awaiting a funeral pyre.

Although Eisenhower came away profoundly affected by what he found in Ohrdruf, it was but a small example of the horrors which would be uncovered in the following days, when the madness that was Nordhausen, Buchenwald, Bergen-Belsen, and the like would shock the world.[4]

C Company's First and Second Platoons, attached to the Third Battalion of the 13th Infantry, attacked northward from Halver that afternoon. They blazed through the small towns of Hurxdahl, Altenbrecherfeld, Holthausen, Filde, Ruggeberg, Muhlinghausen, Homberge, and finally rolled into Altenvorde just before midnight. No enemy tanks stood in their way during the rather wild ride, but several concentrations of withering ground fire took its toll on the accompanying infantry and the tankers' lines of supplies.

Technician Fifth Grade Rudolph D. Bridges and Private First Class A. B. Cook of Service Company, ran into a hotspot as they were hauling gas and ammunition to forward elements of C Company tanks. Their 2 1/2-ton truck was struck by enemy artillery shells and instantly set afire. They both tumbled out of the cab before the ammunition exploded, but quickly realized that the burning truck could blow up at any minute and block all road traffic behind them. Bridges climbed back into the driver's seat, and with Cook guiding him, drove the blazing truck off the road and out into the middle of a field, where it exploded shortly thereafter.[5]

Still, some seven hundred prisoners were taken during the day, and the tankers cleared the deck of the two enemy truck columns that blundered across their path.

Similarly, the Third Platoon of C Company, hooked up with the Third Platoon of D Company, rolled out from Ockinghausen with the Second Battalion of the 13th Infantry, and took a wild ride against light resistance through Carthausen, Flasskamp, Breckerfeld, Konigsheide, Kalthausen, and on into Voerde. They, too, caught and destroyed a number of wheeled and track vehicles along the way, and picked up about four hundred prisoners.

When the column entered Kalthausen at high speed, firing as it advanced, Staff Sergeant Alton N. Fleming's tank was hit by enemy tank fire and burned. Four rounds went into the turret. Sergeant Fleming, Corporal Cecil B. Brown, and Corporal Robert W. Prillaman, were killed.

Corporal Wayne Lowe said that the enemy tank was a Tiger Royal with an 88mm cannon. There wasn't a rocket scientist in the bunch, but they all knew that that Tiger was too much for them. What was left of the column scrambled as best they could for cover. Any cover. Anywhere.

Lowe's tank, commanded by Sergeant Thomas P. Reiley, was fourth in line and the last to find cover—belatedly backing in behind a red brick building they later learned had been the German CP. Of course, that drew the Tiger's fire, which missed them by inches, said Lowe. Then a round came right through the brick wall of the building, showering them all with red dust. Somehow, they made it out of that one all right. "Thank the Lord," said Lowe.

It was too late for his buddies in the column's lead tank.[6] Sergeant Reiley took command of the platoon, reorganized it, and pushed on to Voerde, where they set up roadblocks for the night.

But the day was not over for Staff Sergeant Roy Parks and his Third Platoon from D Company. His tank was clobbered by anti-tank fire as it approached the city of Hagen. Both he and Sergeant Walter H. Ford were seriously wounded and evacuated.

COMPANY "C"
740th TANK BATTALION
APO 230, c/o Postmaster
New York, N. Y.

Germany
9 May 1945

Mrs. Mable Fleming
    Route (2)
       May, Texas

Dear Mrs. Fleming:

       I wish to extend the sympathy of the Officers and
Enlisted Men of this Organization the death of your son
Staff Sergeant, Alton M. Fleming, 38371532, killed in action
near Kotthausen Germany on 13 April 1945.

       Your son has been a member of this organization
through all of our many missions and his loss will be felt
by his many freinds.

       Staff Sergeant Fleming was in the lead tank of his
platoon attacking the enemy near the town of Kotthausen Germany
when his tank was hit by shells from a concealed and well
camouflaged enemy tank and he died instantly.

       Alton was buried in the Breuna (1) Cemetery in
Germany and the appropriate Religious Services were held by
an Army Chaplain.

       If there are any other questions regarding your
son's death, his personal effects, I suggest you write to the
Quartermaster General, Army Service Forces, Washington, D. C.

       I hope I have been of some assistance and comfort
to you in your bereavement.

                Sincerely,

                James D. Berry
                JAMES D. BERRY
                Captain Co "C"
                740th Tank Battalion
                Commanding

42. Letter courtesy of David F. Fleming, nephew of Alton Fleming

Captain "Red" Berry's letter to Mrs. Mable Fleming following the death of her son.

Chapter 23

Closing out the Ruhr

The population center of the Ruhr valley originated at Winterberg, and most of the entrances to the primary manufacturing area were heavily guarded.

Company A rolled out early on April 14 to blast its way into Winterberg, and reported that about one hundred roadblocks were "neutralized" that morning between Winterberg and Schwelm. On a roll, the First and Second Platoons roared off to the east and overran Milspe. Gevelsberg, just to the northwest, was next. Even though it was in the 86th Infantry Division's zone, the 86th was nowhere in sight, and there was Gevelsberg to be had, just a half-mile or so away.

It just so happened that two heavy German tanks, waiting patiently for some American tanks to clank into range, stood watch at the northern edge of the town. Company A tankers, in their highly mobile, but still comparatively thin-skinned Shermans, shrewdly scattered before the ponderous Germans could score a direct hit. It was unanimously agreed that the intelligent course of action was to bypass the two monsters and roll on towards their river objective.

When First Sergeant Charles W. Edwards from Headquarters Company moved into the supposedly "clear" town of Milspe to set up shop, his billeting group from the Reconnaissance Platoon was greeted by burp gun fire. The houses they were taking over for the Battalion Command Post turned out to be a nest of SS troops, and they had a brief skirmish on their hands before taking the Germans prisoner. Of course, it's never over 'till it's over, and when incoming artillery fire flared, the prisoners fled in the confusion. Edwards and his hard-nosed crew went after them and sent all that could be found back to the POW cage.

B Company's First and Third Platoons hit Hagen that same day, shelling the city from the south. Heavy concentrations of artillery, flak, and sniper fire kept them on the outskirts of the city. The Second Platoon attacked from Werdohl and rolled through several small towns into Wiblingwerde, with very little opposition. Things were looking up.

With the Third Battalion of the 13th Infantry Regiment, the First and Second Platoons of C Company jumped off from Altenvorde, —2nd Lt. Tompkins' tank spearheading the attack—and took Delle, Hegte, and Volmarstein. Against light resistance, they rounded up about three hundred prisoners. Infantry patrols were sent out from Volmarstein that evening to make contact with the 75th Infantry Division, which was on the north bank of the Ruhr River.

The Third Platoons of C and D Companies rolled out of Vorde, and took Jellinghausen, Westenbauer, Tucking, Haspe, Vorhalle, and Eckesey, with Corporal (later Sergeant) Floyd E. Bickel's tank leading the way. They destroyed a column of German trucks and picked up five hundred prisoners by the time darkness closed in.

The battalion closed to the Ruhr River at Wetter by the end of the day, where new orders awaited them.

Anxious to get back, Lt. Col. Rubel rejoined the 740th's *Daredevil Tankers* in Milspe at noon on Sunday, April 15, and promised hospital authorities to return when time permitted. Overnight, the battalion received notice that the 8th Infantry Division, along with the 740th tankers, was to begin a massive turning movement to the west that morning, in an attack on the city of Dusseldorf, the great Ruhr industrial center. The attack was to parallel the Ruhr River, and the division was to spread wide to the south, taking in the northern part of Wuppertal—a division front more than ten miles wide.

The colonel knew his tankers had their work cut out for them "because we had driven a great number of enemy troops and a considerable number of their mobile anti-tank weapons up against the river. The enemy troops fighting at this point were mostly German paratroopers and remnants of SS Divisions who had backed up rather than surrender," Rubel said.[1]

In fact, when the giant pincers of the First U.S. Army from the south, and the Ninth U.S. Army from the north, clanged shut in this area of the Ruhr River just the day before, the Ruhr Pocket was effectively split in two. The bulk of the German Field Marshal Walter Model's Army Group B was cut off in the western half, in and around Dusseldorf and Wuppertal.

From a start line about a mile north of Milspe, Company A's Second Platoon had moved out earlier, on schedule. The tanks almost immediately faced a fierce barrage of anti-tank fire from long-range. With armor piercing rounds whishing viciously through their column, they scrambled for cover as best they could behind and between buildings.

Before he could find safety, Sergeant Charles D. Kilgore's tank was hit and burned. As the company's First and Third Platoons rushed up to reinforce their besieged brethren, they drew fire from their rear, big guns now firing high-explosive ammunition, and blowing huge holes in the buildings that were supposed to be protecting them.

43. Photo credit: 740th Tank Battalion Association Archives

Lt. Col. Rubel knew his tankers had their work cut out for them.

The Germans infiltrated back into the area which the infantry had cleared the night before, and were coming at the tankers from every direction.

As the 740th tanks recovered from the surprise ambush, and all three platoons began to find targets of their own, the Germans gradually disengaged. Still, it was not a very successful mission.

That night, as the company advanced toward the town of Herzkamp, the Third Platoon was cut off from the rear by still more infiltrating German infantry — some with those wicked self-propelled guns they constantly dragged about. These tanks were then pretty well stuck where they were for the night, unable to move forward or back until C Company was able to move up and reinforce them the next day, April 16. Herzkamp was finally taken.

But Herzkamp took its toll. Staff Sergeant Hendrix's tank was hit that night and immediately caught fire. Private First Class Angelo J. DeLuca was killed. And Sergeant Hendrix, after incredibly losing his second tank in three days, was severely wounded.

After his tank was hit, Technician Fourth Grade Clell W. Mott crawled back into the turret of the burning tank, dragged his platoon sergeant out, and carried him to safety — in spite of continuing enemy fire.[2]

To their surprise, resistance was unbelievably weak as the 740th tankers began the turn toward Dusseldorf. Elements of B Company rolled out of Hagen with the 341st Infantry Regiment, up to the Ruhr River, then back down to Ludenscheid, moving fast and facing only occasional sniper fire. Other elements met only sporadic artillery fire as they advanced to Hohenlimburg.

The First and Second Platoons of C Company, with the 13th Infantry Regiment, rolled through Volmarstein, Esborn, Holz, Kol, Bomerholz, Ham, and Holthausen. By the time they pulled into Hattengen after dark, they were so far out front they figured they'd better set up a full perimeter defense for the night. They had no idea who or what was up ahead, back behind, or on their flanks.

At least six hundred prisoners were sent back during their fifteen-mile advance that day, and a number of artillery emplacements, flak guns, wheeled vehicles, and horse-drawn cannons had been destroyed.

C Company's Third Platoon, after being released from the 13th Infantry and sent over to the 121st Infantry, spearheaded the attack from Ullendahl to Hasslinghausen, and caught only occasional artillery fire.

Meanwhile, D Company light tanks were protecting fuel and ammunition truck convoys, staving off a number of minor ambushes, and were involved in the final clearing of some stubborn clusters of enemy diehards in Hagen.

Most of the battalion held in place, or was shuffled back and forth between outfits on April 16—SNAFU, as it were. But C Company action, with the 121st Infantry, collected more than one thousand prisoners as they pushed from Herzkamp through Horath, Kloberg, Neviges, and Tonisheide, winding up in Rohdenhaus after dark. Resistance was so scattered as to seldom slow the advance during the day.

The 740th reassembled in the vicinity of Neviges on April 17 and spent the day rounding up prisoners.

As the tankers spread out to clear the surrounding villages on the 18th, one three-man patrol—Corporal Walter D. Stengel, Technician Fifth Class Lloyd P. Wright, and Private First Class Lester E. Derby—returned with Colonel General Karl Hollidt, in Field Marshal Model's high command. Lt. Col. Rubel quickly sent the German general on his way through division, and thence to XVIII Airborne Corps Headquarters.

Although more prisoners were coming in, there were still pockets of resistance that all too often reared up to strike from the rear. The German Field Marshal Model would not, could not, surrender. German soldiers were bound unto death by their oath of allegiance to Hitler.[3] Not even field marshals were exempt from the wrath of the Führer. Model knew that both he and his family could be imprisoned, even executed, because of his actions. And all that aside, "A German Field Marshal does not surrender," said Model.[4]

Gen. Omar Bradley, the 12th U.S. Army Group commander, was a proud man. He had just been promoted to full general, with four stars. As his First Army fought its way up from the southeast, and his Ninth Army stormed in from the west, the Ruhr Pocket was effectively split in half. Model's situation was futile; he had lost control of his armies, and even contact with some of his generals. Bradley wanted the German group commander. "He promised the Bronze Star to any American soldier who brought in the little, monocled German Field Marshal, whether dead or alive."[5]

Nevertheless, it was not to be. Model, from his headquarters outside Dusseldorf, rejected a personal appeal to surrender from Gen. Matthew Ridgeway, XVIII Airborne Corps Commander, and came up with an ingenuous plan to thwart Hitler's order to remain in the Pocket, and fight to the end. The wily little field marshal ordered that troops under his command—who were born before 1898 and after 1926—be formally separated from the German army. In other words, older men over age 47, and young boys under 18, were discharged and sent home, saving their lives and sparing them "the humiliation of surrender." Soldiers between ages 18 and 47 had three choices: (1) head for home and take their chances, (2) surrender individually, or (3) keep on fighting and try to break through to the German lines.[6]

He simply dissolved his armies. Certainly, no formal surrender could be asked of a command that did not exist. Further destruction of the Ruhr was avoided, and Model believed every life saved would be invaluable in rebuilding the Fatherland when the war was over.

The only problem with Model's big plan was that the Americans were left out of the planning. Overwhelmed by the flood of prisoners, they arrested and put behind barbed wire every man who appeared to be of military age, whether in civilian clothes or carrying official discharge papers.[7]

And Model? Having fled Dusseldorf, and after an uncomfortable night in the woods, the field marshal asked his adjutant to join him for a walk on Saturday, April 21. In a shadowy glade near a big oak tree, Model's last words were, "You will bury me here." Then he put his pistol to his temple and ended his life with his own hand.[8]

The battle of the Ruhr Pocket was over for the *Wehrmacht,* the German regular army, and they came pouring in with torn pieces of old sheets, table linen, handkerchiefs, anything white with which to give themselves up. Some 317,000 of them—young and old, arrogant and dejected, infantrymen and generals, nurses and technicians, teenagers in the Hitler youth. Most, of course, wearily on foot, bedraggled and downcast. But some were in vehicles, riding stiffly at attention. Others were on horseback and on bicycles. Some with a loaf of black bread or a bottle of wine, and carrying all kinds of personal stuff, even accordions and guitars. Many with tears in their eyes.[9] Most had to walk a long, long way to find an American who would take them.

Armed bands of Volkssturm, the Waffen SS, and the Hitler Youth still roamed, using delaying tactics and inflicting what damage they could. These armed bands had to be eliminated, and the lead American tank in the column never knew what to expect around the next corner. But here, it was over.

"In many ways it had been a steeplechase—[but for the tankers] it was a hundred miles of spearheading and a grueling, exhausting battle. We had lost as many tanks here as we had lost in the Battle of the Ardennes," said Lt. Col. Rubel.[10]

Chapter 24

The Occupation of Dusseldorf

One by one, the major industrial cities concentrated north of the Ruhr River, had fallen to the Ninth U.S. Army. Some cities and towns were heavily defended, and others abandoned without a fight.

The First U.S. Army had come up south of the river, in the region known as the Sauerland. The sector was not as industrialized as that to the north, but the area was about three times as large. The terrain was rugged, with steep hills and valleys, and was heavily forested. It was here that the 8th Infantry Division and the 740th Tank Battalion nestled and awaited what was to come.

It had been tough going for the tankers from their very first day in the Pocket, as they pushed north out of Siegen. The Germans had concentrated in the south for a possible breakout and were defending every stream and ridge along the way. However, their tank-supported counterattacks and stubborn resistance gradually eased against the 740th, as the tankers thrust hard ahead for several miles every day. Soon, the Germans were holding only in towns and villages, then just along the main roads—roadblocks with maybe a tank, a self-propelled gun, or even a 20mm flak wagon.

The once beautiful, but now badly battered city of Dusseldorf on the Rhine, was the last remaining German stronghold in the Ruhr. Germans were killing Germans. A resistance group wanted to surrender and save what was left of the city, but the *Gauleiter* (regional party leader) and his SS cohorts had never lost faith in the Führer, and were determined to fight on.[1]

Two of the resistance leaders courageously made their way through the German positions to the closest American outposts at Mettmann, just north of the city, and led elements of the 13th Armored Division into Dusseldorf. The column of American tanks, half-tracks, and trucks, along with several hundred infantry, rolled into the city with the resistance leaders on the turret of the lead tank. The city and its defenders surrendered without a shot being fired. It was too late for some key resistance members who had been brutally murdered earlier that day. But it was in time to arrest the Gauleiter and the SS murderers who had not escaped, and pack them off to special camps for hard-core Nazis.[2]

Meanwhile, the 8th Infantry Division had been assigned responsibility for the province of Dusseldorf, along with an adjoining province to the east. The 740th Tank Battalion was assigned to the 13th Infantry Regiment for occupational duty, and Lt. Col. Rubel was informed that the 644th Tank Destroyer Battalion, along with the infantry's Cannon and Anti-Tank Companies, would be attached to the 740th to assist with the task. His orders were to gather his small task force and move into Dusseldorf.

The colonel was told that "This is a great honor to you. This will make you Lord Mayor of Dusseldorf." Chuckling, the infantry commander added, "The last Lord Mayor of Dusseldorf was killed a few days ago, you know—don't let it become a habit."[3]

Rubel made a quick reconnaissance of the area, then called together the commanders of the units assigned to him, outlined their sectors on the map, and instructed them to move in and take control of their sectors on April 19. He selected the City of Dusseldorf for the 740th, subdividing it into sectors for each company. "Our main job was to establish law and order and to gather up prisoners of war, as well as enemy weapons and munitions," he said.[4]

Reconnaissance had located thousands of vehicles, anti-tank guns, some ammunition dumps, and a number of German soldiers hiding in the woods of the heavily forested area of Erkrath, a tiny village at the eastern edge of Dusseldorf. Company A was moved in to handle that situation. D Company was billeted at the Dusseldorf City Jail to guard prisoners brought in.

Before Rubel could get all his resources in place, however, the usual breakup and scattering of companies was beginning to occur. B Company was detached from the battalion and sent to the 28th Infantry Regiment in Pernze. C Company was detached and sent to the 121st Infantry Regiment in Cologne. Service Company had its hands full repairing tanks in Neviges, and still had to continually scour the area for enemy soldiers and weapons.

The occupying tankers of the 740th took over houses on the eastern edge of the city on April 19, before finally setting up headquarters in the Park Hotel on the 21st. The hotel had been bombed, but what remained had been cleaned and was in fairly good repair. About seventy of the original two hundred fifty rooms were habitable. The German manager and staff, including cooks, waiters, and chambermaids, were still on hand. All in all, with the hot water, a number of bathtubs, and a great wine cellar, the hotel was an enviable place to be.

Apart from the growing number of German soldiers surrendering each day, the wretched mass of foreign slave laborers was a major administrative problem for the American and British authorities. As they were turned loose, they wandered, desperate, hopeless, living off the land. They were French, Dutch, Belgian, Czech, Poles, and Russians, and came to be called "displaced persons."[5]

Several dozen such refugee camps dotted the area around Dusseldorf, each filled with hundreds, to many thousands, of these displaced persons. One such camp, just east of the city, held some 2,500 French soldiers as prisoners of war. Nearby, another was crowded with up to 10,000 Polish refugees who had been doing forced labor for the Germans. By this time, a lot of the Poles were on the loose and out of control—armed bands prowled from small farm to small village demanding food, water, and clothes. They took what they wanted, more often than not. They burned and killed and thoroughly terrorized the outlying population. The besieged Germans regularly came into the city seeking protection, and were just as regularly sent back to reap what they had sowed.

Although they lived well there in the city, the tankers were really spinning their wheels as they awaited the arrival of the permanent occupation force. Lt. Col. Rubel requested relief from occupation duty in order to get the men and the tanks ready for the next action, which was due within ten days or less. He also asked that B and C Companies be returned to battalion control so that they, too, could get ready for the fight. No such luck.

The 740th occupied Dusseldorf in exactly five days. In that time, they filled the division stockade with five thousand prisoners, the majority of whom were SS troops. Large numbers were in civilian clothing and carried the unacceptable discharges given out by their German commanders. All were checked for the telltale SS tattoo mark under their left arms. As more and more of western and central Germany came under American occupation, the Combined Chiefs of Staff, through General Eisenhower, ordered a policy of non-fraternization. American soldiers were told they could not even talk to a German except on official business. It was an illogical order, unreasonable in the face of human nature, and was therefore impossible to enforce.[6]

The policy inevitably broke down. It was just completely contrary to the quality and character of the young, healthy American and Allied soldiers, especially when children and women were involved.[7]

On April 25, orders came down from the XVIII Airborne Corps, through the 8th Infantry Division, for the 740th Tank Battalion to move to the vicinity of Uelzen, Germany, by the 27th. All that was known was that the battalion was detached from the U.S. First Army, attached to the U.S. Ninth Army, and assigned to the Second British Army for operations. *Now what?*

Field Marshall Montgomery's 12th Army Group was holding at the Elbe River, girding for a massive "set piece" crossing. To the American generals, Monty's slow and laborious buildup was gradually becoming "another Rhine-like extravaganza." The British mission was to protect the Ninth U.S. Army's left flank and cross the lower Elbe below Hamburg, then advance rapidly to Lubeck/Wismar on the Baltic Sea, intercepting retreating Germans and effectively blocking the Russians from driving on into Denmark.[8]

By this time, the Russians were not only encircling Berlin, but were also moving rapidly toward Lubeck and the Danish border. To underscore the importance of immediate action, General Eisenhower flew to Montgomery's headquarters just southeast of Hamburg on April 20, and offered Gen. Ridgway's XVIII Airborne Corps to assist in the operation.[9]

The British Field Marshal finally agreed, and Gen. Bradley transferred Ridgway's corps from the First to the Ninth U.S. Army "for administrative purposes." However, he placed the American Corps "under control" of Gen. Sir Miles C. Dempsey, commanding the British Second Army. "No one could build a fire under Monty better than Ridgway," Bradley said.[10]

Montgomery's broad directive to Ridgway was to insert his XVIII Airborne Corps between Simpson's Ninth U.S. Army and Dempsey's Second British Army, to protect the British army's right flank in its advance across the Elbe to the Baltic Sea.[11]

Chapter 25

Across the Elbe River

Lt. Gen. Matthew Bunker Ridgway was given the highest priority to draw forces for his XVIII Airborne Corps from the divisions holding the Ruhr. He selected his favorite division, the 82nd Airborne; then the 8th Infantry Division, which had performed so well in the Ruhr campaign and which included the 740th Tank Battalion; and finally, the 7th Armored Division, which had fought closely with the 82nd in the Battle of the Bulge under his command. In addition, he was assigned the 6th British Airborne Division, which was already in the assembly area near Lauenburg at the Elbe.

As he came to know the details of the British plan of attack, Gen. Ridgway realized that his American divisions would be stuck behind the Elbe, chomping at the bit for days while the British crossed first. It would be slow going for the Brits against the concentration of enemy forces waiting for them, and then, dammit, they'd probably stop for tea. By then, the Russians would undoubtedly be through Wismar and Lubeck, and probably occupying Denmark. His job was to "build a fire," speed up the action, not wait for it to happen.

Montgomery's directive to him had been broad and rather wide open, he believed. He flew up to the Elbe, surveyed the possibilities, and decided to turn his divisions toward Bleckede, southeast of the British crossing. There were a lot of Germans there, but obviously not massed to defend against a river crossing. He'd build his own bridges before the Germans could organize a defense, and try to beat the British across. Then he'd be on his way to the Baltic Sea. Ridgway messaged his XVIII Airborne Corps divisions to assemble at Bleckede instead of Lauenburg, and then and there decided that the 82nd Airborne would lead the American assault across the Elbe.[1] *And what of the Daredevil Tankers?*

For the 740th Tank Battalion, it was another three hundred mile trip. This time the tanks would march overland, stopping only for gas. They moved out early morning on April 28. Halted to refuel at the halfway point just west of Braunschweig. Had a hot supper. Ate a quick breakfast in the dark at 4:00 a.m., then pushed hard to reach Bohlen by midafternoon on the 29th.

On arrival, the battalion was immediately attached to the 82nd Airborne Division, which was to lead the assault across the Elbe, and was then alerted to move out the next day to Bleckede. Into the breach, again.

The 740th moved to Bleckede on April 30, and the big split was on again. Company A was attached to the 82nd's 505th Parachute Infantry, with C Company going to the 504th. B Company was attached to the 8th Infantry Division's 121st Infantry Regiment.

44. Photo credit: From the files of Harry Miller

These tanks are believed to belong to the 740th Tank Battalion, shown here crossing the Elbe River, April 30, 1945.

The plan was for the 82nd Airborne to force a crossing of the Elbe at Bleckede and establish a bridgehead, including building a pontoon bridge at Bleckede, then another one five miles south at Barskamp. The 8th Infantry would secure the bridgehead, then attack toward Schwerin, veer to the left, and go all the way to the Baltic Sea at Wismar.[2] The 740th tankers were to be smack-dab in the middle of it all.

As the shadows lengthened on April 29, the 82nd's 505th moved into position at the Bleckede ferry site, and troopers could see the Germans digging in and preparing defenses on the other side of the Elbe. Gen. Gavin decided to go for broke before the Germans became entrenched, and crossed stealthily in the middle of the night with an assault force of boats and amphibious vehicles. With flashlights and M-1 rifles, the troopers had a field day routing the Germans out of their foxholes. The veteran 505th Parachute Infantry consolidated the bridgehead by daylight, and the 504th followed them in on April 30.[3]

"The 82nd Airborne Division engineers did the fastest job of bridge building I have ever seen, and at 2010 hours on the 30th, it was ready for operation," Lt. Col. Rubel said.[4]

The 740th's First Platoon of A Company crossed immediately to link up with the 505th, and the Second Platoon of C Company followed, joining the 504th in preparation for the mission—to enlarge the bridgehead and locate another pontoon bridge in the vicinity of Barskamp.

"Thus closed the month of April 1945," Lt. Col. Rubel said. "The Battalion had moved a total of seven hundred sixty miles, and had fought under three armies—the 1st and 9th United States Armies, and the 2nd British Army."[5]

Chapter 26

The Death of Hitler

By this time, Hitler had lost control of events, was heavily medicated, and sinking evermore into depression. He ranted and raved at his generals in daily briefings, and at times became hysterical over the treasonous behavior and failures of those who had deserted him. He never left his bunker, fifty feet below the Chancellery buildings in Berlin.

On April 20, Russian forces surrounded the city, and block by block, fighting began. It was Hitler's fifty-sixth birthday, and that afternoon he met with some teenagers from the Hitler Youth, ready to take their place with the SS, the Wehrmacht, and the aging Volkssturm, in the last-ditch battle for their Fatherland and their Führer. Then he met with all of the Nazi leaders and military chiefs, together for the last time.

As they came, the Red armies took revenge for the suffering of their people, as the Germans scorched the Russian earth all the way to Moscow in 1941. The Russians not only fought, but killed indiscriminately, raped, looted, and burned their way through the cities and countryside of eastern Germany. Their thirst for revenge and pillage could be expected to reach its peak when they broke into Berlin. The German people would pay the price for the unspeakable crimes the Nazis had committed.[1]

The news that flowed into Hitler's bunker worsened day by day. On April 28, telephone communication with the OKW, the German High Command, failed. Then, it was confirmed that Mussolini had been arrested by Italian partisans. On April 29, Hitler learned that the Italian dictator and his mistress had been executed and strung up by their heels shortly after their arrest.[2]

On April 30, the day that the 740th Tank Battalion crossed the Elbe, Adolph Hitler proclaimed the German people unworthy of their Führer, and killed himself, having named Grand Admiral Karl Doenitz as his successor. Thus, Doenitz, the Commander in Chief of the German Navy, suddenly became both President of the Reich and Supreme Commander of the Armed Forces.

By late morning on the 30th, an advance Russian unit was reported nearing the Chancellery bunker. After a quiet lunch, Hitler began his goodbyes to Borman, Goebbles, and the others, telling his personal pilot that he wanted "He was the victim of his generals!" written on his tombstone.

Around 3:30 that afternoon, in his suite, he placed his Walther pistol at his right temple and pulled the trigger. Eva Braun Hitler, whom he had married near midnight just the night before, had already taken a poison capsule.

Following Hitler's instructions, aides placed the bodies in a shallow ditch just outside the bunker entrance, and even as Russian shells exploded amid the rubble of the Chancellery, gallon after gallon of gasoline was splashed on the bodies and torched repeatedly. Later, the charred remains were brushed into a canvas and placed in a shell hole, then covered with dirt. Hitler was buried in "the rubble of defeat."[3]

The war in Europe would end on May 8th. The countdown began.

On Tuesday, May 1, most of the 740th Tank Battalion maneuvered into position in the vicinity of Neuhaus and Suckau, in preparation for the big push on Schwerin the following day. However, at 5:00 a.m., C Company's Second Platoon was sent on a little "mopping up" mission with elements of the 504th Parachute Infantry Regiment. They attacked southeast along the Elbe from the bridgehead at Bleckede.

Against occasional artillery, but hardly any small arms resistance, the little task force took the towns of Wendischthun, Stiepelse, Nevgarge, Viehle, Popelau, Dachau, Kuhren, and eventually Zeetze. Mission completed, with little evidence of any concentration of enemy forces. Then, they received orders for one section of tanks to turn northeast five or six miles to Jessenitz, to see if contact could be made.

Lt. Tompkins, the tank platoon leader and mission commander, took two tanks, with seven or eight troopers on the back of each, and roared off toward Jessenitz, which they encountered without incident. However, about five hundred yards farther on, they ran into trouble. During a fierce firefight that lasted over an hour, Tompkin's tank was hit by a Panzerfaust and knocked out. The bow gunner, Corporal Ray T. Merritt, was killed.

Tompkins said he saw some Jerries a couple hundred yards ahead and ordered his gunner to get on them, and his driver to stop. "I saw a blinding flash to my immediate front and knew [it was] Panzerfausts. I ducked my head just as the explosion came and was knocked about halfway out of the turret," Tompkins said.

There was no immediate fire, and as he dropped back into the turret to survey the damage, the gunner and loader scrambled out. Up front, he could see the driver and bow gunner struggling to get out. He then left the tank and took cover in a ditch, only to find Corporal Merritt mortally wounded.[4]

Technician 4th Grade Charles D. Hoover was the driver of the tank. He said,

"The concussion knocked me out for a few seconds. It seemed as though something had torn half of my neck away. But, I found it was only burned pretty badly. I dismounted and took up a prone position behind a tree. As I lay there I saw several more *Panzerfausts* hit the tank—and found myself closer to the Jerries than any of the doughboys.

"In the meantime, the other tank was firing on the enemy. I then crawled to the other tank. The tank commander was trying to contact the other tanks of our platoon, but unfortunately they couldn't be contacted."[5]

When Tompkins' tank was put out of action, Sergeant Harold G. Bradley, commanding the second tank, immediately pulled into the lead position and opened up with a torrent of fire. He kept the beleaguered force from being encircled until two of his .30 caliber machine guns jammed.

As luck would have it, just a few days before, the crew had a third .30 caliber mounted in the rack on top of the turret. Bradley's loader, Private First Class T. J. Woodress, jumped to it and blazed away while both he and Bradley were exposed to heavy small arms, automatic, and flak fire.

"We couldn't fire our cannon with our guys spread out all around us." Bradley said. "But Woodress must have fired thirty boxes of ammo keeping the Jerries pinned down while our infantry scrambled for cover. I don't believe I'd be around to tell this story today if it hadn't been for T. J. Woodress."[6]

The hour-long firefight went back and forth until the tankers and troopers were finally able to regroup well enough to withdraw, bloody but unbowed.

That same day, Tuesday, May 1, the 740th Tank Battalion was detached from the 82nd Airborne and reattached to the 8th Infantry Division. Lt. Col. Rubel and Maj. Floyd stood near the bridge at Bleckede, spotting gun flashes as battalion tanks continued to receive fire as they crossed the river. As they split up and walked away, Rubel went across the field toward Service Company and Floyd went down the road to the C.P. They heard the angry scream of an incoming artillery shell coming their way. As they watched and waited anxiously, the mound of rocks on which both had been standing just minutes before blew sky-high in a cloud of smoke. Close.

The 121st Infantry Regiment was split into three task forces for the rolling breakthrough attack. Task Force Adams was composed of the 740th's B Company tanks and Assault Gun Platoon, the 121th's First Battalion of infantry and Cannon Company, along with elements of the 644th Tank Destroyer Battalion, the 12th Engineer Battalion, the 83rd Armored Field Artillery Battalion, and the 89th Chemical Battalion.

Task Force Kunzig utilized the balance of the 740th's tanks, the 121st's Second Battalion of infantry, and elements of the 644th T.D. Battalion, the 12th Engineers, the 83rd Armored Field Artillery, and the 89th Chemical.

Task Force Hogan was the reserve force and had the 121st's Third Battalion of infantry riding in trucks, the 121st Anti-Tank Company, and the 56th Field Artillery Battalion.

The attack was made in two columns, with Task Force Adams as the left assault column, Kunzig the right assault column, and Hogan following two hundred yards behind Kunzig, assisting and protecting.

Patrols were to maintain contact between the two columns and clear out lateral roads using the 644th T.D. Battalion Reconnaissance Company. Artillery liaison planes flew over each column, locating roadblocks, craters, blown bridges, and enemy troop and armor concentrations.

With infantry loaded on the backs of their tanks, and with no recon out front, the 740th *Daredevil Tankers* were to just take off down the road until the lead tanks were stopped by a wrecked bridge, or were simply blown away by an entrenched concentration of fire.

With the attack slated for the next morning, Rubel, and his counterpart with the 121st Infantry's Second Battalion, Lt. Col. Kunzig, struggled through the night planning how in heaven's name they were going to get Kunzig's entire Second Battalion of infantry on the back of Rubel's tanks. As the 740th's C.O. checked around to ascertain the strength of his tank companies and to make sure they were ready to go, he learned that C Company's Second Platoon had still not returned from the firefight at Jessenitz. At 4:00 a.m., he sent a recon peep out to look for them.

Finally, at 5:00 a.m., just as Capt. Red Berry was lining up his C Company tanks for the big attack, his Second Platoon clanked tiredly in, looking for a hot meal and a good bed—beat up, worn out, and bedraggled, but praise the Lord, back with their outfit at last. Berry waved them down and grinned up at them. "Gas 'em up, boys," he said, "and get in line. We're moving out!"

At 5:30 a.m., Wednesday, May 2, C Company tanks moved out, loaded with infantrymen and leading Task Force Kunzig, hell-bent for Schwerin, some forty miles to the northeast. At Gromitz, hundreds of American and British POWs were liberated, along with thousands of French, Italians, and Poles in a forced labor camp. They literally tore down their cages and swarmed the column in excitement and relief. The Americans handed out cigarettes, candy, and food — whatever they had. But they had to roll. Others would take care of these poor souls.

As the road finally cleared, the column eased forward. Ten miles an hour. Twenty. Rumbling through village after village.

It was the job of the tanks to keep on the move, and Lt. Col. Rubel and his driver, Corporal LeRoy C. Meyer, ranged up and down the column, stopping at a building here and a house there, to start the German soldiers down the road. Follow-up elements of the task force would gather them up.

The column hit some trouble spots as it pulled into Hagenow, but a blanket of machine gun fire generally smothered them on the run. Enemy airplanes took off from a large airfield as the column moved through and to the northeast outskirts of town. C Company's tanks stopped where they were on the road and leveled cannon and machine gun fire on the planes as they scrambled to take off. It was a shooting gallery. More difficult as the planes lifted off for sure, but the ones on the ground waiting their turn were sitting ducks. In minutes, some thirty or forty planes were on fire.

In an effort to get the column moving again, Lt. Col. Rubel ordered D Company up into the airport where they shot up fifty to seventy-five more airplanes and collected several thousand prisoners.

As Task Force Kunzig moved out again, Rubel and Meyer took out after them in their peep and passed every tank in the column, including the spearhead tank, until an enemy machine gun drew down on them as they entered a patch of woods. "This taught me a lesson," the good colonel said. "I let tanks do the spearheading from then on."[7]

It was good he did. The spearhead tank ran head-on into an angry roadblock several miles south of Warsow. It was heavily defended by several German *Panzerfaust* teams who apparently had not yet heard the war was over for them and opened up on the tanks. The initial melee became a tragedy, as it became necessary to burn the little village to get them out and the column moving again.

Word of the task force's attack must have preceded the column as it advanced. As the lead elements approached Schwerin just before noon, they could see thousands of German soldiers, and they prepared for the worst.

"Here we go!" one of the tank commanders was heard to holler. With grim faces and hearts pounding, they hit the town at top speed.

Enemy planes could be seen taking off from a large airfield just to the west of the city. Lt. Col. Rubel quickly called on C Company's Third Platoon to peel off and blow the threat away. Timing was everything. The tankers had a field day catching planes taking off and shooting them down, just as they cleared the ground.

Meanwhile, the main column tightened and roared into the city. To the tankers' complete surprise, there was no fight left in the enemy there in Schwerin. Broad grins broke out where only tight faces had been seen before. The tanks rolled right through without major incident and the division commander called the task force to a halt at the northern edge of the city, stopping the left assault column, Task Force Adams, in place as well.

Totally unbelievable. The shocked tankers and infantrymen were immediately inundated by what had to be tens of thousands of German soldiers wanting to surrender. An urgent call for help brought all the military police and other available soldiers in to control the situation. No way could they handle the masses of POWs by themselves. In fact, they wanted out.

In the middle of all this confusion, Lt. Col. Rubel and the task force commander, Lt. Col. Kunzig, learned of an enemy corps headquarters in Klein Trebbow, a village no more than ten miles away. They immediately took off through the German lines to try to effect a widespread surrender of enemy forces in the area, and decided to split up and take separate routes in case one or the other didn't make it.

In a patch of forest off the main road, Lt. Col. Rubel and his driver, Cpl. Meyer, ran their little peep right into the middle of an SS ack-ack battery, which fired at American planes just as they rolled in. As the Germans lowered their guns on them, Rubel said he had visions of his wife collecting his insurance money. Talking fast, and with more bravado than he felt, he somehow managed to convince the Germans that they were surrounded and were his prisoners, and had them destroy their guns then and there.

Rubel then ordered one of the German officers onto the hood of his peep, and he and Meyers took off for the German corps headquarters in Klein Trebbow, arriving just as Col. Kunzig turned the corner to greet them coming in.

Entering the building, they introduced themselves and demanded the Germans' surrender. Producing maps and troop dispositions, the two sides eventually reached an agreement. The German corps commander would not surrender under any condition, but he instructed his chief of staff to order his five divisions, along with some thirty- to forty thousand other troops under his command, to begin an immediate "withdrawal" to the southwest into the American lines.

He then radioed his Army Group Headquarters regarding his action and recommended their "withdrawal." When the German commander failed to receive an answer, Lt. Col. Rubel had him send notification by airplane to Kiel, just south of Denmark, where Grand Admiral Doenitz, the new head of the Third Reich, had convened his advisers. His thinking was that word of the mass surrender in the Wismar area might help cause the disintegration of die-hard German troops in the extreme northern German operations.

Most of the German general staff spoke English quite well, and Lt. Col. Rubel and Kunzig decided to stay the night at corps headquarters to help facilitate the massive surrender. In the meantime, they received orders from their own XVIII Airborne Headquarters that "under no circumstances was anyone allowed to negotiate surrender with German 'units.' The 'units' were to be dismembered and the surrender was to be as individuals."

They showed the German commander the message, and told him to continue an orderly withdrawal as planned, but to consider it strictly as "unconditional surrender" on the part of individual soldiers.[8]

Not more than a dozen miles to the north, elements of the British 6th Airborne

Division had moved into Wismar on the Baltic Sea. The U.S. XVIII Corps commander, Gen. Ridgway, had positioned the 6th so that they would have the distinction of being there to greet the Russians when they arrived.[9]

When the first few light tanks loaded with Canadian paratroopers on the back rumbled into the city without opposition, they immediately became suspicious and more than a little uneasy. There was no movement anywhere in the town. Only an unsettling quiet. Still, they knew the Germans were there, hiding. Was it a trap? No. Wismar was undefended, its inhabitants behind locked doors — listening, waiting, deathly afraid. Afraid it was the Russians who had arrived first and would soon be knocking on their doors.[10]

Hours later, when the first ragtag group of Russians from the Belorussian Army raced in from the east, a lot of handshaking, backslapping, and vodka guzzling ensued. However, it was not long until the Russians had constructed a massive roadblock on the outskirts of Wismar. The tension tightened and trouble began — almost as if the Iron Curtain had already begun to close down.[11]

With the 740th on the move again, the tankers rolled on past Klein Trebbow to Mecklenburg, just two and a half miles south of Wismar. But with the British now firmly in control of that city, and the German armies in the extreme north of the country completely cut off, the 740th circled right, back down south to Moltrow, and then to Hohen Viecheln, holding there temporarily on the shores of Schweriner See, Lake Schwerin.

By then, the roads were jammed with German soldiers seeking refuge in the American lines, away from the Russians. Massive columns of foot troops were interspersed with every kind of vehicle imaginable — Wehrmacht trucks, cars, trailers, wagons and horse-drawn carts, bicycles, and now and again, a battle wagon or a tank. Some came with their women and children and pathetic little hoards of personal possessions. At Schwerin, more than 155,000 Germans surrendered that day to the 8th Infantry Division alone.[12]

By Thursday, May 3, the division had all its military police up and down the road, and both the 740th tankers and the 121st's Second Battalion of infantry were scattered strategically about, directing prisoners. "We marched them out under the control of their own officers until they hit the main highway leading from Wismar to Schwerin, where they deposited their weapons," Lt. Col. Rubel said. "After that, they became 'individuals,' and their officers led them on down to the prisoner stockades at Schwerin."[13]

The Germans left behind an astounding array of weapons: every kind of knife and sword, rifle and hand gun, artillery piece, and other such military equipment. Even an armored railway train pulled up.

Two lone C Company tankers in a jeep, ranging far and wide out ahead of the pack, watched in shocked disbelief as the train hove into sight. When the train pulled to a screeching halt just off to their right, nervous would hardly describe their condition. They didn't have a lot of choices. No way could they outrun the big guns on that train.

Hearts in their throats, they could barely draw in enough air to whisper to one another. Still, the Germans had been giving up all around them and they had been sending them on their way down the road to the prisoner cages.

Standing tall in their flimsy little vehicle, they put on big welcoming smiles and waved and pointed down the road, as hundreds of German soldiers poured off that train with their weapons on their shoulders and their hands in the air. What do you know? It worked.

On Friday, May 4, at Luneburg, Germany, Field Marshal Montgomery accepted the unconditional surrender of forces facing his 21st Army Group, including all German soldiers in north Germany, Denmark, the Netherlands, and all islands—effective at 8:00 a.m. the next day. General Eisenhower had ruled that the German surrender of Norway would have to wait since it was a "political" rather than a "tactical" surrender and would require the presence of the Russians. [14]

On Saturday, May 5, the German delegation proceeded to SHAEF forward headquarters at Reims, France, to negotiate total capitulation. Admiral Hans-Georg von Friedeburg, the German navy commander, and his group, met with SHAEF staff and called for a "phased surrender" in the west, stalling for time in order to move additional units into the American and British zones to save their troops from the Russians.

General Eisenhower, however, refused to authorize a separate surrender on the Western Front and would not allow negotiation. Surrender immediately, unconditionally, on all fronts, or face the consequences.

Sunday, May 6. Learning of Eisenhower's stand, Admiral Doenitz sent General Alfred Jodl, Chief of the Operations Staff of the German High Command of the Armed Forces (OKW), with full authority to sign but claiming lack of control over all German troop movements and the need for more time. Ike was adamant and would have no more of it. He sent word to the Germans that they had twenty-four hours to settle the matter or he would break off negotiations and seal the Western Front, allowing no more German soldiers or civilians through Allied lines. Jodl notified Doenitz of Eisenhower's determination and received authority to surrender on all fronts. [15]

At 2:41 a.m., Monday, May 7, "In the War Room of General Eisenhower's headquarters in a red brick boys' school at Reims, Jodl signed the surrender." [16] This Act of Military Surrender to be effective at 11:01 p.m., Tuesday, May 8, 1945.

Afterward, Jodl asked to speak to General Eisenhower and was led upstairs to the second floor office. Ike, with RAF Air Chief Marshal Arthur Tedder at his side, "stood behind his desk at attention in Army service dress uniform, without sword or pistol." He warned Jodl that he and his colleagues would be held "officially and personally responsible" for any violations of the surrender, then dismissed him.[17]

The United States, Great Britain, France, and the Soviet Union were represented at the ceremonies. It is interesting to note that Russian General Ivan Susloparoff had been in Reims since mid-March serving as an observer in surrender talks and as a contact between SHAEF and STAVKA, the Soviet High Command. Both Susloparoff and an aide attended the surrender.

It is apparent, however, that Stalin was not happy with what happened at Reims. General Susloparoff, late on May 7, left Reims for Moscow and got a "harsh reprimand for allegedly participating in the surrender ceremony without permission." He was never heard from again.[18]

At the insistence of the Russians, a second surrender ceremony was reenacted for the Russian press and people in the rubble of Berlin on May 8. Wilhelm Keitel, General Field Marshal, and the Chief of Staff of the German High Command signed the documents in place of Jodl. General Eisenhower did not attend.

Both Keitel and Jodl would eventually hang as war criminals.

Chapter 27

The War Ends in Europe

Victory in Europe Day was cause for tremendous celebrations across most of the world. In Washington, D.C., President Truman announced Germany's unconditional surrender in a radio broadcast to the American people. Thousands upon thousands packed Times Square in New York in a boisterous demonstration. Thankful, cheering, hugging and kissing, proud to be Americans. The war had revitalized the U.S. economy. The boys would be coming home now —most of them.

In London, the Royal Family, along with Winston Churchill, appeared before the cheering crowds at Buckingham Palace. The excited Londoners could not believe the terrible war was over, and they were proud to see the future Queen Elizabeth II in uniform. The British were flat broke, their ranks depleted, and they had given up some sixty thousand dead to the German bombing of their homeland. God Save the Queen.

In Paris, the people of the magnificent old city literally came unwound. The nightmare was over. There were "crowds and singing and cheers and lots of Cognac and girls. People stopped work, and the airplanes of all the Allied forces buzzed the Champs Elysees."[1] *De Gaulle et "La Marseillaise."*

In Moscow, victory celebrations did not come to the people until May 9. The happy, milling throngs watched a mighty armada of Soviet power parade through Red Square in a hard rain. That night, they were rewarded with a fireworks display the likes of which had never before been seen in the communist state. Stalin, hero of the "Great Patriotic War." What could America expect from him now?

In the Pacific, the Allies and the Japanese were still killing one another, bringing that war ever closer to the American soldiers who had survived the war in Europe. Would the *Daredevil Tankers* be called into the fray over there?

Back in Germany, the celebration was somewhat muted among the tankers of the 740th Tank Battalion. There was a certain disbelief that the end was really at hand. A lot of silent prayers. *Thank you, God.* Tears, yes. Battle-hardened GIs who literally broke down and cried, but mostly handshakes and hugs and congratulations, along with, "Well, we made it." That was about it.

A Russian outfit, just across the lake, shot off a lot of flares in what amounted to a huge fireworks display. The Seaforth Highlanders, with the British just to the north, responded by firing what was left of their flares. Not having any flares to light up the sky, the 740th tankers just skimmed a few hand grenades out across the sea with resounding explosions and a lot of water spray.

Of course, there was great relief. The tankers had been party to the horror of war, and had witnessed the gradual disintegration of a once powerful enemy in the process. A welcome, but not a joyous feeling, and more of a letdown if the truth were known. It had been a grueling, nerve-wracking, welded-in-the-memory experience. They had lost close friends. Fatigue set in. They were so tired. What was next? The ever-present rumor mill ground on.

They were headed for the Pacific. Was such a thing really possible? After all of this?

The battalion quickly became so busy rounding up the thousands of German prisoners of war and displaced persons, that there was little time to dwell on what might never be.

If they had to be somewhere in Germany right then, the Schwerin Sea was about as good a place as any. The City of Schwerin was near at hand and provided stage shows and movies, with German, and later, Russian casts. The tankers didn't always understand what was going on, but it was fun to get away and not think too much about it. The duke of Mecklenburg's castle was a sight to see, and not more than a mile away on a high cliff overlooking the sea.

The Schwerin Sea was the main attraction. There were hundreds of sailboats, power boats, and rowboats in marinas along the shore, and these provided a lot of exciting, if unique, recreation. Not that many tankers knew much of anything about sailing, but they had the gas, and they knew about engines. It wasn't that long before they got a "Yacht Club" going with the 6th British Airborne guys.

The Russians were just across the lake at Regensdorf, and a lot of interesting contacts were made back and forth. Sergeant Herschel B. Wall from B Company met the Russians rather unexpectedly just after the war ended. Wall and four of his buddies decided to take a "little cruise" in a beautiful sailboat harbored at the Leubsdorf Marina. They threw in some K-Rations, smokes, and .45 automatic pistols, then checked the oil in the auxiliary engine, filled the gas tank with gas from their Sherman tank, and eased slowly out along the shoreline. Just a little joyride with the small, four-cylinder auxiliary engine driving the boat along at about five miles an hour. They didn't need to know about sails and keels and stuff like that. They had their little engine and had no intention of going out into the open water. Occasionally, they would stop, strip down, and dive into the cold water for a quick swim. After a couple of hours, they headed back toward the marina.

Suddenly, the propeller snapped a screw and shut down. Only one paddle in the boat. No problem. After all, this is a sailboat. Just figure out how to crank up the sail, and head for home.

That big sail really caught the wind, and the boat started moving rapidly. The rudder was useless. The wind was driving them sideways across the lake.

Two Russian officers stood on the far shore at Regensdorf with binoculars, watching with mounting curiosity as the near naked sailors approached.

"Fellows, we better get into our uniforms or they'll think we're Germans," Wall said nervously, noticing what appeared to be at least a platoon of Russian soldiers camouflaged among the trees in the background.

Quickly, they struggled into their uniforms and buckled on their .45s. Desperately, they sought to lower the big sail. All of a sudden, the boat whacked sideways up against the shore. Wall held up his hand, palm outstretched (the old Indian "We come in peace" gesture), and called out, "Americanski soldaten!"

One of the Russians rushed toward him, while Wall struggled to keep his hand away from his gun.

The Russian broke out in a big grin, grabbed Wall's hand in a bear grip, and said excitedly, "Ruski soldaten!" The other Russian came up, and they shook hands all around. When the tankers offered cigarettes, the whole gang of Ruskies broke out of cover and rushed toward them.

This made things a little uneasy until they learned that the Russians were only after their American cigarettes. Fortunately, they had enough to go around.

It seemed that every one of the Russians had a canteen full of schnapps, about the same type of stuff Wall used to call "White Lightning" back home. The toasts began. Wall distinctly recalls the Russian who took two tin cups and filled them half-full of lake water, added enough schnapps to fill both cups, and handed one to him. He said he'll never forget how the schnapps turned the lake water milky white.

The Russian put the cup to his mouth and drained it, and Wall realized that it would be downright insulting if he didn't do the same. It literally took his breath away, and tears came to his eyes. But now the two of them were buddies, and the Russian wanted to fire Wall's .45 pistol.

Feeling absolutely no pain himself, Wall figured *Why not?* and handed him the pistol. The Russian tossed his tin cup into the water and put two big holes in it before it sank.

Then they traded money. Wall had an American one dollar bill with George Washington on it, and the Russian had a three ruble bill with Nikolai Lenin on it.

When the time came to worry about getting back across the lake, the Russians came up with an idea. They had a German prisoner, and if he knew how to sail a boat, they would give him to the Americans.

Of course the German knew how to sail a boat. They all said their goodbyes and piled in the boat. The German grabbed the lone paddle to move them out from shore. And he rowed. And rowed. And rowed. West, against the wind. All the way to Leubsdorf. That German knew nothing about sailing a boat, they quickly learned. He just wanted to get away from the Ruskies! Wall and his buddies got a huge laugh out of that, along with the German, who really put his back into that oar.

When they finally got to the other shore, the German POW looked up questioningly. *Now what?* Wall and his buddies broke into big grins, gave him all the food they had, and told him that wherever home was, he was free to go there. The enemy soldier thanked them over and over, and backed slowly away until the darkness closed in around him.[2]

On May 27, a solemn and impressive ceremony and memorial service was held in Schwerin for the 740th tankers who had fallen in battle. The entire battalion was present, and memories flooded the ranks. As taps sounded, and that star spangled banner waved from across the field, few were able to hold back the tears—especially when the names of their comrades were called. The division chaplain paid homage to the honored dead who had given their lives in the service of their country. Lt. Col. Rubel spoke "of these gallant men," saying, "To live in hearts you leave behind is not to die."[3]

A few days later, the formal parade was the 740th's first in the European Theater of Operations. Brig. Gen. Bryant E. Moore, Commanding General of the 8th Infantry Division, presented Distinguished Unit Badges to the members of C Company, the First Platoon of A Company, the Second Platoon of B Company, and a number of other men who were attached to C Company when the 740th stopped the German breakthrough in the Battle of the Bulge.

"It can truthfully be said that nearly every man in the Battalion deserved a medal for valor for his part in the defeat of Germany," said Lt. Col. Rubel. "There are innumerable deeds of heroism that will go unrewarded and unheralded."[4]

Zones of Occupation

As the zones of occupation gradually took shape, the British took over the Mecklenburg area the first week in June, and the 8th Infantry Division, along with the 740th Tank Battalion, were ordered to the vicinity of Kassel, Germany. No one was happy about leaving the great duty on the Schwerin Sea, but word was that Schwerin would soon become part of the Russian zone anyway.

The 740th packed up on June 5 and rolled nearly two hundred miles southwest to two villages just north of Kassel, Humme, and Schoneberg, wearing out twenty sets of tank tracks. Within days, the 8th Infantry Division was ordered to the port of embarkation, headed for the war in the Pacific. The tankers simply could not believe it. Was this really happening? To them?

They lucked out. When the 8th Infantry moved out, the 740th was immediately attached to the Artillery Brigade of the 78th Infantry Division, which, for the time being, was to remain in occupation duty in and around Kassel. This was happening to them.

The battalion was moved to Hofgeismar, a little closer to Kassel, into much nicer quarters, relieved from the Ninth U.S. Army and assigned to the Third U.S. Army. At that time, the 740th Tank Battalion officially became Category 1, Army of Occupation.

Relocation began again, twenty-five miles southwest to Witzenhousen, on the border of the U.S. occupation zone. The adjoining areas were occupied by the British to the north, including their old friends, the Seaforth Highlanders, and by the Russians to the east.

As the "Governor" of the Landkreis Witzenhausen, Lt. Col. Rubel named Capt. Sheppard as town mayor of Witzenhausen, and Capt. Prevatt as Landkreis estate agent. These two officers and their staffs worked around the clock to get utilities going again, and to reorganize governmental operations. While C Company remained in Witzenhausen, A and B Companies were quartered just to the south in Bad Sooden, and D Company was just to the north in Eichelberg.

The battalion went on guard on the border to the Russian zone. One tank and crew manned each guard post three days at a time, or until relieved. Their responsibility was to interdict and control the flow of traffic, and check for appropriate passes.

Refugees by the thousands were intercepted, grouped by nationality, and sent home—if they had good claim, or professed energetically that they lived west of the border. If not, they were sent back to be handled by the Russians.

Meanwhile, the battalion was shuffled from the 78th Infantry Division to the 3rd Infantry Division, and in the first week of July, the Third Battalion of the 3rd

Infantry relieved the 740th of most of its guard duty responsibilities.

The Army Intelligence and Education Program was inaugurated, and activities organized in three disciplines. The Educational Platoon taught academics, along with on-the-job courses such as welding, motor vehicle mechanics, animal husbandry, and farming. The Special Services Platoon operated out of a privately owned theater, appropriately renamed "Daredevil Theater," where they trained and booked the battalion orchestra, and edited the weekly newspaper, the 740th Tank Battalion "Police-Up." The Athletic Platoon provided physical training, baseball leagues, field events, and other sporting activities.

As the time passed, the 740th *Daredevil Tankers'* thoughts turned more and more towards home. They had been lucky, but when word came down that soldiers would not be released from the army if their services were required in the war against Japan, the noose tightened a little. They had fought one war, but there was yet another war to be won.

August 6th and the Bomb

When President Harry Truman ordered the atomic bomb dropped on Hiroshima, and another three days later on Nagasaki, America was losing one thousand men a day in the Pacific islands. The Japanese were well known to prefer death over surrender, and would undoubtedly fight fiercer than ever on their own homeland.

"It was a question of saving hundreds of thousands of American lives," said the President. "The casualty estimates [for an invasion] called for 750,000 American casualties—250,000 killed, 500,000 maimed for life. I couldn't worry about what history would say about my morality. I made the only decision I ever knew how to make. I did what I thought was right."[5]

Japanese casualties were estimated to have been two million men, women, and children if an invasion had in fact been ordered.

"The Japanese surrendered five days after the bomb was dropped on Nagasaki, and a number of major Japanese military men and diplomats later confided publicly that there would have been no quick surrender without it," President Truman said.[6]

45. Photo credit: Harry S. Truman Library

Their war was really over. The men of the 740th Tank Battalion could begin to breathe again, and dream again, of home, of families and girlfriends, Mother and Dad, clean sheets, hamburgers and ice cream — the American Way. How long had it been?

These "Citizen Soldiers," as Stephen Ambrose called them, could, at last, stop living on the edge and now consider what was next in their lives. After all of this——so much tension and fear, heartbreak and brutality, and yes, valor and daring, there was still a grim satisfaction in what they had done.

With the 30th Infantry Division, they had stopped lead elements of *Kampfgruppe Peiper* dead in its tracks in the powerful Nazi breakthrough in the Ardennes. The Belgians later placed a monument at that very spot on the road near Stoumont Station. It stands there today.

Both tankers and infantrymen involved in this engagement received the prestigious Presidential Unit Citation for "outstanding performance of duty in action against the enemy" in the first days of the Battle of the Bulge.

As the Allied counterattack built up steam, the 740th joined the 82nd Airborne Division and pushed the Germans back to the heavily fortified *Siegfried Line,* attacking day and night and finally breaking through at Udenbreth. Then, following attachment to the 8th Infantry Division, the tankers drove across the Ruhr River at Duren, the Erft Canal at Modrath, and all the way to Cologne in heavy, and at times, desperate fighting.

That done, they loaded their tanks on railway flatcars and shuttled south to crack the *Siegfried Line* again, this time with the 63rd Infantry Division at Ensheim. Following this action, the call came down from the 8th Infantry Division to go back up north to Siegen to help split the Ruhr Pocket. Elements of the 740th were briefly attached to the 86th Infantry Division.

Quickly then, they were called back to the 82nd Airborne Division to help in the drive across the Elbe River. At the end, the *Daredevil Tankers* returned to their old friends of the 8th Infantry, in the defining drive to the Baltic Sea, to meet the Russians, as World War II in Europe drew to a close.

Meanwhile, a "Point System" had been devised in the European Theater of Operations for the discharge of eligible American soldiers. Points were given for the total number of months of service, total number of months overseas, number of awards and decorations, and the number of dependents. Those with the most points went home first.

And so, the *Daredevil Tankers,* individually and in small groups, gradually made their way home to put their lives back together. They had made and lost a lot of good friends along the way. Of course, things would never be the same.

The 740th Tank Battalion was deactivated on July 23, 1946, at Limburg/Lann, Germany. Those 740th tankers who remained in Germany were assigned to the 9th Infantry Division, 1st Division, U.S. Constabulary, or Military Government.

Afterword

And so the war was over for the *Daredevil Tankers* of the 740th Tank Battalion. In order, according to their standing in the point system in 1945 and 1946, the men—at first individually and then in groups—shook hands, hugged close friends who remained, shed a few tears, and said their goodbyes. Then they began the long trip home.

From the seaports of France, it was a five-day voyage home, and an incredible experience quite unlike the eleven torturous days going over. When that magnificent lady known as the Statue of Liberty came into view, with the great City of New York sparkling in the background, there was hardly a dry eye on deck.

Interestingly enough, all that emotion for at least one boatload of GIs with which the author is familiar, was, on their arrival, momentarily short lived. That ship pulled up to the docks in the midst of a massive docker strike. Strikers, with their ubiquitous signs, roamed all up and down the docks.

As the impassioned heroes of the war in Europe crowded the ship's rails, totally caught up in the thrill of being home, a strident voice flew up at them from out of the crowd down below: "What are you guys doing home? There's no jobs for you!" It was one of those unique ironies of war and peace in America.

Most of the returning GIs on board had, in fact, been on hold in France for six weeks or more because of the strike, anxiously awaiting the arrival of a ship to come for them. It was not as if they had been caught unaware, so they figured, *Oh well, this is America after all*.

Although the army had become a way of life for a certain few of the tankers who chose to stay in the service, separation from the army could hardly come quickly enough for most of them. And it usually came within days, as they were rotated out to their different states, and on to separation centers as near to their homes as possible.

It was here that the welcome began with more often than not, Mother and Dad, if both were still living by then. Wives and girlfriends. Brothers and sisters. Dear God, what a blessed comfort and relief. Endearing hugs and kisses. Then, finally home. Home at last. Back where it all began.

Of course, it took some getting used to. The war had entangled sixty-seven nations around the world, with some twenty-three million soldiers killed, along with approximately fifty-seven million civilians.[1] The United States military lost 407,000 killed,[2] and hundreds of thousands of soldiers were wounded or still missing. A great shadow was cast over the land.

The good old USA was a different place from the way the returning tankers remembered it. The small towns smaller. The big cities bigger. And even though the homeland was all still pretty much in one piece—unlike the destruction wrought throughout battleground Europe—it still took a lot of getting used to.

The strikers were right about the job situation around the country. And some commodities were still scarce. But rationing had ended.

The 35 mph speed limit imposed during the war was pretty much a thing of the past. Spiffy new cars were beginning to be seen now, but cost over $1,000. Gas was up to 15 cents a gallon. The average rent was $60 a month. A new two-bedroom frame house with bath could cost over $4600. All pretty tough with an average annual income of less than $2400.[3]

The return to civilian life was not going to be easy. And a rather severe housing shortage had developed in the cities. But they were confident that opportunity was there, and they accepted the responsibility. They had seen the world. And there was certainly no place like home, like America. Freedom— life, liberty, the pursuit of happiness—all seemed rather incredible after what they had seen.

So they went to work. They stuck their uniforms in the back of the closet and went back to their old jobs, or became craftsmen, insurance salesmen, or real estate agents. Some became big-city cops or small-town firemen. Some of the mechanical, carpentry, plumbing experts, truck drivers, or other entrepreneurial types began their own businesses.

The new GI Bill, America's commitment to the future, provided tuition and a small amount of spending money to those who would go back to the universities to pick up on chosen careers, or to enroll in higher education for the first time. It was a godsend.

As the returning *Citizen Soldiers* followed their dreams, they became proud laborers and engineers, farmers and ranchers, scientists, school teachers, accountants, lawyers, doctors, merchants, chiefs, even politicians—all the kinds of people who make America the great and diverse country that it is.

Tom Brokaw has called them The Greatest Generation, but individually they had no such concept of greatness. They married and raised their families as law-abiding, God-fearing Americans had always done. In the main, they worked hard, enjoyed or suffered the breaks as they came, and moved gradually ahead in life in the American way.

In the process, the vast wartime machine, which was America in World War II, became the most dynamic and influential peacetime economy in the world, helping to rebuild the countries and institutions of their former enemies, then hanging as tough as need be against the tyranny of their former ally, the Soviet Union, until democracy won out in the end. There is a lesson in there somewhere.

The Star Spangled Banner still sends shivers down their spines, and brings tears to the eyes of the old *Daredevil Tankers* who have made it this far. They are proud to pledge allegiance to the flag of the United States of America now as then, the magnificent stars and stripes they have always revered. They are quite simply unable to understand those who would dishonor it in any way.

More than sixty long years have come and gone since the *Daredevil Tankers* plunged into the breach to help throw back the Nazi juggernaut in the Battle of the Bulge in World War II. Peace is still not assured. Perhaps it never will be. There will always be those whose hearts are cold to our prosperity and way of life, and who would take us down.

America must remain vigilant. And, although our armies exist only to protect and defend democracy, our freedom is not necessarily free, and must be defended even as we strive to keep the peace.

May God continue to bless America.

Part IV

Addendum 1
740th Tank Battalion Memorials & Monuments
The Return to Belgium in 1999

Addendum 2
Whatever Became of Jochen Peiper?

Addendum 3
"Freedom Isn't Free" – Speech by Mathilde Schmetz

Notes and Documentation

Bibliography

Addendum 1

740th Tank Battalion Memorials and Monuments
The Return to Belgium in 1999

Battalion monuments and memorials that are emplaced around the country and across the seas:

- ❖ A stone monument in Memorial Park, adjacent to the Patton Museum at Fort Knox, Kentucky.

- ❖ A small metal plaque, and a massive German Mark VI King Tiger tank, captured by Staff Sergeant, later Second Lieutenant, Glenn D. George, inside the museum.

- ❖ A large brass plaque at Bouse, Arizona, at the old World War II railroad siding location.

- ❖ The Armor Monument at the Arlington National Cemetery in Washington, D.C.

- ❖ An engraved brick at the Patton Museum in Chiriaco Summit, California.

- ❖ Citation with other units on a rock plaque in front of City Hall at Malmedy, Belgium.

- ❖ A large plaque in the World War II Museum in La Gleize, Belgium, along with a large white cloth signed by members of the battalion.

- ❖ Numerous artifacts and photographs in Marcel and Mathilde Schmetz's Remember Museum in Clermont, Belgium.

- ❖ An imposing monument of granite and stone in Aubin-Neufchateau, Belgium.

The Return to Belgium in 1999

The men of the 740th Tank Battalion Association are quite proud of these memorials, and a number of the tankers have traveled far and wide to visit them. A few have reminisced at all of them. For most of the men, the memories of the return to Belgium for the dedication of the magnificent monument in Aubin-Neufchateau, Belgium on April 24, 1999, will linger forever.

Following a return to Europe to retrace their tracks in World War II, several members of the Association came back enthused about the possibility of an appropriate monument in Belgium dedicated to the Belgian people who had befriended the battalion in so many ways during the war, and at the same time, honor the battalion's fallen comrades. The project was put to the Association at their 25th annual reunion in 1997, was determined to be way past due, was then immediately approved, and a fundraising campaign was endorsed by the membership.

Marcel and Mathilde Schmetz of the **Remember 1939–1945 Museum in Clermont, Belgium**, were instrumental in the coordination and ultimate success of the project, along with Gaspard Schyns and a number of other dedicated citizens.

The choice site was, of course, the rural Belgian villages of **Aubin-Neufchateau** and **Mortroux**, whose townspeople had taken the battalion into their homes, and into their hearts, when they first arrived in the war zone in November 1944, just prior to their being thrust into the breach in the **Battle of the Bulge**. The villagers agreed, and the Honorable Mayor of Dalhem/Neufchateau, J.C. Dewez, designated the ground in Neufchateau's town square. An imposing monument was constructed in memory of the citizens of Neufchateau and Mortroux who were there at the time, and in honor of those in the 740th Tank Battalion who gave their lives in the battles of the Ardennes, the Rhineland, and Central Europe campaigns.

The names of the fallen heroes are engraved on the monument, along with the dedicatory inscription. The names of those members of the battalion whose contributions helped fund the memorial are at both sides. Some of those named were so honored by families and friends.

The monument's main structure stands nine feet tall and ten feet wide. It is cut of Belgian blue stone and black granite, and was constructed by Pesser Pierres and Marbre of Aubel, Belgium. The protectors of the monument are Monsieurs Desiré and Charles Wiels of Dalhem/Neufchateau. It's so impressive that it left the old tankers awestruck as it was unveiled. They were overcome with emotion.

So many memories brought back the tears.

46. Author's collection
The monument, with the village of Neufchateau in the background.

On the morning of the dedication, members and family of the battalion were loaded into vintage World War II American army vehicles and taken to the dedication in convoy. Children lined the way as the convoy arrived, cheering, clapping their hands in delight, waving American and Belgian flags, and giving out candy, just as the Americans had done for their parents and/or grandparents so many years ago. All manner of flags were hoisted about—here, there, everywhere.

Both Belgian and U.S. Military honor guards snapped to attention as the St. Barbe Band from Warsage struck up a tune. It was a moving experience.

The cheering crowd, estimated at close to one thousand, finally settled down, and the ceremony got underway. In addition to the twenty-nine members of the battalion and their families, numbering more than one hundred, a number of dignitaries were there: representatives of the King of Belgium, the U.S. Embassy in Brussels, the U.S. Army and Department of Defense, the Belgian Governor of the Province of Liege, the Minister of International Relations for the Province of Liege and the Walloon Region, and the Belgian Commandant of the Military in Liege, along with Mayor J.C. Dewez, Commune de Dalhem/Neufchateau, Mr. Hubai, the Superintendent of the U.S. Military Cemetery Henri-Chapelle, the Reverend Father Simons of the Church in Neufchateau, General Van Aubel, and Mrs. Hilda Rubel, widow of Lt. Col. George K. Rubel, commanding officer of the 740th Tank Battalion.

Following the speeches and ceremonies, a sit-down luncheon was served in relays in a huge tent the length of the square while the band played on. Later, the Belgian people called the tankers up by name, and presented them with medals of appreciation, inscribed "740th Daredevil, 1944-1999, THANK YOU, Neufchateau, 04.24.99."

The group of Belgians, headed by Marcel and Mathilde Schmetz and Gaspard Schyns, hosted the tankers and their families for the next several days. They guided the group in large see-through buses to the various towns and villages in the area that the 740th had fought their way through so long ago.

One of the most impressive moments came that first day after the dedication of the monument when the group visited the **Netherlands American Cemetery in Margraten, Netherlands**, where at least three of their own were laid to rest in these hallowed grounds, among the 8,301 headstones. Beautiful white crosses in perfect unison, stretching out as far as the eye could see. Tankers and families alike searched for loved ones or close friends known to be buried there.

It is a sanctuary. Sixty-five acres of gently rolling farmland. Memorials everywhere.

O Lord / Support us all the day long / Until the shadows lengthen / And the evening comes / And the fever of life is over / And our work is done. / Then in Thy mercy / Grant us a safe lodging / And a Holy Rest / And peace at last.

At the chapel: *Honor*Faith*Valor.*

And at the tower, which rises 101 feet above the Court of Honor, a bronze sculpture group: *New life from war's destruction proclaims man's immortality and hope for peace.*

The observation platform was reached by 149 steps: *In memory of the valor and the sacrifices which hallow this soil.*

And at the north wall: *Here are the names of Americans who gave their lives in the service of their country and who sleep in unknown graves.*

At the last, on top of the hill, at the axis of the mall, is the flag.

The Henri-Chapelle American Cemetery is in Homberg, Belgium. It's a magnificent fifty-seven acres at the crest of a ridge. An inspiring site. Seven of the 740th's fallen tankers are buried here, along with 7,982 other brave soldiers, most of whom died in the Battle of the Bulge. The group was met on site by the loyal Belgians, who had planned the trip so carefully, and who had come out early this day to locate the seven 740th graves, darken the print on the crosses, and place flowers and flags. Remarkable people, those Belgians.

On the plaque at the Henri-Chapelle Chapel: *1941–1945 In proud remembrance of the achievements of her sons and in humble tribute to their sacrifices this memorial has been erected by the United States of America.*

In the auditorium of the Schmetz's **Remember Museum** in Clermont that evening, the scheduled meal at the hotel fell through, and the Belgians pitched in with drinks all around, heaping stacks of sandwiches, and Belgian waffles for dessert. The Belgian Gaspard Schyns raised his glass and offered the first clinking of glasses and a simple toast: "Here we are to America and Belgium." He passed out candy bars, saying, "This is for all the chocolate you gave us kids when you were here during the war."

The fellowship and festivities that followed provided an evening of pure delight. An impromptu talent show of singing, dancing, music, hijinks, and whoopee had the crowd cheering all the way through. All MC'd by the inimitable Douglas Tanner.

The Remember Museum is filled with mementos and memorabilia left by Americans of the 1st Infantry Division who liberated the village of Clermont in late fall, 1944, when Marcel Schmetz was a boy of eleven. He recalls breaking into tears when they were called into the Battle of the Bulge. During occupation by the Germans, Clermont was split down the middle, Schmetz said—the Belgians on one side, the Germans on the other. "They came to our house and said we were now Germans and gave us new passports. Had I been seventeen, I would have been drafted into the German Army."[1] They were given German schoolbooks.

"We had curfews and black-outs of our homes. If a German soldier was walking down the street and saw a light, he would shoot through the window at the bulb. We listened and watched for the planes and buzz bombs during the days, and slept in the cellars at night. Even if we had coupons, there was not much in the shops. Everything had to go to the German Army," said Mathilde Schmetz.[2]

A completely restored Sherman tank stands guard beneath the Belgian and American flags, just outside the museum. Although it was a challenge getting up and down, the old tankers swarmed the tank, inside and out. Inside the museum, the tankers were encouraged to scrawl their names on a masterfully restored GI truck. Pictorial displays and representative dioramas utilize dummy figures and authentic World War II field gear and equipment to depict times as they were then.

The museum is private, near the Henri-Chapelle American Cemetery, and is open by appointment only. "If you're American, you visit for free," said Mathilde. "You just need to call first." To arrange a tour, call civ 087-44-6181.

The Remember Museum is a labor of love for the Belgian couple. They have poured their hearts and souls into the endeavor through the years. Belgian school children are frequent visitors for the guided World War II historical tours and lectures.

The tankers' tour rolled into **Sprimont** the next day and gathered for a picture on the spot where the maintenance depot stood on December 18, 1944. It's where they worked through the night preparing a ragtag group of tanks to plunge into the breach at the German breakthrough in the Battle of the Bulge. **Remouchamps**, the jump off point. Then down into the **Valley of the Ambleve**: **Targnon**, where Teller mines blew the author's C Company tank on the second day of combat. **Stoumont**: where the 740th had left four shot-up tanks in the road, three of them afire. A lot of memories were made around the embattled St. Edouard Sanatorium.

The tour backtracked to the monument **Ici** (Here) that stands at the farthest point of the German advance in 1944, the spot where the 740th had helped to blunt the *Kampfgruppe Peiper* spearhead. There, the American and Belgian flags stood side by side. Shockingly, the American flag flew upside down. The tankers piled out of the buses, uprooted the twenty-foot pole, and righted the American flag. A cheer went up from the crowd. It was quite a moment.

While at a luncheon provided by the **City of Stoumont** in their honor at the **Chateau de Froidcourt**, the tankers could hear echoes of long ago as Lt. Col. Rubel's "borrowed" 155 mm gun pounded **La Gleize** from the terrace of the castle during the Battle of the Bulge. **The Chateau**, not open to the public, was made available to the 740th that day by the owners, Monsieur et Madame Charles-Albert de Harenne.

Belgian children waving American flags came out with their families to greet the 740th caravan as it made its way into **La Gleize**. One of those monster Tiger tanks, No. 213, stood menacingly outside the **December 1944 Historical Museum**. Inside, there were more pictorials, displays, and dioramas of the time. The narrator of a documentary film there noted, "Tanks from the 740th Tank Battalion destroyed three German tanks in a matter of minutes."

Then they went on to **Spa**, where the U.S. First Army had its headquarters—the "resort" where the 740th moved into two hotels for a respite from the fighting just after Christmas 1944, only to be called back on line with the 82nd Airborne the very next day.

The next morning, on a tour of the **Pesser Pierres et Marbres** monument factory in Aubel, the tankers were given souvenir bars of granite used in the monument in Neufchateau. At an unusual ceremony at the City Hall, the Mayor of Aubel presented an Honorary Diploma to each tanker as he was called forward, and then pictures were taken. Following the ceremony, a luncheon was provided at the **Restaurant Jean Deguelle**, a delightful get-together with the Belgians.

Later, at the **Mardasson Memorial in Bastogne**, honoring the American soldiers of the Battle of the Bulge, the tankers were awestruck by the beauty of the monument, and literally felt chills run up and down their spines as they read an inscription: *Think for a moment: what if, not too long ago, heroes had not stood where you stand?*

The magnificent memorial is laid out in the form of a star and is engraved with the story of the Battle of the Bulge. In the Bastogne Historical Center, the course of the battle is traced on an illuminated model, and the group watched scenes filmed during the actual fighting.

Nearby, a German cemetery stretched out a great distance. The grass was green, but the dark gray crosses were in sharp contrast to the crisp white crosses of the American cemeteries, and gravesites were spaced widely apart, each holding three or more soldiers. The tankers spread out across the area, noting names and dates, and remembering that these were boys—sons, brothers, friends—just like those they left behind years ago.

The visit to **Udenbreth, Germany,** was an emotional experience for them all. Weather and gunfire had taken a heavy toll on the tankers there. Casualties were high, and the 740th had attacked day and night. This was the place where they had first broke through the *Siegfried Line.* A long line of massive dragon's teeth still snaked across the hillside and ran through the trees, clear out of sight. It was crusted with rust and mold, heavily nicked, and even shattered. It stood waist- to shoulder high, and it was still there. Unbelievable.

The tankers piled out of the buses and roamed through the formidable, top-blunted, cone-shaped stones, conversing excitedly, or quietly, in groups of twos and threes. Remembering.

As they wandered afield, they spread out and approached the concrete and steel pillboxes where the Germans had zeroed their big guns on the most vulnerable breakthrough points in the line—pillboxes where they had locked in their soldiers so they *had* to fight to the death. A few of the tankers still had the keys to those pillboxes they had confiscated at the time.

The next stop was the **Memorial American**, and the long, curved rock wall at **Baugnez**, where the **Malmedy Massacre** took place:

USA – BELGIUM / To the prisoners of war of overseas / Who liberated the east-districts / And were the victims / Of Nazie's [sic] cruelty.

It was a poignant reminder of the inhumanity of that war. Bob Cole and Dwight Davis, who had been there searching for tankers among the frozen bodies just after the massacre, stood this day at the edge of the field, and were overcome with emotion.

A quick tour through **Camp Eisenberg, a Belgian military camp and museum.** Then at the end of the day, on to **Malmedy**, where the tankers and their families spread out around the square to buy some Belgian candy and visit the lovely little shops.

The Americans were all too recognizable in their white 740th caps and were stopped on the sidewalk, or while crossing the street, and at almost every shop by a Belgian man who just wanted to shake hands and chat; or a mother and child who wanted to thank them and hug or kiss cheeks; or boys and girls who just wanted to touch them or hold out a limp hand to shake. Those too shy to come up to visit just bowed acknowledgement as the Americans walked by. It was a brief, shining moment for the tankers and their families, not ever to be forgotten.

And so it was that the dedication of the Monument at Neufchateau and the tour of their triumphs and heartbreaks in the Battle of the Bulge ended that week in 1999 for the old tankers, who are all in their 80s now. Still, the memories linger on—the absolute horror and agony of war itself, the stench of the killing field, the fear of failure, the consequences of defeat, the freezing cold, the closeness of friends made and lost, and the tragic plight of the people caught up in the tragedy of it all.

Was it worth it? All the blood, sweat, and tears? Would such sacrifice of free men in the defense of a free country make a difference?

Yes. Yes, of course.

Addendum 2

Whatever Became of Jochen Peiper?

With his right hand raised, and in front of a skull-and-crossbones banner, Jochen Peiper pledged his life to Germany's new ruler. "I swear to you, Adolf Hitler, as *Führer* and Reich Chancellor, loyalty and bravery. I vow to you, and those you have named to command me, obedience unto death. So help me God."

It was 1935. Peiper was 20 years old, and it was here that he became a member of Hitler's new Praetorian Guard, the *SS Leibstandarte Adolf Hitler*.[1]

Peiper's given name was actually Joachim, but he preferred the more common German nickname, Jochen. Early on in his career, he was selected to serve on the personal staff of *Reichsführer* SS Heinrich Himmler, where he quickly became a favorite. Here, in 1939, he married a secretary to Himmler, and they would have a son and two daughters. After returning to active duty, he was soon called back on a second attachment to Himmler, where he apparently developed powerful friends, even coming to Hitler's attention. As the war evolved, he was wounded in action in France in 1940, and in Russia in 1941. In several tortuous tours of duty, he distinguished himself on the Eastern front against the Russians, fought in Italy following the Allied invasion of Sicily in 1943, and rose steadily in influence and rank.[2]

47. Photo Credit: Wikipedia
Public Domain

Jochen Peiper

Peiper was headstrong, but he was recognized as a superior tactician in battle. He won the Knight's Cross of the Iron Cross with Oak Leaves, and other prestigious medals along the way. Heads wagged, and many people believed he was headed for general by age 30.

Well-versed in the social graces, Peiper could be quite charming in polite company. However, he was a ruthless warrior and demanding of his troops, as well as himself, and he had a rough-edged reputation for arrogance within the SS and among his superiors.

Hitler's last offensive exploded into the Ardennes at 5:30 a.m. on Saturday, December 16, 1944. But it was not until the early morning hours of Sunday, December 17, that the 29-year-old *Obersturmbannführer* (SS Lieutenant Colonel) Jochen Peiper, commanding *Kampfgruppe Peiper,* launched his tanks out of

Germany's Eifel, and through the *Siegfried Line* into Belgium.

Peiper's battle group included his own heavily reinforced 1st Panzer Regiment, and was the main striking group, and arguably the most powerful of the four *Kampfgruppen* out of the *Leibstandarte Adolf Hitler 1st SS Panzer Division.*

The weather was desperately cold, foggy, and misty. The forest was heavily wooded and blanketed with snow. The narrow, winding roads, clogged with traffic. His column of tanks, half-tracks, and other vehicles, including horse-drawn artillery, reached back for miles.

Crossing into Belgium, the *Kampfgruppe* began to stretch out and break loose. Although he had had four tanks shot out from under him, Peiper was standing in his own Panther when he entered the first little village of Lanzerath, already in German hands. Still, his column balked there. The Germans had given up for the night and gone to bed. Peiper was furious, ran roughshod over their colonel, and ultimately routed the recalcitrant troops into a pre-dawn attack on Honsfield. There was little opposition moving into the village, where the German surprise caught most of the Americans in their sleep, all too often finding themselves prisoners before they could get their defenses up. And, although the Americans pulled themselves together enough to disrupt the latter parts of the column, Peiper rolled relentlessly on.

By dawn on Sunday, December 17, the German spearhead was on its way to Büllingen, where the column apparently ran into bazooka fire and suffered some losses. Resistance was scattered and quickly crushed by the Kampfgruppe's superior numbers and firepower. An American fuel dump was captured, providing an incalculable opportunity to refuel. The column did catch damage, and was slowed considerably just outside of Büllingen when they ran afoul of some American Thunderbolts on the prowl.

Well behind schedule, Peiper took off across open fields from Büllingen to Moderscheid, then on through Schoppen and Ondeval. The going got tough as the heavy German tanks began to slip and slide, and often sunk in the slushy ground, having to be towed. The situation became confused and disorganized. But the *Obersturmbannführer* stormed and prodded up and down the line, and finally shoved the column on into Thirimont, deep into American territory.

He made a false start out of Thirimont, however, heading for the Ambleve Bridge at Ligneuville, which he understood was an American headquarters of some kind. The big panzers became stymied by a little stream in the valley, and had to backtrack and turn north to the tiny settlement of Baugnez, just south of Malmedy. It was here at the Baugnez crossroads that his *Kampfgruppe* ran into B Battery of the 285th Field Artillery Battalion, precipitating the infamous Malmedy massacre. Interestingly enough, Peiper is purported to have left the area before the shooting of the American prisoners took place. Still, the massacre would be his final undoing.

From Baugnez, the *Kampfgruppe* tracked back south to Ligneuville, having made nearly a full circle to get there. The Ambleve Bridge was secured after a brief firefight, and Peiper was on his way to Stavelot, which appeared to be well defended by now. And, with his battle group spread out all the way back to Ligneuville, he decided to hold his attack on Stavelot until morning.

Monday, December 18: The *Kampfgruppe* opened up with mortars and artillery, then Peiper launched his panzers across the bridge, and a hot firefight ensued. As the Americans gradually withdrew from the overwhelming force of the attack, Peiper pushed his panzers west to Trois Points. Here, the Americans were dug in, fought tough, and quickly blew the two main bridges. Peiper then turned north to La Gleize.

There was no American opposition in La Gleize, although some Belgians were killed as the panzers machine-gunned the town. Still, more Belgians were shot at the Cheneaux Bridge as the column moved on Cheneaux and Rahier. The battle group paid a goodly price for this strip of ground as it was hammered by a series of allied air strikes.

Peiper pushed on and was soon headed west for a bridge at Lienne Creek, hoping to turn north from there and hit Werbomont. However, the Lienne was flooding, and his lead tanks were unable to make it across. He decided to withdraw, backtrack to cross the Ambleve at Cheneaux, then advance to Stoumont.

That night, from his headquarters in the area of the Chateau de Froidcourt, Peiper prepared for the attack on Stoumont the next morning. Having learned that Stavelot was now being threatened, he immediately dispatched reinforcements there to help secure the town and keep the communication and supply route open. With the fuel situation fast becoming a problem, other units were ordered to occupy La Gleize for the same purpose. The troops and tanks designated for the advance on Stoumont encamped in the forest area of the Chateau for the night, and braced themselves for the morning attack, thankful for the brief respite.

Meanwhile, the American defenses facing this breakthrough in the Battle of the Bulge had begun to stiffen. The 30th Infantry Division was gradually regrouping on the right (Spa) side of *Kampfgruppe Peiper's* planned advance, and the 82nd Airborne Division had arrived to strengthen the left (Werbomont) side of the advance.

Tuesday, December 19: Heavy, misty fog oozed up and down the valley that morning, so there was no mortar nor artillery barrage announcing the *Kampfgruppe's* coming. Instead, the German panzer grenadiers and infantry filtered in around the village roadblocks and defenses as Peiper's panzers hit Stoumont all out. A couple of Panthers were accounted for, but it was really no contest, as the *Kampfgruppe* was all too quick and powerful. American casualties mounted, and a large number were taken prisoner and back to the Chateau de Froidcourt, which now served as both a holding compound for prisoners and an emergency aid station for the wounded.

From Stoumont, the *Kampfgruppe* continued its menacing mile march over the narrow, twisting road west, through a tiny settlement called Targnon —where trouble began to spark. Heavy American artillery fire greeted them as they emerged from the village, driving them back briefly. But they rallied and began to drive forward once more toward Stoumont Station, just a few bends in the road dead ahead.

In the face of such force, American tanks and troops on the scene began a fighting retreat. It was touch and go. The 740th Tank Battalion, along with elements of the 30th Infantry Division's 119th Infantry Regiment, was ordered into the breach.

There are varying accounts of exactly what happened then, seemingly dependent upon timing, according to Michael Reynolds in his book, *The Devil's Adjutant: Jochen Peiper, Panzer Leader.*[3] But timing is a unique thing in war, and there is complete agreement that Peiper's panzers were stopped dead in their tracks just past Stoumont Station.

Into the Breach details this action, with firsthand accounts in Chapter 11, as the 740th Tank Battalion and Old Hickory's 119th Infantry, smashed headlong into *Kampfgruppe Peiper,* driving the German spearhead attack back through Targnon, Stoumont, and La Gleize. The 740th *Daredevil Tankers* continued the attack until they were relieved from attachment to the 30th Infantry, and then assigned to hook up with the 82nd Airborne Division near Werbomont on December 29, 1944. The 740th's Lt. Col. Rubel said it was the first good news to come out of the Battle of the Bulge. Major elements of the battalion received the Presidential Unit Citation for a job well done.

On January 16, 1945, patrols from the U.S. First and Third Armies linked up in Houffalize, cutting off the leading edge of the German penetration through the Ardennes. It was the beginning of the end for the Battle of the Bulge, which was officially ended on January 28, 1945.

Into the Breach provides some detail regarding the retreat of *Kampfgruppe Peiper* from Stoumont Station, Targnon, Stoumont, and La Gleize. There is no doubt that the heavy loss of men and material, and the stress of the withdrawal took its toll on Jochen Peiper. Back in his own lines, he appeared to have a nervous breakdown, requiring convalescence.

In a matter of weeks, however, he was back as a *Standartenführer* (SS Colonel), commanding a panzer group in Hungary, and later in Austria. Germany was under continuing pressure from all sides.

Hitler had become disenchanted with his *Leibstandarte,* and in a moment of unreasoning fury, ordered his SS division stripped of their armbands. This angered Peiper and his troops, and the Imperial Guard broke off with their *Fuhrer*.[4] It would not be long now.

With the unconditional surrender of Germany on May 8, 1945, the *Leibstandarte* was quickly dismantled — vehicles and the troops were ordered west to become prisoners of war, hopefully escaping the devastating Russian advance. Peiper and a handful of henchmen took off for home in Bavaria, and Peiper very nearly made it.

Unhappily for him, he somehow caught the suspicious eye of an American patrol a couple of days later and was taken to a POW encampment. In time, his true identity became known, and among other crimes, he was charged as a suspected war criminal involved in the killing of American POWs near Malmedy. He was considered arrogant and not to be trusted.

Peiper was moved from camp to camp, from interrogation center to interrogation center, confronted with survivors of the Baugnez shootings, kept in solitary confinement for weeks at a time, and finally in April 1946, was officially charged with war crimes.

At the military trial in Dachau, the court was composed of six American military officers, with a brigadier general in charge. There was tremendous news coverage around the world.

Peiper and his commanding generals, along with seventy members of his *Kampfgruppe*, stood charged with the deaths of hundreds of Americans, more than one hundred Belgians, and the American soldiers at the Baugnez crossroads in the Malmedy Massacre. Witnesses told of his orders "to drive on relentlessly, give no quarter, and take no prisoners."[5]

On July 16, the court sentenced forty-three of the accused, including Peiper, to death by hanging. Twenty-two got life imprisonment, and the others got between ten and twenty years in prison.[6]

As the commander of his *Kampfgruppe*, Peiper accepted responsibility. American Major Hal McCown testified for the defense that Peiper had treated the American prisoners quite well in La Gleize, and the chief American defense counsel, Lt. Col. Willis Everett Jr., was ultimately convinced that there had been a miscarriage of justice.

In time, all of the death sentences handed out at Dachau were commuted, and all the prisoners were eventually released. After more than eleven years as a prisoner, and nearly five years in solitary confinement, Peiper was the last of the accused to be paroled, in December 1956.

In 1958, Peiper was released from parole. By 1969, he owned a small plot of land in Traves, France, doing translation work on military and historical books to make his living.

Eventually, he was identified by the French Communist Party on information from the East German authority. The known Nazi war criminal became an embarrassment to the French authorities. A hate campaign began. Peiper got letters and phone calls telling him his house and dogs would be burned. He sent his wife away for safety. He never saw her again.

On Bastille Day, July 14, 1976, flames spewed from Peiper's house. The authorities found charred remains inside. Dental records tended to prove it was Peiper.

The evidence: a grotesquely shrunken body, and nearby, an old .22 rifle and a .38 Colt pistol. On the terrace, a 12-gauge shotgun. All with shots fired. No shots appeared to have been fired into the house, and the police believed that Peiper had fired from inside and outside of the house in an attempt to fight off fire-bombers. Several Molotov cocktails were found in and about the old wooden house, which had evidently burned furiously.[7]

Peiper was 61 years old.

Addendum 3

The following is an excerpt of a speech given by Mathilde Schmetz. It was presented at the 740th Tank Battalion Reunion Memorial Service on Saturday, September 5, 2015.

740th Tank Battalion Association
70th Anniversary Victory in Europe 1945-2015
42nd Annual Reunion Memorial Service
September 5, 2015

"FREEDOM ISN'T FREE"
Mathilde Schmetz

"It is an honor for us to be here with all of you for the 42nd Reunion of the 740th Tank Battalion Association, and especially for this Memorial Service . . .

I would like to thank the 740th Tank Battalion Association and the members of that unit who generously paid for all the expenses of our trip. If it wasn't for them, we would not be here today.

For those whom we have not had the pleasure of meeting, we are Mathilde and Marcel Schmetz from Belgium, nicknamed by our American friends: 'The Belgian M&Ms.' We are the creators of the Remember Museum 39–45 of Thimister-Clermont in Belgium.

Belgium is a small country, especially compared to Texas! It has eleven million people, and three languages are spoken: French, Dutch, and German.

In 1933, when Hitler became the Leader of Germany, Belgium realized that something was again going on. Even though Belgium was a neutral country, the Germans built a defense fortification line a few miles inside the German border, and it was called the Siegfried Line. On May 10th, 1940, the German Army invaded Belgium and took back the villages they had lost after WWI. The German Army was very powerful, and after eighteen days of fighting, the Belgium King surrendered with his soldiers, becoming Prisoners of War for the next five years.

In 1940, near the end of October, the German Army advanced the borders once again, this time annexing ten more villages. Clermont, where we live, was part of those villages. The newly annexed villages became German, while the rest of Belgium was living under German rules.

Marcel, my husband, was 7 years old when the area where his family lived was annexed to Germany. He was forced to attend primary school in a small, neighboring village where only German was allowed to be spoken.

He and the people of the annexed areas were not trusted by the Germans. They lost all their freedoms and were very controlled. For example, one major freedom they lost: the ability to lock their doors. To most people, a key is just a little piece of metal, but it was a big freedom lost, as the SS were allowed to come into their homes, day or night, without permission or knocking on the door.

The German Army took from the civilians anything they could use. First, they took the homing pigeons, and it was forbidden for the civilians to have pigeons. Then they took the horses. Horses in their army were more important than men, as a man cannot pull a cannon! They even had gas masks for the horses, just in case somebody would use gas like in WWI. They confiscated, also, everything you had made of copper, such as doorknobs, decorations, and all the bells in the churches. They melted the metal to make ammunition.

They knew everything about you. If you had many chickens, you were required to bring to the German Commandatur Officer that many eggs. If you had that many cows, you should bring so much milk to the Commandatur. That's why a war is not just difficult for soldiers but also involves civilians who will suffer because of war. War is just hell. Any war!

On September 11, 1944, the whole area where we live was liberated by the soldiers of the First Infantry Division, thus 9/11 is a very sad day for America, but was once a very happy day for Belgium.

The American soldiers fought then around Aachen in the Hürtgen Forest. With winter approaching, some soldiers took a break at Marcel's parent's farm, which had been transformed into an enormous camp for 110 G.I.s, belonging to the 1st I.D. 26th Regiment 'Delta Company.'

This was a paradise for the 11-year-old boy who had been deprived of everything the previous four years, and changed him for life. Marcel was impressed and transformed by the contrast existing between the previous restrictions and bad treatment during the German annexation, in contrast to the generosity of the American G.I.s.

In the meantime, the tankers of the 740th Tank Battalion were taken into the homes of the people at Aubin-Neufchateau, a little village near Marcel's family farm. The next [few] weeks were a dream until the beginning of the Battle of the Bulge, when soldiers or tankers left in a hurry for new battles, leaving all their personal items behind. As a result, the Schmetz family, and many other families, were in front of a real 'Ali Baba Cavern.' While some families used or sold off the G.I.s' items, Marcel kept them in respect and in memory of those who had left.

Over the next forty years, Marcel taught himself to restore vehicles and opened his own body shop. In 1991, thanks to a car accident that I made (which some friends say on purpose), he and I met. Together, we established the Remember Museum with all the items left on his parent's farm. Touched and impressed by the respect we have shown these items, more and more American WWII Veterans and family members chose to donate their belongings, confident their donated items and their military service would never be forgotten.

We have so many friends because of our dedication to the former American soldiers, but also because of our concern for the future, and living our life as a bridge between the World War II veterans and veterans of the wars that have occurred since. We are not caught in one time, but we are moving into other wars and sacrifices.

Over the years, our visitors have been mainly Americans, but we have more and more Germans visiting. The Germans seem more reserved but also appreciate the very personal nature and sensibility of the way in which the museum has been set up. At our place, there is no judgment or resentment. Only REMEMBER! We don't ask for recognition. It is just a labor of love and respect for the Americans!

As proof of our dedication, a few years ago we were honored to receive the Outstanding Public Service Award from the Supreme Allied Commander in Europe. Last week, we were honored again with a 'Proclamation" by the City Council in Farmersville, Texas, (the hometown of Audie Murphy) proclaiming Saturday, August 29th (2015) as Marcel and Mathilde Schmetz Day. The Proclamation submitted by the Gerens was presented to us by the mayor. The main reason for these awards is that we operate the Museum, we organize ceremonies, and host free of charge, WWII American Veterans, WWII American Orphans, and young American Veterans of the wars in Iraq and Afghanistan.

Of course, we have less WWII Veterans coming, but more and more WWII Orphans. They still miss their father[s]. These children were never able to have closure or express their feelings in The States, as that war happened in Europe or in the Pacific. To us, it's a forgotten generation, and we hope it helps when they are able to come and see where their father[s] fought and died. They can also realize that someone needed to free us from the Nazi Dictatorship and that their father[s] came and made the ultimate sacrifice for all of us. I feel that after their visit, they can better understand, and they seem to be very proud of their fathers. We strive also to let the young, wounded warriors of today know that we will always love the Americans, and that we are also touched by what they have done.

We will never be able to know the horrors endured by those who gave their life, and we will never have a chance to look them in the eyes and simply say 'thank you!' to the families, and those veterans who fought for us, we offer our thanks for their spending countless hours, days, months, and years far away from loved ones, often in extreme and dangerous conditions. We are thankful to these veterans for fighting for our freedoms, and especially for those who made the ultimate sacrifice for all of us.

Now, regarding the ceremonies we organize, there is one closest to our heart, which is the *Ceremony for the Adoption of American Grave Sites*. Every year, we hold a ceremony at which we give out the 'Certificates of Adoption' to those wishing to adopt a grave site. We personally have adopted fourteen graves of young American soldiers who died for our freedom. Adopting a grave doesn't mean we work or maintain the crosses, but we go as often as possible to pray over them and lay flowers. Of course, all the graves of the 740th Tank Battalion men who are resting forever at the American Cemeteries in Belgium are adopted by local, dedicated friends.

To finish my speech, on behalf of my husband and myself, I would like to thank again, very warmly, the 740th Tank Battalion friends, especially Mark Hatchel, and all the American friends for their support of the Remember Museum, to help us keep the memory alive, and to remind all of us to 'Never Forget.'

We love you, and may God bless America, and may God bless Belgium."

Notes and Documentation by Chapter

Part I

Chapter 1: America at War, 1944

1. Allied casualty figures from MacDonald, *The Mighty Endeavor*, 308.
2. For the complete story, see MacDonald, *The Mighty Endeavor*, 328-330.
3. Average income indicated here and prices quoted for a new car and a loaf of bread in the following paragraphs from KardLetts, *1944 Pages of Time, A Nostalgia News Report*, 13.
4. Casualty figures from Bradley, *A General's Life*, 304.

Chapter 2: The 740th on the Move
And FDR's Re-Election

1. For the complete story of the president's day, see Bishop, *FDR's Last Year*, 177-180.
2. Ibid., 180.
3. First and Ninth Army losses during the Fall Campaign from MacDonald, *The Mighty Endeavor*, 386.

Chapter 3: Counteroffensive: In the Ardennes

1. Ambrose, *Citizen Soldiers*, 185.
2. Numbers and odds from MacDonald, *The Mighty Endeavor*, 397.
3. Anecdotal material from Whiting, *Skorzeny*, 96.
4. Dupuy, et al, *Hitler's Last Gamble*, 65.
5. In March to Victory, edited by Tony Hall, Stephen Dietrich in Chapter Seven, "The Ardennes Counteroffensive," states that Peiper's men murdered 111 Belgian civilians and 353 U.S. soldiers in a dozen separate incidents, 115.
6. Bradley, *A General's Life, 356.*
7. Ibid., 359.
8. MacDonald, *A Time for Trumpets*, 432.
9. Ibid., 431.
10. Ibid., 434-436.
11. Ibid., 441. See also Rubel, *Daredevil Tankers*, 56.
12. MacDonald, *A Time for Trumpets*, 441.

Chapter 4: Into the Breach

1. Telephone interview with C.B. Seay 7-21-03, personal interview 9-24-04, and

     follow up calls and correspondence.

2.   Telephone interview with Harold Henry 7-21-03 and subsequent calls and correspondence.

3.   Personal interview with Charlie Loopey at his home in Sanger, Texas, 9-19-03.

4.   The story of the 740th's C Company's "bastard tanks" smashing headlong into Jochen Peiper's lead column in the Ambleve Valley in their first few minutes of combat was first told in Lt. Col. George Rubel's history of the 740th, *Daredevil Tankers,* 57-58, right after the war. It was later recounted in some detail in MacDonald's *A Time for Trumpets,* 441-442, and in various other military histories. The 740th's Charley Loopey, C.B. Seay, and Henry L. Harold were there, involved in the action, and quoted here. In his book, *The Devil's Adjutant,* 147-151, Michael Reynolds puts forth a contrary point of view based on a detailed analysis of the element of timing.

5.   Rubel, *Daredevil Tankers,* 58.

Part II

Chapter 5: The 740th Comes Alive

1.   Rubel, *op. cit.,* 9.

2.   Ibid.

3.   Kennett, *G.I. The American Soldier in World War II,* 6.

4.   Ibid., 4-7.

5.   Statistics were drawn from Kennett's excellent treatise on "The Draft" in Chapter 1 of his book, *G.I.: The American Soldier in World War II,* 3-23.

6.   Kennet, *op. cit.,* 37.

7.   *Chronological History of 740th Medium Tank Battalion (Special),* War Department Records Branch, A.G.O., 1.

8.   Ibid.

9.   Ibid., 2.

10. Ibid.

Chapter 6: On the Home Front

1.   *KardLets,* 1943 Pages of Time, (A Nostalgia News Report), 20.

2.   Bailey and the Editors of Time-Life Books, *The Homefront: USA,* 107.

Chapter 7: Special Training Group

1.   *Chronological History of 740 Medium Tank Battalion (Special), op. cit.,* 2.

2.   Rubel, *op. cit.,* 13.

3. CAMA history and statistics from "General Patton's Desert Training Center," by Brigadier General David C. Henley, one page, printed in the *740th Tank Battalion Association Newsletter,* no date, Harry F. Miller, Secretary.

4. Rubel, *op. cit.,* 17.

5. *Chronological History of 740 Medium Tank Battalion (Special), op. cit.,* 2.

6. Ibid., 3.

7. Ibid.

8. Rubel, *op. cit.,* 20.

9. *Chronological History of 740 Medium Tank Battalion (Special), op. cit.,* 3.

10. Rubel, *op. cit.,* 20.

11. *Chronological History of 740 Medium Tank Battalion (Special), op. cit.,* 3.

12. Report of *The General Board: United States Forces, European Theater, Armored Special Equipment,* "CDL Tanks," 35.

13. Fuller, Maj. Gen. J.F.C. "The Strange Story of the CDL Tank," *Marine Corps Gazette,* April 1952, 15.

14. Rubel, *op. cit.,* 22.

15. Ibid., 25.

16. Ibid., 29.

17. Bishop, *FDR's Last Year,* 27-28.

18. Laffin, *Hitler Warned Us, 63.*

19. *Adolf Hitler,* a paste-in picture album, 123.

Chapter 8: Return to Fort Knox

1. Rubel, *op. cit.,* 30.

2. *Chronological History of 740 Medium Tank Battalion (Special), op. cit.,* 4.

3. Rubel, *op. cit.,* 33.

4. David Eisenhower, *Eisenhower: At War 1943-45,* 296-297.

5. Ibid., 297.

6. Bradley, *A General's Life, 255.*

Chapter 9: "We're Going Over . . ."

1. Correspondence with C.O. "Chigger" Webster, 11/24/2000, and subsequent personal follow-up interviews.

2. MacDonald, *The Mighty Endeavor,* 320-321.

3. Rubel, *op. cit.,* 34-35.

4. C.O. Webster correspondence and personal interview.

5. Rubel, *op. cit.,* 39.

6. C.O. Webster correspondence and personal interview.

7. Reynolds, *The Rich Relations: The American Occupation of Britain 1942-1945, xxiv.*

8. *Mosley and the editors of* Time-Life Books in The Battle of Britain, 102.

Chapter 10: Marching as to War

1. Bishop, *FDR's Last Year,* 113.

2. In a cooperative venture of appreciation and long-lasting friendship, the 740th Tank Battalion Association dedicated on April 24, 1999, and the citizens of Neufchateau, Belgium, agreed to maintain in perpetuity, a monument in the town square. *See Part IV, Addendum 1, 740th Tank Battalion Memorials and Monuments: The Return to Belgium in 1999,* 265.

Part III

Chapter 11: Breakthrough in the Ardennes

1. MacDonald, *The Mighty Endeavor,* 397.

2. Excerpted from "Dark Moments" by Billy C. Ritchie in Rubel, *op. cit.,* 243.

3. Excerpted from "Dark Moments" by John A. Thompson in Rubel, *op. cit.,* 242.

Chapter 12: Into the Breach

1. Rubel, *op. cit.,* 238.

2. Bradley, *A General's Life,* 361.

3. MacDonald, *A Time for Trumpets,* 446-447.

4. Ibid.

5. Ibid.

6. Rubel, *op. cit.,* 62. See also David Oglensky's Silver Star citation, same reference, 281.

7. Excerpted from "Dark Moments" by Robert Russo in Rubel, *op. cit.,* 241-242.

8. Rubel, *op. cit.,* 63. See also James Flowers Bronze Star award, same reference, 289.

9. MacDonald, *op. cit.,* 456-457. See also James D. "Red" Berry's Silver Star citation in Rubel, *op. cit.,* 277.

10. See Charles Powers' and Charley Loopey's Silver Star citations in Rubel, *op. cit.,* 281-282 and 280 respectively.

11. Toland, *Battle: The Story of the Bulge,* 197.

12. Personal interview with Lloyd P. Wright, 8/30/02, and subsequent meetings.

13. Toland, *op. cit.,* 206.

14. Eisenhower, Dwight D., *Crusade in Europe,* 354-355.

15. Joe Hatchel's son, Mark Hatchel, tells this story and knows it to be a defining moment in his father's life, bringing home to him the incredible inhumanity of

war. The incident was the subject of nightmares and a nervous breakdown at one point in his father's later years. But Joe Hatchel, the tanker, eventually came to terms with his part in the war and related the incident to family and close friends on numerous occasions. Mark Hatchel, the son, is now the secretary of the 740th Tank Battalion Association—the first non-tanker to hold an office in the association. In addition, he has developed through the years an impressive and unique collection of original World War II uniforms, medals, guns, and memorabilia donated to the museum by the men of the battalion. *The 740th Museum is on display at the annual meetings of the association and other historical occasions.*

16. MacDonald, *op. cit.*, 459.

17. Whiting, *Jochen Peiper*, 81.

18. Ibid., 82-83.

19. Excerpted from "Dark Moments" by J.D. Kirkpatrick in Rubel, *op. cit.*, 239-240

20. See John Early's Bronze Star award in Rubel, *op. cit.*, 288.

21. See Gerald Lange's Bronze Star award in Rubel, *op. cit.*, 292.

22. See Joseph Salvestrini's Bronze Star award in Rubel, *op. cit.*, 300.

23. Excerpted from "Dark Moments" by Frances Rebel in *Rubel, op. cit.*, 237-238.

24. MacDonald, *op. cit.*, 462.

25. Whiting, *Jochen Peiper*, 91.

26. Rubel, *op. cit.*, 67.

27. Personal interviews with Frank Cole, 10/15/01, and subsequent meetings.

28. Personal interviews with Dwight Davis, 10/15/01, and subsequent meetings.

Chapter 13: Christmas at Home

1. Bailey and Editors Time-Life Books, *The Home Front, USA, World War II*, 107.

2. Ibid., 103.

3. Ibid., 77.

4. Ibid., 76-77.

5. Strahan, *Andrew Jackson Higgins and the Boats That Won World War II*, 1.

6. Larrabee, *Commander in Chief: Franklin Delano Roosevelt, His Lieutenants, and Their War*, 6-7.

7. Bailey and Editors *Time-Life Books, op. cit.*, 77.

8. Krull, *V is for Victory: America Remembers World War II*, 18.

Chapter 14: And to the South: Bastogne

1. Dupuy, *Hitler's Last Gamble*, 194.

2. MacDonald, *A Time for Trumpets*, 524.

3.   Ibid., 525.

Chapter 15: With the 82nd Airborne Division

1.   Young (editor), *The World Almanac of World War II: The Complete and Comprehensive Documentary of World War II, 315.*

2.   "740th Battle Report for the Month of January 1945," 1.

3.   Ambrose, *Citizen Soldiers,* 370-371.

4.   *Time Magazine,* January 1, 1945, 23.

5.   Irving, *Hitler's War,* 724.

6.   Ambrose, *op. cit.,* 384.

7.   "740th Battle Report for the Month of January 1945," 1.

8.   Ibid., 2. See also Ambrose, *Citizen Soldiers,* 384-385, for more details of the action.

9.   Ibid.

10. Personal interview with Joseph Schooley, 11/11/2000, and subsequent meetings. See also Rubel, *op. cit.,* 78, and Silver Star citation, 282.

11. Excerpted from "Dark Moments" by Arthur McBrayer in Rubel, *op. cit.,* 245-246.

12. Excerpted from "Dark Moments" by George Wright in Rubel, *op. cit.,* 247.

13. See Carl Miller's Bronze Star citation in Rubel, *op. cit.,* 297-298.

14. "740th Battle Report for the Month of January," 3. See also Rubel, *op. cit.,* 79, for an account of the action; 289 and 292 for the Bronze Star citations for Fasoli and Kilgore respectively; and 283 and 284 for Tribby's Silver Star citation and his oak leaf cluster to the Silver Star.

15. C.R.I.B.A., *504th Infantry Regiment,* 2. (*Original quote from Center of Research and Information in the Battle of the Bulge: no longer included*).

16. Personal interview with John Tullier, 10/15/01, and subsequent meetings. See also "Dark Moments" by Tullier in Rubel, *op. cit.,* 246.

17. Dupuy, *Hitler's Last Gamble,* 322.

18. Rubel, *op. cit.,* 81-82.

19. "740th Battle Report for the Month of January 1945," 5.

20. Rubel, *op. cit.,* 85-86. See also "740th Battle Report for the Month of January 1945," 5. A conflicting account of this battle appears in Gregory Orfalea's book, *Messengers of the Lost Battalion: The Heroic 551st and the Turning of the Tide at the Battle of the Bulge,* 310-311. The 551st commander at the time was Lt. Col. Wood Joerg. Tragically, he was killed in the action. Orfalia makes the case that there was only one tank during the incursion and that Rubel's account of the situation "simply does not square" with the situation nor with the 551st commander's actions during the battle at Rochlinval.

21. "740th Battle Report for the Month of January 1945," 5. See also Rubel, *op. cit.,* 86.

22. Rubel, *op. cit.*, 87.

23. Montgomery quotes excerpted from MacDonald, *A Time for Trumpets*, 611-612. The press conference is reported in numerous accounts of World War II in Europe. However, MacDonald's version is perhaps the most informative, complete with events leading up to the sticky situation and the repercussions following, including the apology from Winston Churchill. For the full story, see *A Time for Trumpets*, 611-614.

24. MacDonald, *A Time for Trumpets*, 614.

25. Jones, *WW II*, 202.

26. Gardner, *The Year That Changed the World*, 76.

27. "740th Battle Report for the Month of January 1945," 6.

28. Telephone interview with Burt Tyler, 5/1/03, and follow-up discussions.

Chapter 16: Inauguration Day, 1945
The 740th's Drive to the West Wall

1. Bishop, *FDR's Last Year*, 243-244.

2. Luce, Henry L., and Gottfried Manfred, editors. *Time: The Weekly News Magazine*, Vol. XLV, January 29, 1945, 17-19.

3. Bishop, *op. cit.*, 247.

4. Luce, Henry L., and Gottfried Manfred, editors. *Time: The Weekly News Magazine*, Vol. XLV, January 22, 1945, 28.

5. Rubel, *op. cit.*, 91.

6. Ibid.

7. Excerpted from "Dark Moments," by Loyd C. Rule in Rubel, *op. cit.*, 246

8. Rubel, *op. cit.*, 92-93.

9. See Charles Powers' Oak Leaf Cluster to the Silver Star in Rubel, *op. cit.*, 284.

10. Personal interview with C.R. Horn, 9/4/04, and related correspondence following. See also Horn's "Dark Moments" in Rubel, *op. cit.*, 245.

11. See Glenn H. Lewis' Silver Star citation in Rubel, *op. cit.*, 279-280, and "Dark Moments," same reference, 244.

12. Ambrose, *Citizen Soldiers*, 393. Ambrose notes that January 1945 was the costliest month of the entire campaign in Northwest Europe for the U.S. Army in KIA and wounded.

13. Hall, editor, *March to Victory: The Final Months of World War II*, 127.

14. Ibid.

Chapter 17: Cracking the Siegfried Line
And a Glimpse of the Yalta Conference

1. Rubel, *Daredevil Tankers*, 101.

2. Montgomery was awarded the Silver Star posthumously for this action. Citation in Rubel *op. cit.*, 280.

3. Excerpted from "Dark Moments" by Maurice Logan in Rubel, *op. cit.*, 247.

4. Rubel, *op. cit.*, 247.

5. Conversations with J.D. Keen through the years, a follow-up letter from Dorothy Keen after J.D.'s ultimate passing, and a personal interview with Mike Smith, 9/2/05. See also Smith's "Dark Moments" in Rubel, *op. cit.*, 249.

6. Excerpted from "Dark Moments by W.A. Nipper in Rubel, *op. cit.*, 248.

7. See Jack Ashby's Silver Star award in Rubel, *op. cit.*, 276.

8. Excerpted from "Dark Moments" by James E. Lewis in Rubel, *op. cit.*, 248-249.

9. See James Windam's Bronze Star award in Rubel, *op. cit.*, 301.

10. Rubel, *op. cit.*, 107.

11. Ibid., 108.

12. Excerpted from "Dark Moments" by Burlin Wilson in Rubel, *op. cit.*, 246–247.

13. Excerpted from "Dark Moments" by Orbie Floyd in Rubel, *op. cit.*, 243.

14. Bishop, *op. cit.*, 269.

15. *Churchill,* Memoirs of the Second World War, 912.

16. Specifics and quotes regarding Big Three goals in this section, "The Yalta Conference," are culled primarily from Chapter 1 of *The Yalta Conference*, edited by Richard F. Fenno, Jr., 3-8. The chapter, entitled "Yalta in Context," was written by William H. McNeill.

17. Ibid., 8.

18. Gardner, *The Year That Changed the World*, 74.

19. Rubel, *op. cit.*, 109.

20. Ibid., 111.

21. Ibid.

Chapter 18: Veritable and Grenade

1. Rubel, *op. cit.*, 115.

2. Ibid., 253.

3. Ibid., 115-118.

4. Excerpted from "Dark Moments" by Corporal Ray F. Newman in Rubel, *op. cit.*, 253.

5. MacDonald, *The Last Offensive*, 81-82. See also Breuer, *Storming Hitler's Rhine*, 30-31.

6. Bradley, *A General's Life*, 393-394.

7. Breuer, Storming Hitler's Rhine, op. cit., *28-29.*

8. Ibid., 35. See Chapter 4, "'Sleeper Patrols' Among the Enemy" in Breuer's *Storming*

Hitler's Rhine for vivid details on the wait at the Roer.

9.   Ambrose, *Citizen Soldiers*, 306-307.

10. Ibid.

11. Rubel, *op. cit.*, 120.

12. Rubel, *op. cit.*, 120-121.

13. Rubel, *op. cit.*, 122-123.

14. Breuer, *op. cit.*, 60-61.

15. Ambrose, *op. cit.*, 408.

16. *740th Battle Report for the month of February 1945, 4.*

17. MacDonald, op. cit., 161.

18. Rubel, *op. cit.*, 128.

19. See Joseph "Buck" Southers' and Morris Copeland's Bronze Star citations in Rubel, *op. cit.*, 295 and 287 respectively.

20. Rubel, *op. cit.*, 259.

21. Amann, *Rite of Passage: The Story of My Service in the U.S. Army 1944-1945, 91.*

22. Rubel, *op. cit.*, 130.

23. Personal interview with Paul Gittings, 8/31/02, and subsequent meetings.

24. Rubel, *op. cit.*, 132.

25. See James Thomas' Bronze Star citation in Rubel, op. cit., 296.

26. Rubel, *op. cit.*, 134-135.

27. See Guy Knight's "Dark Moments," in Rubel, *op. cit.*, 251, and Bronze Star citations for Knight on 292 and for Wolverton on 301.

28. Rubel, *op. cit.*, 137.

29. Breuer, *op. cit.*, 82-83.

30. "Journal and Worksheet," 740th Tank Battalion, March 1945, 7.

31. Rubel, *op. cit.*, 139. Specific details found in A Company's Action Report, February 6 to March 8, 1945, 3. See also Mumford's Silver Star citation, 281; and Bronze Star citations for Graves, 290, and Shores, 301, in Rubel's *Daredevil Tankers.*

32. Rubel, *op. cit.*, 143.

33. See "Dark Moments" by L.C. Dunn in Rubel, *op. cit.*, 259.

34. Rubel, *op. cit.*, 145.

35. Rubel, *op. cit.*, 144-145.

36. Gen. Moore, previously assistant commander of the 104th Infantry Division, had just replaced Gen. William G. Weaver as commander of the 8th Infantry, following Weaver's fourth heart attack a week earlier.

37. "740th Journal and Worksheet," March 4, 1945, 12.

38. Rubel, *op. cit.*, 146. Details in Homer Tompkins' Silver Star citation, 282.

39. Breuer, *op. cit.*, 76.

40. Ibid., 116.

41. Rubel, *op. cit.*, 153.

42. Breuer, *op. cit.*, 159-160.

43. Ambrose, *op. cit.*, 342-344.

44. Rubel, *op. cit.*, 154.

45. MacDonald, *The Last Offensive, 236.*

46. Breuer, *op. cit.*, 160-161.

47. Rubel, *op. cit.*, 160.

Chapter 19: Operation Undertone

1. Eisenhower, David. *Eisenhower at War: 1943-1945, 686.*

2. Bradley, *A General's Life, 403.*

3. Amann, *Rite of Passage: The Story of My Service in the U.S. Army 1944-1945, 130.*

4. Ibid, 138.

5. "After Action Report, March 1-31, 1945," 7. See also Rubel, *op. cit.*, 162-163, and Silver Star citations for Glenn George and William Hamilton in the same reference, 279.

6. Rubel, *op. cit.*, 163.

7. Excerpted from "Dark Moments" by Ernest Swanson in Rubel, *op. cit.*, 262.

8. Excerpted from "Dark Moments" by Bill Shaw in Rubel, *op. cit.*, 261.

9. Excerpted from "Dark Moments" by Rex P. Taylor in Rubel, *op. cit.*, 261.

10. Excerpted from "Dark Moments" by Alfred A. Giangregorio in Rubel, *op. cit.*, 260.

11. Rubel, *op. cit.*, 167-168.

12. Bradley, *A Soldier's Story, 522.*

13. Eisenhower, Dwight D., *op. cit.*, 389. See also Breuer, *op. cit.*, 222-223, for additional details.

Chapter 20: Into the Ruhr Pocket

1. Ambrose, *Citizen Soldiers, 451.*

2. Ibid., 451-452.

3. Excerpted from "Dark Moments" by Douglas F. Greenwalt in Rubel, *op. cit.*, 263.

4. Personal interview with Frank Quick, 8/28/03. See also Bronze Star citation in Rubel, *op. cit.*, 299.

5. Personal interviews and correspondence with C.O. "Chigger" Webster. See also "Dark Moments" in Rubel, *op. cit.*, 262, and Bronze Star citation, 296.

6. Excerpted from "Dark Moments" by Herman R. Beard in Rubel, *op. cit.*, 263. Beard went on to receive a Silver Star for gallantry in action and a Bronze Star with Oak Leaf Cluster for heroic achievement in the service of his country.

7. Rubel, *op. cit.*, 180-181.

8.   Excerpted from "Dark Moments" by Earnest Abney in Rubel, *op. cit.*, 265.

9.   Rubel, *op. cit.*, 182.

10. Ibid., 186.

11. Ibid., 189.

12. See George Merritt's Silver Star citation in Rubel, *op. cit.*, 280.

13. See Oren Blakely's Silver Star citation in Rubel, *op. cit.*, 277.

Chapter 21: The President Is Dead

1.   Selective details and quotes regarding President Roosevelt's last days were drawn from Jim Bishop's superb book, *FDR's Last Year*, 490-540. Complete and unique details of FDR's last days, the conflicted emotions around the world, the family and the funeral, and President Truman's first days can be found in the last chapter, "April 1945."

2.   Bishop, *FDR's Last Year*, 554-557.

3.   Ibid., 556.

Chapter 22: Friday the Thirteenth

1.   Rubel, *op. cit.*, 191.

2.   See Jesse Hendrix's Bronze Star citation in Rubel, *op. cit.*, 291.

3.   Eisenhower, Dwight D., *op. cit.*, 408-409.

4.   Eisenhower, David, *op. cit.*, 762.

5.   Personal interviews with R.D. Bridges on several occasions. See also Bridges' Silver Star citation in Rubel, *op. cit.*, 278, and A.B. Cooks' Bronze Star citation in the same reference, 287.

6.   Excerpted from "Dark Moments" by Wayne Lowe in Rubel, *op. cit.*, 265.

Chapter 23: Closing Out the Ruhr

1.   Rubel, *op. cit.*, 197.

2.   See Clell Mott's Silver Star citation in Rubel, *op. cit.*, 281.

3.   John Laffin in his book, *Hitler Warned Us*, 115, says that within one hour of President Paul von Hindenburg's death on August 2, 1934, Hitler took over full power of the Third Reich. In ceremonies that followed throughout Germany, servicemen took the following oath to the new head of state and supreme commander: *I swear by God this holy oath, that I will render to Adolf Hitler, Führer of the German Reich and people, Supreme Commander of the Armed Forces, unconditional obedience, and I am ready, as a brave soldier, to risk my life at any time for this oath.*

4.   Whiting, *West Wall*, 183.

5.   Ibid.

6.   Kessler, *The Battle of the Ruhr Pocket*, *194-195*.

7.   Ibid., 201.

8.   Ibid., 209. Kessler goes on to explain the note of mystery surrounding Model's death. Model's adjutant called another officer and the two of them dug a shallow grave, wrapped Model's body in a greatcoat, and placed it in the ground. Then they filled the hole and left the scene with no attempt to mark the grave. However, someone unknown later returned and carved the letter "M" on the oak tree, which 10 years later lead Hans-Georg to his father's grave. Page 210.

9.   MacDonald, *The Last Offensive: WWII*, 370-372.

10.   Rubel, *op. cit.*, 202.

Chapter 24: The Occupation of Dusseldorf

1.   Kessler, *op. cit.*, 192-193.

2.   Ibid, 197-198.

3.   Rubel, *op. cit.*, 203.

4.   Ibid.

5.   Gardner, *The Year That Changed the World*, *121*.

6.   Ambrose, *The Victors*, 334.

7.   MacDonald, *The Mighty Endeavor*, *515*.

8.   *Blair,* Ridgway's Paratroopers: The American Airborne in World War II, *579-581*.

9.   Bradley, *A General's Life*, 433-434.

10.   Blair, *op. cit.*, 581-582.

11.   Blair, *op. cit.*, 581.

Chapter 25: Across the Elbe River

1.   Blair, *op. cit.*, 581-583.

2.   Rubel, *op. cit.*, 208.

3.   Gavin, *On to Berlin*, 284-285.

4.   Rubel, *op. cit.*, 211.

5.   Ibid.

Chapter 26: The Death of Hitler:
  The Incredible Race to the Baltic Sea

1.   Bullock, *Hitler and Stalin*, 884-886.

2.   MacDonald, *The Last Offensive*, *459*.

3.   Toland, *Adolf Hitler*, 1000-1004. Vivid details.

4.   Excerpted from "Darkest Moments" by Homer Tompkins in Rubel, *op. cit.*, 267. See also Tompkins' Silver Star citation, 282.

5.   Excerpted from "Darkest Moments" by Charles Hoover in Rubel, *op. cit.*, 268.

6. Personal interview with Harold Bradley, 8/30/03, with follow-up meetings and correspondence. See also Silver Star citations for Bradley and Woodress in Rubel, *op. cit.*, 277 and 283 respectively.

7. Rubel, *op. cit.*, 218.

8. Ibid., 219-221. See also George K. Rubel's Silver Star citation in Rubel, *op. cit.*, 282.

9. Bradley, *A General's Life, 434.*

10. Whiting, *The End of the War – Europe: April 15–May 23, 1945, 99–100.*

11. Ibid., 100.

12. MacDonald, *The Last Offensive, 465.*

13. Rubel, *op. cit.*, 222.

14. MacDonald, *op. cit.*, 465.

15. Eisenhower, David, *op. cit.*, 800-801.

16. MacDonald, *op. cit.*, 474-475.

17. Eisenhower, David, *op. cit.*, 802.

18. Ibid, 803.

Chapter 27: The End of the War in Europe

1. The Editors, *Yank: The Story of World War II as Written by the Soldiers, 142.*

2. Excerpted from a paper entitled, "The First Escape from the Iron Curtain," by the 740th's Sergeant Herschel B. Wahl, undated, 2-5.

3. Rubel, *op. cit.*, 230.

4. Ibid.

5. Truman, "Why I Dropped the Bomb," *Parade Magazine*, December 4, 1988, 11.

6. Ibid.

Afterword

1. Wikipedia: The Free Encyclopedia, http://en.wikipedia.org/wici/World_War_II_casualties

2. Ibid.

3. "Remember When, 1945: A Nostalgic Look Back in Time," 13.

Part IV

Addendum 1: 740th Tank Battalion Memorials and Monuments
The Return to Belgium in 1999

1. Larscheid, Tom. Editor and writer. "Unique museum dioramas show GI life of 55 years ago," *The Benelux Meteor,* unofficial Army newspaper, September 3, 1999, 5.

2. Correspondence from Mathilde and Marcel Schmetz.

Addendum 2: Whatever Became of Jochen Peiper?

1. Whiting, *Peiper*, Introduction, IX.

2. Reynolds, *The Devil's Adjutant: Jochen Peiper, Panzer Leader*. Relevant historical details from Chapter I, "The Man and His Regiment," 21-35.

3. In his book, *The Devil's Adjutant*, Michael Reynolds has done an exhaustive study on Jochen Peiper. Regarding Peiper's entrance into the Ardennes offensive and movements from the *Siegfried Line* to Stoumont in Belgium, the author has drawn specific details from Reynolds' extensive maps and narrative. Since the 740th Tank Battalion entered the battle at Stoumont Station, *Into the Breach* details events as they were recorded by after action reports in Lt. Col. Rubel's history of the 740th Tank Battalion as well as personal accounts of Daredevil Tankers who were there.

4. Whiting, *op. cit*, 108.

5. Ibid, 131.

6. Reynolds, *op. cit.*, 253.

7. Details regarding Peiper's trial, imprisonment, and death are from a number of sources. Just type in "Jochen Peiper" on your computer, and you will see the wealth of information available. However, Reynolds' *The Devil's Adjutant* is most often quoted and ultimately provides the most definitive accounting of the SS Colonel's tragic ending. See Chapter XXXIX, "The Trial and Prison," 252–259, and Chapter XLI, "Murder," 264-269, for a complete and intriguing analysis.

Bibliography

Ambrose, Stephen E. *Citizen Soldiers: The U.S. Army from the Normandy Beaches to the Bulge to the Surrender of Germany, June 7, 1944–May 7, 1945.* New York: Simon & Schuster, 1997.

_____. *The Victors: Eisenhower and His Boys: The Men of World War II.* New York: Simon and Schuster, 1998.

Bailey, Ronald H. *The Home Front: U.S.A.* Alexandria, Virginia: World War II: Time-Life Books, Inc., 1978.

Baty, Roger M. and Maddox, Eddie M. Jr., editors. *Where Heroes Trained: 736th Medium Tank Battalion (Special): From its formation through secret battle training in the Desert Training Center and California-Arizona Maneuver Area, February 1943–April 1944.* Tucson, Arizona: Fenestra Books, 2004.

Bishop, Jim. *FDR's Last Year: April 1944–April 1945.* New York: William Morrow & Company, Inc., 1974.

Bradley, Omar N., and Clay Blair. *A General's Life: An Autobiography.* New York: Simon & Schuster, 1983.

_____. *A Soldier's Story.* New York: First Rand McNally & Company printing, 1978.

Breuer, William B. *Storming Hitler's Rhine.* New York: First St. Martin Press mass market edition (paperback), 1986.

Brokaw, Tom. *The Greatest Generation.* New York: Random House, 1998.

Bullock, Alan. *Hitler and Stalin: Parallel Lives.* New York: Alfred A. Knopf, 1992.

Churchill, Winston S. *Memoirs of the Second World War.* A paperback abridgement of the six volumes of *The Second World War.* Boston: Houghton Mifflin Company, 1959, 1987.

Cole, Hugh M. *The Ardennes: Battle of the Bulge.* Old Sayrbook, CT: Konecky & Konecky, undated.

Cooper, Belton Y. *Death Traps: The Survival of an American Armored Division in World War II.* Novato, California: Presidio Press, Inc., 2001.

Cross, Robin. *The Battle of the Bulge 1944: Hitler's Last Hope.* Havertown, PA: Casemate, 2002.

Dupuy, Trevor N., David L. Bongard, and Richard C. Anderson, Jr. *Hitler's Last Gamble: The Battle of the Bulge, December 1944–January 1945.* New York: Harper Collins, 1994.

Eisenhower, David. *Eisenhower: At War, 1943-1945.* New York: Random House, Inc., 1986.

Eisenhower, Dwight D. *Crusade in Europe.* New York: Doubleday & Company, Inc., 1948.

Eisenhower, John S.D. *The Bitter Woods.* New York: G. P. Putnam's Sons, 1969.

Fenno, Richard F., Jr., editor. *The Yalta Conference.* Massachusetts and London: D.C. Heath and Company, 1972.

Folkestad, William B. *The View from the Turret: The 743rd Tank Battalion During World War II.* Shippensburg, Pennsylvania: Burd Street Press book, printed by Beidel Printing House, Inc., 2000.

Gardner, Brian. *The Year That Changed the World: 1945.* New York: Coward-McCann,

Inc., 1963.

Gavin, James M. *On to Berlin: Battles of an Airborne Commander 1943-1945*. New York: The Viking Press, 1978.

Gies, Joseph. *Harry S. Truman: A Pictorial Biography*. Garden City, New York: Doubleday & Company, Inc., 1968.

Goering, Goebbels, Hoffmann, et al. *Adolf Hitler: Bilder Aus Dem Leben, Des Führers*. Leipzeg, Germany: Herausgegeben Vom Cigaretten/Bilderienst, Hamburg/Bahrenfeld, 1936.

Green, Michael. *M4 Sherman: Combat and Development History of the Sherman Tank and All Sherman Variants*. Osceola, Wisconsin, 1993.

Gérgoire, Gérard. *Les Panzer De Peiper Face A L'U.S. Army* (English Translation). La Gleize, Belgium, 1989, (2nd edition).

Hall, Tony: editor. *March to Victory: The Final Months of WWII, From D-Day, June 6, 1944, to the Fall of Japan, August 14, 1945*. New York: Crescent Books, 1994.

Hugh Lauter Levin Associates, Inc. *The Stars and Stripes: World War II Front Pages*. New York: Bonanza Books, distributed by Crown Publishers, Inc., 1987.

Irving, David. *Hitler's War*. Condensed paperback version. New York: Avon Books, 1990.

Irwin, John P. *Another River, Another Town: A Teenage Tank Gunner Comes of Age in Combat–1945. New York: Random House, 2002*.

Jones, James. *WWII*. New York: Ballantine Books, Mass market format in paperback, first printing, 1977.

Kershaw, Alex. *The Longest Winter: The Battle of the Bulge and the Epic Story of World War II's Most Decorated Platoon*. Cambridge, Massachusetts: Da Capo Press paperback edition, 2004.

Kennett, Lee. G.I.: *The American Soldier in World War II*. New York: Charles Scribner's Sons, 1987.

Kimball, Warren F. *Forged in War: Churchill, Roosevelt and the Second World War*. Hammersmith, London: HarperCollins Publishers, 1997.

Krull, Kathleen. *V Is for Victory*. New York: Alfred A. Knopf, Inc., 1995.

Laffin, John. *Hitler Warned Us*. London-Washington: Brassey's, 1995. (Brassey's Inc. is now Potomac Books Inc.)

Larrabee, Eric. *Commander In Chief: Franklin Delano Roosevelt, His Lieutenants, and Their War*. New York: Simon & Schuster, First Touchstone Edition, 1988.

MacDonald, Charles B. *Company Commander*. New York: Ballantine Books, Inc., revised edition (paperback), 1961. Reprinted by arrangement with the Association of the United States Army.

_____. *The Last Offensive: WW II*. New York: BDD Special Edition. First printed in 1973 by the Center of Military History, United States Army, Washington, DC.

_____. The Mighty Endeavor: The American War in Europe. *New York: Da Capo* Press paperback edition, 1992.

_____. *A Time for Trumpets*. New York: William Morrow and Company, Inc., 1985.

Megellas, James. *All the Way to Berlin: A Paratrooper at War in Europe*. New York: Ballantine Books, A Presidio Press Book, Published by the Random House Publishing Group, 2003.

Moody, Sidney C. Jr. and the Photographers of The Associated Press. *War in Europe*.

Novato, CA: Presidio Press, 1993.

Morin, Relman. *Dwight D. Eisenhower: A Gauge of Greatness.* An Associated Press Biography, 1969.

Mosley, Leonard – and the Editors. *The Battle of Britain.* Alexandria, Virginia: World War II Time-Life Books, 1977.

Nordyke, Phil. *The All Americans in World War II: A Photographic History of the 82nd Airborne Division at War.* St. Paul, MN: Zenith Press, an imprint of MBI Publishing Company, 2006.

Orfalea, Gregory. *Messengers of the Lost Battalion: The Heroic 551st and the Turning of the Tide at the Battle of the Bulge.* New York: The Free Press, 1997.

Pallud, Jean Paul. *Battle of the Bulge: Then and Now.* After the Battle, The Mews, Hobbs Cross House, Hobbs Cross, Old Harlow, Essex CM17 ONN.

Reynolds, David. Rich Relations: *The American Occupation of Britain, 1942-1945.* London: Harper Collins (paperback edition), 1996.

Reynolds, Michael. *The Devil's Adjutant: Jochen Peiper, Panzer Leader.* New York: Sarpedon, 1995.

Rubel, George K., Lt. Col. *Daredevil Tankers: The Story of the 740th Tank Battalion, United States Army.* Edited by First Sergeant Charles W. Edwards, with illustrations by Private Tats B. Hirasuna. Werk Gottengin, Germany: Muster-Schmidt Ltd., 1945.

Strahan, Jerry E. *Andrew Jackson Higgins and the Boats That Won World War II.* Baton Rouge: Louisiana State University Press (paperback edition), 1998.

Toland, John. *Adolf Hitler: Volume II.* Garden City, New York: Doubleday & Company, Inc., 1976.

_____. *Battle: The Story of the Bulge.* New York: New American Library, First Meridian Printing (paperback), 1985. Published by arrangement with Random House, Inc.

Whiting, Charles. *The End of the War: Europe April 15-May 23, 1945.* New York: Stein and Day, 1973.

_____. *Jochen Peiper: Battle Commander, SS Leibstandarte Adolf Hitler.* Barnsley, South Yorkshire, S70 2AS: Leo Cooper, an imprint of Pen & Sword Books, revised edition, 1999.

_____. *Skorzeny: Ballantine's Illustrated History of the Violent Century, War Leader Book No. 11.* New York: Ballantine Books, Inc., 1972.

_____. *West Wall: The Battle for Hitler's Siegfried Line.* Pan Grand Strategy Series. London N1 9RR: Pan Books, an imprint of Pan Macmillan, Ltd., 2002.

Yank: The Story of World War II, As Written by the Soldiers. New York: Greenwich House, distributed by Crown Publishers, Inc., 1984.

Yeide, Harry. *Steel Victory: The Heroic Story of America's Independent Tank Battalions at War in Europe.* New York: Ballantine Books-A Presidio Press Book, published by the Random House Publishing Group, 2003.

_____. *Weapons of the Tankers: American Armor in World War II.* St. Paul, MN: Zenith Press, an imprint of MBI Publishing Company, 2006.

Young, Peter, Brigadier, Editor. *The World Almanac of World War II: The Complete and Comprehensive Documentary of World War II.* New York: World Almanac: An Imprint of Pharas Books, A Bison Book, First Revised Edition, 1986.

National Archives at College Park, MD

Chronological History of 740th Medium Tank Battalion (Special): February 27, 1943 to October 20, 1944.

740th Tank Battalion Action Against Enemy Reports for January through May 1945.
Summary of Action Report for 740th Company A, January 6, 1945 to March 6, 1945.
Journal and Worksheets for 740th Tank Battalion for March, April, and May 1945.
740th Tank Battalion Reports of Operations for August 1945–March 1946.
General Orders, 740th Tank Battalion: March–December 1943; January–July 1944; January–November 1945; and January–April 1946.

Pamphlets, Unpublished Papers & Manuscripts

Amann, John A. "Rite of Passage: The Story of My Service in the U.S. Army 1944–1946." Unpublished manuscript by the late John Amann, First Platoon, Company B, 740th Tank Battalion. Undated.

Cash, William R. "Diary." Unpublished diary of Bill Cash, Service Company, 740th Tank Battalion, covering his period of service from July 19, 1944, when the battalion left Fort Knox for the port of embarkation to England, Camp Kilmer, N.J., through November 9, 1945, at Fort McPherson, Georgia: "The day I had been looking for 4½ years—'Honorable Discharge, U.S. Army.'"

KardLets Pages of Time: A Nostalgia News Report. Millersville, Tennessee. KardLets, from Pages of Time: 1943, 1944, & 1945 editions.

Miller, Harry. *The 740th Tank Battalion Monument: Dedicated April 24, 1999.* Printed in the U.S.A., 1999.

Remember When—A Nostalgic Look Back in Time, 1945. Seek Publishing, undated.

Wall, Herschel B. "The First Escape from the Iron Curtain." Excerpted from the unpublished writings of that 740th Daredevil, "Herk" Wall, in which he tells the stirring story of how he and his B Company buddies virtually drifted into a sea of trouble with the Russians at war's end. Undated.

About the Author

October 1923 – April 2009

Paul L. Pearson grew up in Wichita Falls, Texas, when hamburgers were six for a quarter, and modern America was just beginning to make its debut.

He was a member of the 740th Tank Battalion from its inception in Fort Knox, Kentucky, in 1943, until linking up with the Russians on the Baltic Sea at the end of the war in Europe, and then the ultimate occupation of Germany in 1945.

He was a Buck Sergeant Tank Commander in Company C, 2nd Platoon, and was awarded the Silver Star and the Purple Heart. Other citations include the Presidential Unit Citation, the Belgian Croix de Guerre, the World War II Victory Medal, and various campaign medals with bronze service stars.

After the war, he became a YMCA youth worker and camp executive, then a teacher, principal, and director in the Fort Worth Public Schools. Although born and bred a Texan, he never was a cowboy.

He lived and wrote in Benbrook, Texas, until the age of 85, with the girl who waited for him to come home from the war, those many years ago, still at his side.